HOTEL IN

by

Nancy Johnstone

The Clapton Press

This edition © The Clapton Press Limited 2022

First published by Faber & Faber Limited, 1938

Cover design by Gruffydd Art

ISBN 978-1-913693-16-9

About the Author

Bored with life in London, Nancy and Archie Johnstone left their jobs and moved to the Costa Brava in 1934 to build and run their own hotel. It sounded like a recipe for disaster but within twelve months Tossa de Mar became the destination of choice for a vibrant group of international writers and artists. *Hotel in Spain* is a light-hearted account of their ups and downs before the Civil War erupted and darkness descended.

Nancy Johnstone's sequel, *Hotel in Flight*—also available from The Clapton Press—continues their story as the couple refuse an offer of evacuation by the Royal Navy and convert their hotel into a refuge for children displaced by the war, eventually escorting them in a terrifying dash for the border as Franco's mercenary army advanced.

The Johnstones emigrated to Mexico in 1939 and later went their separate ways. In January 1951 Nancy was seriously injured in a car crash in Guatemala, in which her friend, Constancia de la Mora, was killed. The same year she wrote to her publisher from Tossa de Mar leaving a forwarding address and was never heard from again.

Contents

Contents

Book I — On Paper

1

'Dear Madam,

I have received your letter with inquiries about our hotel in Tossa de Mar and I will answer them in order. I must first of all explain that the hotel is still under construction, but we are confident that it will be ready by Whitsun—which by the way is the weekend of the 9th June, not, as you state, the 29th. However, in case of any unforeseen difficulties arising, would you be prepared to stay in a Spanish hotel (which I can thoroughly recommend from personal experience) until our hotel is finished?

Now with regard to your questions:

1. The Casa Johnstone is situated on the south side of a hill overlooking the sea, the village, and surrounding hills.

2. I admit quite frankly that it is absolutely safe to walk about alone anywhere in Catalonia.

3. The milk is goats' milk. Butter from cows' milk is always obtainable and it has none of that peculiar taste you say you found in Sardinia.

4. There are practically no mosquitoes. I do not recognize the creature you describe, but can only assure you I have never seen anything approaching your description.

5. The bathing is absolutely safe. I did not quite understand your query about "natives" bathing. Of course the local people use the beaches as much as the visitors, but there are no coloured people here.

6. No, there are no life-guards on the beaches. Doubtless local fishermen would oblige if anyone found himself in difficulties, but the whole coast is absolutely safe.

7. The cooking . . .'

The telephone rang in the hall. I tilted back the packing-case upon which I had been sitting and moved my legs gingerly between it and the larger packing-case where my typewriter was balanced. There was no other furniture at all in the room, which was stripped even of curtains and carpet. The telephone was on another case in the empty hall.

It was an old school-friend who had recently married and from whom I had not heard for months. She was evidently settling down for a long chat, but I found little comfort telephoning on a packing-case.

'My dear, I can't stop now, but I must see you somehow this week. We are up to the neck. We are off in a week to start an hotel in Spain.'

I had expected the usual gasp of amazement with which most of our friends greeted this statement, but there was only a tiny pause. Kate was always the kindest-hearted creature.

'What an odd place to start an hotel,' she said at last.

'Odd? I don't think so. The weather is always so lovely and lots of people go there—'

'Yes, of course, there must be a great many people passing through,' said Kate hopefully. Then, as if determined to look on the bright side: 'It will be lovely to have you near us, anyway!'

It was my turn to be surprised. 'Why, are you thinking of going to Spain too?'

'Spain!' Kate's gasp of relief was audible. 'My dear, I thought you said Staines!'

I had just got back to my letter when the telephone rang again.

'Hello!' It was a man's voice and I did not recognize it.

8

'Hello! May I speak to Mrs Johnstone? '

'This is Mrs Johnstone speaking.'

'My name is Brooke. I have just seen your advertisement about your hotel in Spain. Have you any accommodation for the last two weeks of August and the first two of September?'

'I am afraid that that is a very full time. For how many would it be?'

'About twenty, but perhaps more. We usually get up a pretty big party to get advantage of the cheap railway fares—'

'I am awfully sorry,' I interrupted, 'I might have squeezed in one or two more for August, but a party would be impossible. But I will send you some particulars if you will give me your address, and perhaps another year—'

I burst into the kitchen, where my husband was cording up some boxes. 'Archie,' I said solemnly, 'I have just turned down twenty people for August!'

Archie and I were working as hard as we could. We had been doing this for the last two months, ever since the building had actually started. On top of looking after our small flat, packing up what we had to take with us, and getting rid of everything else, I was overwhelmed with correspondence from the few small advertisements that we had put in various periodicals. Apparently everyone had been putting off going to Spain until some English person designed an hotel with all the accustomed English comforts.

Archie, besides having developed a hitherto unsuspected and astonishing commercial astuteness that would have shamed a moneylender, was still working on the *News Chronicle* as 'night-sub' which meant his being at the office from 9 pm until 4 am, with consequent somnolence until about two the following afternoon. However, he was very wide awake when it came to coping with agents for moving our belongings and the thousand other expenses entailed. I had almost closed with an offer from a firm of professional packers and shippers to transport things to Barcelona for about thirty pounds. Archie found that if we packed the things ourselves we could send them for ten pounds from our flat in Hampstead to Tossa de Mar, which is fifty miles north of Barcelona. He dug up a friend who knew someone who 'did things' in the wholesale world, and we got all our cutlery, spoons, and forks (which are much better in England than in Spain) and various other things we had decided to take with us, at 33 1/3 per cent discount. People were so interested in our project that we found many friends who had unsuspected talents for saving us money. And we needed to be economical.

The whole project developed so quickly that we were able to start off gaily, quite unaware of possible pitfalls that might have deterred most people from attempting such a thing as starting an hotel in a foreign country. We had no experience, no business training, a very sketchy knowledge of Spanish, and very little money—which had quite unexpectedly come to me from my erratic father. We felt it rather a waste to invest this money safely and to have just a bit added to our usual income. Also, our dream—the journalist's dream—was to retire to the country and run a pub—somewhere in England, we thought vaguely, but that was before we saw the Costa Brava and Tossa.

We had found Tossa by accident. Archie, with his usual method of choosing a place for his holiday, thought of the Costa Brava because he had never heard of anyone going there. We set out with a small suitcase each and eventually arrived at Gerona. We saw the name Tossa written somewhere, thought it had a good sound, and went there. We were actually staying there when we got the news of the windfall. Unfortunately, we had to go home almost immediately, but we left with the firm conviction that if we really got the money, which seemed too good to be true, we would come back and start a pub somewhere on the Costa Brava. That was in the spring of 1933, and it was not until the end of September of that year that I was able to get back to Catalonia to see what chances there were of getting land on the Costa Brava.

I left my flat with a small attaché case and stood waiting for the 28 bus on my way to King's Cross for the Hillman Airways' coach. My greengrocer, Mr Wyer, whose shop is at the bus stop, greeted me and asked where I was off to.

'To Spain,' I said. He was enormously interested.

'For two pins I'd come with you,' he said. 'Fine lot of fruit in those parts.'

'I'll bring you back an orange,' I said. 'I'll be back in a week or so. I'm off to find some land to start a pub.'

'Well, now, if that don't beat everything. Hey, missus! Mrs Johnstone's off to Spain to start a public house.'

'I hope you'll both come out when it really is started.'

Mrs Wyer smiled. 'I think we're a bit old to start travelling around. But the boys will be interested. Cyril is all for going abroad on his motorbike this year. You must have a talk with him.'

'I will,' I promised, and leaped for my bus.

I left with no fixed idea of going to Tossa. My intention was to explore the whole coast, to look for likely spots, and to inquire locally about land, prices, etc. My Spanish was appalling, my Catalan absolutely nil, but I have always been a believer in luck. And at this time it did not let me down. The first bit of luck was on arrival at Gerona, where one changes for Tossa or Palamós. I had intended to go to Palamós and use it as a centre for explorations. I was rather vague about the exact way, and so was the only porter at Gerona, so I said to hell with it and went to Tossa instead, where I knew the route and the hotel.

The Hotel Rovira was almost as lucky a find as Tossa when we went on that first important holiday. We had then no experience of Catalan hotels and had the usual idea that everything Spanish must be dirty. We were surprised to find a spotless room with a red-tiled floor, whitewashed walls and sky-blue beams, and greatest surprise of all, running water. From one side the room looked down on a patio full of scarlet geraniums, and the front windows looked over the narrow village street to the hills beyond. The food was heavenly, but the best thing about the Hotel Rovira was Rovira himself. He was definitely a person to keep on the right side of, but luckily he adored Archie. He would talk to him in floods of Catalan; Archie would retaliate with a broad stream of Aberdeen. Less fluent dialecticians stood by and marvelled.

This time Rovira rushed out to greet me, calling to his wife. They were bitterly disappointed to find only me and were profuse in their inquiries about 'the *señor*'. However, they decided to make the best of it, gave me our old room, and were as charming as ever. When Archie and I were at Tossa in the spring we had not spoken to a soul, we just lazed about all day, swam and walked, and went to bed at nine or earlier.

I had been there half a day on my own when I knew everyone in the place. A large blond Austrian called by everybody Carlos, who practically lived in the place, recognized me from the spring visit, and he proved to be invaluable. He spoke perfect Spanish and knew everyone. I had no intention of telling the world about our project, but I told him, and then had another piece of luck.

A friend of his, Fritz Marcus, ran a bar in Tossa—and Marcus was a well-known German architect who had left Germany because he was a Jew. I went to his bar, which impressed me very much. He had renovated an old Catalan cottage and had somehow managed to keep the atmosphere both of a Catalan cottage and of a bar. His clever wife had painted tiles with caricatures of local celebrities and had had them set in the whitewashed walls. Marcus himself presided at the bar, immensely dignified and like some youthful patriarch. His wife, Riehm, whose sketches are well known in Paris, smiled at her guests in all languages, looked charming in baggy trousers and saucy little jackets and occasionally

12

favoured someone with a dance on the tiny dance floor. This opened out into a patio roofed with a huge vine, from which hung great bunches of Malaga grapes, a great temptation to the people sitting below. I had a long talk with Marcus. Luckily, I had not forgotten what German I had learnt during a year's stay in Berlin. He was most helpful, and promised to come with me to look for a site.

We hired a car and started a tour of the coast. We drove along miles and miles of hair-raising roads, with a sheer drop hundreds of feet to the sea on one side and a deep ditch on the other, bordering great crags which towered above us. Pine-trees and cork oaks clung to crevices in the rocks, and everywhere heather and arbutus fought a winning battle with the bare sandstone. The road twisted down to small bays of yellow sand and then rose up again in a series of twists. I decided to live at each small bay as we came to it, well knowing that little things like accessibility, water, electric light, etc were of paramount importance in running an hotel. Eventually we came to Palamós, where Marcus knew someone who had some land for sale. We picked up a man who, I have since realized, was a perfectly normal Catalan, but who appeared to me at the time to be a cross between a bandit and a small boy at the seaside. He directed us for miles over a series of cart-tracks, and at last we came to a hill overlooking the sea. He ran up the hillside like a mountain goat and we followed hopefully. I had on only a cotton frock and Marcus shirt and trousers, but we were really hot by the time we reached the top. The owner seemed to be lost in admiration of his view, which was certainly magnificent. On one side was the deep blue of the Mediterranean and on the other the far-off Pyrenees just showed across miles of sweeping plain. A purple-black cloud seemed to be exactly above us.

I looked at Marcus, to find him shaking his head wisely. I myself felt that it was hardly the spot on which to build anything. At that moment there was a tremendous flash, a roar, and the rain came in torrents. It was so sudden that we just stood there and in two seconds were wet through. The most beautiful forked lightning seemed to play all around us. I could see Marcus was saying something, and I faintly heard him above the thunder. 'Perfectly useless place. No light, no water,' said the architect, the rain streaming down his large nose and lightning playing round his head. I shrieked with joy and looked for our host, but he had disappeared. We went down that mountain at the double. In a few minutes the sun was out again; in a few minutes more we were dry. We never saw the owner of the land again. It occurs to me as I write that perhaps the poor man was struck by lightning!

We saw one place that I loved, El Paradis, but it had so many disadvantages that I reluctantly gave up the idea of building there. It was very shut in and one could only reach it after a three-kilometre car drive. I had visions of unexpected guests and the nearest village three kilometres away, and decided against it. The only other piece of land that seemed possible was a very lovely garden going down to the beach, but it already had a large house built on it. However, I thought it might be possible to alter it into an hotel. After driving for miles to locate the owner we found he was willing to let only half of it, and he intended living in the other half with his family. He had six children. We decided that we had done enough for one day and returned to Tossa.

There is a point just before reaching Tossa where the road turns in one of its usual hairpin bends, and quite suddenly there is Tossa lying at its foot. The brilliant sea cuts two sapphire curves, edged with diamonds, into beaches of amber sand, which in turn vanish into emerald trees. On the farthest side of the large beach a line of ancient great fortifications has been built into the rocky headland. Aged cottages cling haphazardly to the hill inside the great battlemented walls, and high above them a ruined church shows glimpses of sky through its arches. The real village lies outside the old town, and grey and white houses cling together and huddle round the church which, like all Catalan churches, rises solid and windowless above the town. The sun was still behind the village and the whole picture was thrown up clearly in the hard light. I suddenly wondered why I had been chasing round the Costa Brava to find a site.

I turned to Marcus. 'Would it be possible to find any building land in Tossa?' I asked. Marcus thought so. He is the sort of person who never makes any definite statement until he is ready to put it in writing. I asked him to find out all about it and to let me know. This would take considerable time, as one must never let anyone know that one wants to buy land. I have never discovered the reason for this, but apparently architects are paid to know these things.

That evening I wrote a long letter to Archie. Among other things I said he must come out at once, as there was a good chance of finding land in Tossa. He had already had his very ample holiday that year, but I thought this was so important that he might as well try to wangle another week. It is often a matter of argument among us that I do the most outrageous things, but I have a theory, which has never yet let me down, that there is no harm in asking for anything. Apparently newspaper men never think of suddenly asking for an extra week's holiday. However, Archie, in the difficult position of either having to do something never done in the annals of Fleet Street or of never daring to face me again, decided to brave the minor terrors of his editor—and got his extra week. There was a slight delay when I found that I had taken our passport—which apparently I was not entitled to use unless accompanied by Archie. We had got a joint passport in a fit of economy a few years before. No one had noticed it on the journey! I had to send it back to him before he could come out. However, that was easily arranged by airmail, although I have since found out that that takes a day longer than the ordinary post from Tossa. At this time I was in happy

15

ignorance of many things like that. By the time he did get to Tossa I had two sites to show him and a wealth of detail to tell him about the possibilities of running an hotel there. Only in the matter of prices was I, and everyone else, completely vague. Actually we never did get any real idea of what things would cost until long after the hotel was built and running and we counted the money we had left. It did not try our arithmetic much.

2

We arranged a party for Archie on the night of his arrival. Some friends who had a cottage in the old town invited us for cognac after dinner. Archie had unexpectedly arrived in the afternoon, instead of at 7.30 pm, by the simple expedient of hiring the station bus and making the journey in solitary state, instead of waiting the four hours for it to leave at its usual time. The bus system from Tossa is peculiar. Buses leave gaily at 6 am for the respective railway stations for Barcelona and Gerona and return in the evening. There are plenty of trains in between, but the buses run only once there and back, for the first train and the last one. Archie arrived dead to the world, having travelled all night and worked all the night previously. He was too excited to sleep in the afternoon and we walked about trying not to look like people looking at sites.

After a gala dinner in his honour at our hotel, where Rovira and his wife Antonia were able to be completely their beaming selves at having both of us at last, we went up to the old town to the party. We had an hilarious evening, starting with brandy out of tumblers and charades. Archie did a ventriloquist turn with Oswald Petersen, the German painter, as the dummy. Petersen spoke no English and Archie no German, so they did it in very bad French. Brignoni, who had forsaken Italy to paint Tossa, did an *adagio* act with his wife, which was the success of the evening. Our host, a Danish banker, finally proposed going to Marcus's bar to finish the evening. Under the mellow influence of that attractive spot a dusky beauty from Canada, who had always hinted darkly in broken English that her mother had been chased by a fleet-footed Cherokee and who wore her black hair parted in the middle and oiled down each side of her brown, not un-squawlike face, suddenly showed an amazing knowledge of Cockney songs, and she and Archie retired to a corner and *Knocked 'em in the Old Kent Road*.

I love bars except that I never quite know what to do in them. I do not smoke and have a secret dislike of the taste of alcohol. In England my problem is solved by bitter, but in Spain the beer is poor stuff. I find that a very little brandy with enormous quantities of soda water generally meets the case, but at Marcus's they have a special brand of orange juice, which is delicious. However, one cannot drink orange juice indefinitely, and I at last decided to drag Archie home. To my amazement I found him almost unable to get back to the hotel. Archie Johnstone, the tough Fleet Street journalist, whom I had never seen even slightly tight in my life, was laid out by a Tossa evening!

In the next few days we found our site. It was a steep hillside which sheltered the village from the north winds. Our land included cork-trees on the top of the hill and a vineyard below. Any house built into the side of the hill would be completely protected from the north and east and have a glorious view to the south over the village and the first bay and, to the west, the foot-hills which lead eventually to the Pyrenees. Marcus was almost enthusiastic and apparently there was water in plenty from our own well, from which it would be pumped up to the house.

Archie and I naturally decided that Marcus as an architect was far more capable of deciding big issues than we were, and we were inclined to leave a great many things to him. He undertook to purchase the land—a lengthy process—and we arranged to send him a power of attorney from England. We had to leave for England the next day, as even I did not intend to try the good nature of the *News Chronicle* further. We asked as many intelligent questions as we could, and I was especially concerned to build as high up the hill as possible.

Marcus was against this and wanted the house at the foot, among the vines. This, of course, was the most economical and sensible idea, but here the first of a series of revolts against expertism stirred in me. I clambered up the hill and pointed to a fig tree. 'I want the house there,' I said. Marcus smiled with a patient smile (how well I got to know that smile and *little woman don't worry your pretty little head about it* expression!) and said he would build it as high as possible. I left it at that for the moment.

That day was Saturday, 6th October. That night at dinner everyone was electrified by a broadcast speech from Companys, the Catalan President. He declared complete autonomy of Catalonia within a Federal Spain. We somehow got stray dishes, but the hotel was in a state of exuberance that was too much for such trifles as food.

We rushed out into the street and found a big procession starting, waving the yellow and red striped Catalan flag—and incidentally several Spanish ones, too. We joined in and went all around the odd narrow streets shouting and cheering. Everyone was thrilled. We went to bed exhausted but happy. We had found our land and we had seen history in the making.

The next morning Antonia came in with our hot water. She looked white-faced and shaken. '*Muy malo! Muy malo!*' was all we could get out of her. We dressed hurriedly and went into the square. Everyone stood round looking pictures of dejection. Several women were crying. I left Archie to try to discover what was wrong and went to see about a car to take us to the station. All I could gather was that nothing would induce the owner or the driver to use the car. Archie came back and said that as far as he could make out Companys had spoken too soon; there had been a reverse and the whole Left Party of the Catalan Government were in prison. There was apparently fierce fighting in Asturias and they were still holding out at points in Barcelona.

Our chief concern was to get home because of Archie's work, although we were intensely interested in the situation. We finally found an obliging German who said he would drive us to the frontier. Apparently all the trains were stopped. We had very little luggage and were soon in the car. My chief concern was a large painting I had bought, a Zügel. I hated the idea of having it riddled with bullets. A Tossa man watched us getting ready, and just as we were going to start he came up. He was very polite, but he advised us not to leave. There was no news of the situation towards the frontier and in any case he was very anxious not to have any bloodshed around Tossa. There was a general strike and our driver would be considered a blackleg. We assured him we should hate to have anything to do with strike-breaking, and went back to our hotel. We neither of us wanted to leave Tossa and it seemed a marvellous excuse, but Archie felt he must do all in his power to get back to work. If he failed we would continue our holiday with a clear conscience and the added excitement of a revolution.

We eventually decided we must try to go by sea. We found an aged fisherman who had not heard about the trouble and who thought we were mad, but agreed to take us to Port Bou. It might take fourteen hours, probably longer. I felt we did indeed suffer for our consciences' and the *News Chronicle's* sake. However, before we could get our things to the boat the fisherman came up to the hotel to say he was sorry, he had just heard about things. So that was that.

The next thing to do was to try to telephone to the paper. The Tossa telephone has its exchange in the kitchen of the operator, so we sat in comfort while he tried to get through. His wife and attractive daughters were fascinated by the pattern of the jersey I was wearing, and I tried to explain the stitch to them. They were far more concerned with that than with the trouble. After two hours' real hard work we heard Lloret, the next village, on the line. And we got there via

Madrid!

Our consciences were at rest and we went back to Rovira's for dinner. We were eating as usual in the patio, and of course the radio was turned on. We heard a speech in Catalan and then there was a long silence. Suddenly a terrific burst of machine-gun fire nearly split our eardrums. Rovira dropped the dish he was carrying. We all gasped, certain that the Spanish Army was in the street. The firing ceased and a very Castilian voice said, in Spanish, that they had just taken over the radio station, and proceeded to read various new decrees. Rovira cleared up the mess on the floor and dinner proceeded. The speaker's voice faltered and finally tailed away, there were some more shots, a crash or two, and someone announced, in Catalan, that there would be a programme of dance music. For some time we listened to last year's records, then the radio was shut off. In about ten minutes the Castilian came back, having finally captured the radio station, and announced a programme of music. We found a slight consolation in the fact that they had to play records of *sardanas*, the Catalan national dance.

For the next few days we could not quite make up our minds whether we ought to lead our usual carefree holiday existence. It seemed wrong to spend hours in the sun on the beach when everyone was so upset and miserable. However, the days seemed to have a wonderful effect on the elastic Catalan spirits, and, despite the bad news from Asturias, where the miners were being incredibly brave in a losing fight, everyone seemed resigned and carried on as usual. The weather was particularly brilliant, even for Spain, and we spent our enforced stay going for long walks and picnics and lying for hours on the beach or in the sea. After five days came the news that the strike was off and trains and buses would be normal the following day.

The village held its usual market for the first time since the revolution started. All the old women were sitting as usual among their heaps of vegetables in the square and the Tossa housewives were clustering round them, doing far more chattering than buying. The town crier came into the square and blew his little trumpet. There was a lull in the conversations. The town crier then read a decree that had been published in Barcelona three days previously, to the effect that no one was to go about the streets in groups, in fact, two people together were considered to be a group and would be shot at sight. The revolution being now over, the decree had just reached Tossa. For a moment there was a stupefied silence as the meaning of the town crier's words sank in. Then an old woman picked up her basket and pointed a bunch of carrots at three other old women who were staring amazed at the town crier.

'Pom! Pom!' she said, threatening them with the carrots.

Rovira saw us off with much handshaking and lugubrious sighs that he might be shot before we came back again, but in any case he would be delighted to see us when we did come back. He looked such an odd little figure, with his bare feet and rolled-up trousers, which were always braced up so high he looked as if he would be hoisted in the air at any minute. We left owing four weeks' hotel bill, a large sum for the picture I had bought, and a hundred pesetas that Rovira insisted that we should take with us, besides odd sums borrowed from Marcus. There was a chance that we might find a bank open in Gerona, but we had no idea what had happened in the town, except rumours of heavy fighting during the first day of the trouble.

We arrived to find the station guarded by soldiers sitting in deck-chairs, with fixed bayonets. The streets were full of soldiers; we hardly saw a civilian. The bank was surrounded by sentries, but it was open. We changed our letter of credit and arranged for money for our debts to be sent to Tossa. This all took a long time, and when we finally emerged into the sunshine again we had just time to catch our train to France.

We both were immediately struck by the fact that there were no sentries outside. Only their chairs remained. The streets were empty. I said at once that there must be a terrific battle going on outside the town. We hurried to the station. Fifteen empty deck-chairs showed where the guards had been. The one porter was standing surveying them absently. Archie asked him what had happened. He did not seem to understand. Then as we pointed to the chairs and the empty street, light dawned. "Ah, that?" He collected our two small cases. "Why, it is *siesta* time now!"

We found the train absolutely packed with people who had been held up in Barcelona, and of course there was the usual amount of hysterical conjecture as to whether the train would be attacked or the bridges blown up. Nothing whatever happened, but it was a relief to get out of the crowded train at Port Bou. We scrummed past the passport officials, who were having a hectic time coping with the crowds, but even so one of them, a beautiful young man with the most stupendous eyelashes I have ever seen, who had stamped my passport each time I had crossed the frontier, was able to recognize me. He stamped our passport, gazing into my eyes—which turned out to be very lucky for us, and bore out another of my theories, to lavish as much helpless sweetness as possible on all officials.

Eventually we reached Cerbère, the French frontier. The moment we were on the platform the lights went out. Everyone thought a revolution had broken out in France, but it was merely an electricity breakdown. After a scene of very French confusion candles were produced and our passports were examined by the light of improvised lanterns. My last vision of the scene before packing into the Paris train was luggage intended for Paris being hurled from the Geneva express as it drew out of the station.

Some time later, people in the carriage began to discuss their adventures. We gathered that one trainload of people had left Barcelona the day before and had arrived at Cerbère, but no one was allowed over the frontier without a special stamp from the military authorities, so everyone had to return to Barcelona. We asked to see it, and fellow passengers showed us a red stamp in their passports. Of course, in Tossa we had not heard a word about this, and if it had not been for my distracted young man at Port Bou we would have been sent back to Barcelona!

3

In London again, we found that the excitement of having actually discovered the land and sent off the power of attorney to Marcus entirely eclipsed the fact that we had been caught in a revolution. The Press had splashed the fighting in Barcelona, and it was as hard to convince people then, as now, that one may be within fifty miles—or even fifty yards—of trouble and not be at all involved in it. But the fact that we had returned safely and were still full of our project finally convinced our friends that we could not have been in much personal danger.

We now began to have some idea of what getting things done in Spain meant. We had thought that one bought land and then started to build on it. This is not at all the Spanish idea. First there were various difficulties about Marcus's power of attorney. Then, when the Spanish lawyer representing the owner of the land was finally convinced that everything was in order, there ensued a long series of delays occasioned by difficulties about a road to the land. It meant negotiating with half a dozen other smallholders, each quite unhurried, and the posts worked overtime between London and Tossa. Marcus nobly took over the Tossa end, and we used the delay to start our publicity campaign.

In this we were doubly lucky. We were, by the nature of Archie's work, right in the heart of 'selling', and we had something easy to sell.

The first thing to be done was to get up a folder about Tossa and ourselves. This nearly led to a divorce. In the end we both wrote the text independently. I thought Archie's was full of information but very dull; he thought mine was colourful and interesting to read but gave no information at all. In the end we managed to combine both efforts, and the results have been successful beyond our fondest hopes. But the crowning success was, after all, Archie's. He was inspired for the introduction. I quote it because it was the cause of so much comment and every guest reacted to it differently.

DO YOU LIKE . . .
Bowler hats? Cannes? Obsequious servants? A Week in Lovely Lucerne? Olde Englishe Shoppes? Crowds? Eastbourne? *The Monarch of the Glen*? Tapioca?
If you do, please leave what follows to those who lack your appreciation of the *Things That Always Have Been.*

We were fascinated by the different things in the 'Do You Like . . .' list that were people's especial hates. One family wanted to come to us, but they spent every holiday on a farm in Scotland, and one of the children simply refused to entertain the idea of coming to Spain. Then he found the folder lying about and read the first paragraph. Tapioca decided him; it was his pet aversion.

Some people wrote from the address of an antique shop and added hastily a postscript. 'This is not an Olde Englishe Shoppe!' and we knew that we should like them. An American couple who had a surfeit of expensive European hotels descended on us with cries of relief; they had read our folder in a glitter of chromium-plate. A very determined person assured us that he never travelled without his copy of *The Monarch of the Glen* and would we object if he put it up in his own room? A delightful couple from Eastbourne said they did not bother about any other details: they knew Tossa must be quite different from their home town. It interested us to notice that all twelve suggestions in the list came in for an almost equal share of comment.

Actually the folder broke most of the rules of advertising which we knew; we would have broken some more if we had

26

known some more. The "Do You Like's" and a reference to whitewashed walls were, we were told, merely inverted snob appeal. Our direct personal request to readers to take our word for it was definitely not done. The sentence 'In our opinion the Costa Brava is the loveliest, friendliest place under the sun, but we do not pretend to be objective about it' was permissible in a letter but not in a folder. And so on. All true, I have no doubt, according to the expert's text-book, but by this time we were prepared to have a knock at expertism every time it raised its head. And we managed, too, to sell Tossa to quite a number of experts in sales and sales-resistance.

I was disturbed in the middle of packing by the usual ring at the door and the usual vacuum cleaner salesman outside. It happened that I was interested not in buying a new cleaner but in disposing of my old one, which was of no use to me in Spain. He came in, complete with paraphernalia, and spread things all over the uncarpeted floor. I explained that I was just moving to Spain. He started a moving address on the usefulness of a cleaner in Spain. I told him a little about Tossa and left a folder with him while I got some beer. I was then bombarded with questions, and the young man finally left with his boxes, several folders, and a conviction that he would spend his next holiday in Tossa. Which he did. One advertising consultant did, however, get one back at us when we were becoming too pleased with ourselves. 'Certainly,' he said, 'your folder sounds completely convincing and cheerful. But that doesn't mean you are so hot as copywriters. Try to sound convincing or cheerful about life insurance.' Naturally we were only too pleased to give Tossa the credit and not ourselves!

Owing to the helpful interest that our printing friends took in the project, the fact that Archie could do all the technical part of the layout, arranging the photographs of Tossa, and the thousand and one things to do with making up a folder, and also that I could design and draw the cover, we were able to produce a folder on the scale of those usually found in travel agencies to advertise an entire country.

We got a step further in our dislike of experts when it came to the actual printing. After repeated battles to convince an infuriating manager that we knew what we wanted we at last succeeded in getting the finished folder, at the cost of a great deal of unnecessary delay and the sack of the manager, but at extremely little cost in actual money.

We were quite unprepared for the enormous interest our project roused in everyone. We were lucky in that we had many friends in many different 'sets'. We knew the skating world well; of course, Fleet Street and Bloomsbury; I was brought up in the country and knew the hunting, fishing crowd; I had many relations in the army; Archie's relations seemed all to be doctors; each contact brought us into another small world. We found someone in each bursting with enthusiasm about the idea, gave them a bunch of folders, and told them to get on with it. However, we found our best ambassador on our own territory. An ex-colleague of Archie's, Jack Cannell, suddenly became a Tossa enthusiast.

That meant that Cannell talked, dreamt, ate, lived the Casa Johnstone. No one was safe. In peaceful pubs people were attacked and buttonholed while Cannell poured out a jerky stream of sentences about the Casa Johnstone. Perfect strangers had folders thrust into their hands and were told to go to Spain next year. Casa Johnstone propaganda flowed from Cannell like a mountain torrent. He exuded Casa Johnstone from every pore. Hair curling wildly over his eyes, hands out-thrust with folders, he strode from bar to bar thundering the praises of the Casa Johnstone. And people listen to Cannell. He has never yet spoken or written two consecutive sentences that a sub-editor would pass unaltered, but every sentence is dynamic and commands attention. One becomes so fascinated by his flow of words, his trick of pointing an accusing finger to emphasize a point and keeping it pointed until the point is driven home, and above all by his own unbounded enthusiasm, that one hangs on his every word. Cannell does at least three jobs, each of which would be a whole-time job for an ordinary man. Besides writing books which are best-sellers he works for the BBC and contributes features to various periodicals as well. But his energies needed an outlet, and Tossa and the Casa Johnstone provided it.

It was through him that we were introduced to the BBC and the Bolivar. We went to the audition room at Broadcasting House to listen to one of Cannell's 'In Town Tonight' series. It was my first visit to the BBC headquarters. Its atmosphere is that of flunkeyism run riot. My first shock was hearing little bell-hops—the place is alive with them—and hall porters all speaking with such beautiful BBC accents. Then the priceless air of solemn importance over everything makes it very difficult not to break out loudly into ribald song. We were conducted by page boys bursting with elocution and eventually arrived at a chaste room with a loudspeaker, a row of chairs, a large tired palm, and a bucket half-filled with sand. We sat at the end of the row of chairs and looked at the loudspeaker. It was very beautiful, pale grey, with scrolls on it.

There were several other people listening raptly to a soprano voice from the grey scrolls. Presently the soprano voice stopped and there was a sudden coming to life of the family. The door opened and Cannell burst in. The atmosphere wakened up, and even the palm drooped less. The door, of course, opened and closed noiselessly, but Cannell seemed to have no reverence for the BBC He told us in his clear voice that 'In Town Tonight' was about to begin, pulled a chair out of line with a noise that made the palm wince, and sat down.

There is something very terrifying about being compelled to listen to anything. The hushed atmosphere and the people sitting in a row as on the deck of a ship had a disastrous effect on me. I hardly heard a word of 'In Town Tonight', I was trying so hard to keep serious. The ship illusion was enhanced when Archie looked wildly round for an ashtray and someone seized the sand-filled bucket and handed it along the row of chairs. I managed to control my now almost hysterical giggles until we were back in the august entrance hall. There we were introduced to several people who were very much interested in the idea of a Tossa holiday, and we all moved over to the Bolivar to discuss the matter further.

The Bolivar is a bar just behind the Langham and definitely belongs to the broadcasters and those of the BBC staff whose spirit has not yet been chilled by the icy respectability of Broadcasting House. It is a fact that the Bolivar is frowned on by the powers that be in Broadcasting House, but only once was any action taken. A commissionaire was deputed to go over to the Bolivar heavily disguised as a frequenter of bars. His job was to make a note of the names of all the BBC staff present during the evening. They could then be ponderously lectured in impeccable English on the undesirability of spending too much of their own time in bars.

Some of the lighter-minded of the staff got wind of this and immediately communicated this truly butler's pantry trick to their friends on the Press. The consequences were unexpected for the butler. Not a single member of the BBC staff turned up, but the bar was full of the more irresponsible of Fleet Street's hard-worked wireless correspondents. The commissionaire had the evening of his life; it was made clear to him that he was the success of the party. Finally he returned, or was returned, to Broadcasting House. Thereafter the Bolivar was merely ignored by the great ones.

It is a curious fact that different sets of people have their own pet pubs. The staff of nearly every big paper has its favourite haunt, generally, of course, the one that wastes the least time between its doors and the office door. While Archie and I knew most of the Fleet Street and surrounding pubs we had never been in the Bolivar and had never met the habitués. Cannell introduced us and immediately collected a crowd in his vicinity round the bar. We left him handing out folders and sales talk and were immediately buttonholed by people eager to hear about the hotel idea. Val Valentine wanted to make a song about Tossa on the lines of The Isle of Capri, but we begged him not to, as we wanted Tossa to remain unspoiled.

We were amused to notice how deeply people got immersed in the folder and how if someone lent his he always insisted on having it back. A rather sad-looking man sat alone at the bar near me. I was having a rest, listening to Cannell. The sad man kept trying to see the folder that was in my hand. Finally I kindly handed it to him, explaining rather uninterestedly what it was. Later I asked Cannell who he was. He was a very important BBC official, whose name I must not mention, owing to the peculiar attitude of his fellow-chiefs with regard to pubs. I have learned this bit of caution from my Scottish sub-editor husband. It is sufficient to say that he controlled a staff of about a hundred, and he went off with pockets bulging with folders to distribute.

We found afterwards that from that one night in the Bolivar we had nearly as many BBC people at the Casa Johnstone as Fleet Street people, and we liked them nearly as well.

4

Our Fleet Street campaign was, to say the least, hilarious. We used to have an early dinner and get to the Falstaff at about eight o'clock. The Falstaff is the least typical of Fleet Street pubs, but it has a deservedly good reputation for comfort and lager beer. If one wants real pub atmosphere and bitter one must go across to the Cheshire Cheese, the Kings and Keys, Mooney's or, at the bottom of Bouverie Street, the Temple, full of *News Chronicle* and *Daily Mail* men or, tucked away up a side alley, the tiny Welsh Harp, where one gets the best toasted cheese in London.

There is a strange migratory instinct among newspapermen that makes it quite easy to find certain people in certain pubs at certain times. It is as mysterious as the gathering of swallows on a given date. At about 8 pm most of the people we knew or wanted to know were to be found in the Falstaff.

For me the chief drawback of the Falstaff is that there is no bitter in the downstairs dive. Also, if I were a newspaper man I would find the almost life size faces of my colleagues which decorate the walls rather trying when I see so much of them anyway. The photographs are well worth hanging, not as examples of modern beauty, but as fine character studies of journalists, ancient and modern.

The two nicest people in the Falstaff are undoubtedly the girls behind the bar. They were very interested in our plans and promised to distribute some folders. We hoped they would be able to come out to Tossa some day and get a new idea of the cost of drinks. Nearly as faithful to the Falstaff as the two behind the bar were Jimmy Foster and Owen Lookyou. They were two to whom the migratory sense did not apply. At almost any hour one or other, if not both, were to be found in the Falstaff. Jimmy did desert it occasionally for one nearer Scotland Yard. He was crime specialist on one of the Big Four, whilst Owen was on its literary staff. Owen was a Welshman and late in the evening the Celtic twilight would descend on him and he would have visions of moonlight beaches, the Little People, and cheap brandy. Tossa seemed to meet the case very well. He and Jimmy decided then and there to come out for their next holidays, which would be around the following September.

The only drawback they could find was that, despite the usual lurid idea of Spanish morals, Tossa was innocent of brothels. I explained that according to Spanish law a town was allowed a house with a red light only when it had a population of two thousand and over. Tossa had only one thousand seven hundred. This seemed an insurmountable difficulty. Owen had an idea that we might import three hundred beautiful girls to make up the number. Jimmy wanted to manage 'Les Johnstone Girls'. We explained that the Costa Brava's red light district's nearest point was San Feliu de Guixols, about twenty kilometres away, and thought we would stick to our idea of trying to run an hotel.

Archie always had to go off to work at 9 pm, and I was generally left to carry on the good work of talking Tossa until closing-time. We found afterwards that our publicity had been on far too large a scale for a small place such as ours. Our official capacity was twenty guests; we had thirty-five our first August because the odd fifteen refused to take 'no' for an answer; we flooded Rovira's with our surplus and still had to write more than a hundred 'House Full' letters.

I have since learned that the normal procedure with a new hotel is to make provision for two fairly lean years until personal recommendations of guests begin to ensure a good flow of business, and that our having an hotel fully booked up for a whole season before the building was finished was something unheard of in hotel history.

Of course, we have had the interviewer's overworked question, 'To what do you owe your success?' put to us hundreds of times, and I must try to answer it here. I think we owed at least 90 per cent of our success directly or indirectly to Fleet Street. Journalists talk far better than they write and we had given them something to talk about. I have never met a journalist who didn't want to run a pub, and running a pub in Spain was almost too much for their imagination. Our pub became their pub. Reporters go everywhere and meet everybody—talking all the time.

Not only did they boost the Casa Johnstone, but they themselves came to us in their scores. Let me say here gladly and gratefully that they were a joy to have around the house. They are the world's best mixers, but they surpassed themselves by the way they overcame such difficulties as complete ignorance of any language except, presumably, English, and had long conversations with Catalans over their beer and brandy. I was most impressed by the wonderful way they mixed with any definitely un-Fleet Street guests who might be there as well. A bewildered elderly lady would think for the first moment that she had arrived in Bedlam, but in a very little while she would be giggling over her wine and water and calling them 'such dear boys'. It used to amaze me sometimes to think that they managed to hold down responsible, highly paid jobs on great national newspapers.

Our idea, too, seemed to have a universal appeal. We found how true that was when we were running the place. Fleet Street toughs liked the idea of a place where brandy was three shillings a bottle and where they could cast off their inhibitions; real hard workers wanted somewhere where they could lie in the sun and do nothing all day, but have plenty of bars and dancing at night; unadventurous people seemed to have been waiting all their lives to go to Spain, but had waited until they found some place run by English people who could understand them when they spoke, and who knew what drains were. Most people were, of course, fascinated by the idea of living for about seven or eight shillings a day and having really hot water on tap. I found that I had to do no salesman stuff, no saying of my little piece. People bombarded me with questions.

Archie's prize bit of publicity was at the *Daily Sketch* dinner. Most newspapers have an annual dinner, to which are invited all the staff and their wives and ex-colleagues and friends. Archie was on the Sketch before he joined the *News Chronicle*, and we went to this dinner to say goodbye to many of his old friends. The first thing that strikes one on looking along the tables at the guests at a *Sketch* dinner is the amazing area of forehead that is visible. If all the *Daily Sketch* foreheads were put side by side, or length to length, they would—but this is too reminiscent of the Queen Mary. Anyway, the Chairman, Jack Greenslade, grandest forehead of them all, welcomed Archie and his project right nobly and referred to it in his speech. Thereupon Archie was called upon. He had never spoken in public in his life, but even the most experienced after-dinner speaker might have found himself in a quandary; it was not possible to get up and give everyone an earful about Tossa and the Casa Johnstone after the marvellous break we had already had from the Chairman and another speaker. I waited, wondering what he would do, and then it came.

'Ladies and Gentlemen,' said Archie (looking very Scotch, and his forehead holding its own very well among the gleaming ones turned towards him, he appeared as if after-dinner speaking was a hobby of his), 'I shan't say a word about Tossa and the Casa Johnstone. The fact that I have been asked to speak to say goodbye to you all and the generous references to our venture in the other speeches prohibits me from doing any more publicity. I won't say a word about the lovely climate, hot and cold water in all rooms, brandy three shillings a bottle, and seven-and-six a day full pension. Nor shall I talk about the beaches, the glorious blue Mediterranean, the amusing bars. I will only say goodbye to my many friends on the *Sketch* and I hope that I shall see many of you again in Tossa!' The end was drowned in the roars of laughter as people realized what he was doing.

There is a definite technique about handing out a folder at the right moment. It is quite all right for someone else to thrust it at people, but we had to be more circumspect. We are sitting, for example, at a table with some people we hardly know. Someone mentions a date the following month. We say casually, 'Oh! Next month we shall be in Spain.' People invariably ask where, and for how long. 'A little, unspoiled place, Tossa de Mar. We are going to start an hotel there.' Immediate interest and request for further information. Presently one fumbles for a pencil, to jot down our address, in case. 'I have a card or, better still, a folder. I believe I had one somewhere—ah, here it is, rather creased I'm afraid.' Immediate silence on receiving folder. Then, with increased interest: 'This sounds just what I have been looking for. I must tell my wife about this.' Starts to give back folder. We say, 'Oh, please keep it,' and settle down to a long inquisition.

The first party we gave to celebrate our departure was on the night Archie handed in his notice to the *News Chronicle*. It started at 6 pm in the 'Falstaff', wandered through various other pubs, and ended in the Temple. Archie had to leave it at nine as usual, but as the Temple was a mere unsteady step from the *News Chronicle* offices he occasionally appeared during the rest of the evening in his shirt sleeves. We were rather concerned in case the next day's late editions came out with a front-page splash about Tossa and the Casa Johnstone.

5

One of the questions that everyone asked us and one which we frequently asked ourselves was: What about our staff? We realized that the first year would be very hard work and that things would be more complicated by the fact that we spoke Spanish badly, that everyone in Tossa spoke Catalan anyway, although most of them spoke a kind of Spanish as well. We had made inquiries when we were there buying the land and gathered that one could employ by the day women who had their homes in the village and who would work by the hour. I decided to do all the cooking and to get someone to do the preparing of the vegetables etc, and the rough kitchen work. We had asked about the possibility of electricity and, according to Marcus, there seemed to be a good chance of it. There was no gas and the only kitchen I had seen was the one at Rovira's hotel, which had a row of strange little charcoal fires which filled me with misgiving and the kitchen with dust. Then, with perhaps two women to do the rooms and beds, we thought we should be able to manage.

The only thing that was worrying me was, oddly enough, the enormous response we were getting to our publicity. That meant we should have to start with the hotel nearly full instead of being able to practise a bit on our long-suffering friends. I was discussing the matter of staff with an acquaintance who had spent some time at a coast village between Tossa and Barcelona at an hotel run by a German. Most of the guests were English, but the only English-speaking member of staff was a twenty-one year old German boy, Walter Leonard, a friend of our informant. Leonard, he told us, had been at the crack hotel school in Lausanne, and he was the real mainstay of this hotel. He did all the foreign correspondence, catering and waiting, was very popular with the guests and, in a word, a paragon. His wages were five shillings a week without a share of the 10 per cent item on every guest's bill, but he was treated as one of the family. He spoke Spanish, Catalan and French perfectly, and he knew Tossa well. Obviously, said our friend, we could offer him a more tempting job; perhaps the bare promise that he would not be treated as one of the family unless he liked would be enough.

Leonard was then on holiday with his parents in Paris. His mother, Lotte Leonard, the well-known singer of German Lieder and oratorios, worked there at a conservatoire. He was coming to London for a few days to stay with our friend, who had liked him tremendously.

We were very much interested. We had not thought of employing an 'expert', but someone so heaven-sent as this seemed worth considering. The chief fact that interested us was not so much that he was a trained waiter—we thought waiting couldn't be so difficult, after all, and Archie would be able to hand round a few plates—but that we would have someone who spoke Spanish and Catalan and who knew the local people.

The upshot was that when he came to London he came out to Hampstead to see us. We have since found that every person has the same first reaction to Leonard. 'What a nice boy!' they all exclaim. We did the same. As a matter of fact, he really is a nice boy. We were enchanted by his charming manners, his good looks—there is something about black hair, very dark sunburnt skin and light grey eyes with thick black lashes that is completely devastating in mid-winter in London—and, despite his southern appearance, his air of efficiency. He was naturally somewhat cautious about accepting a job out of the blue with apparently rather mad foreigners, but he said he would discuss it with his parents on his return to Paris and if he decided to come in with us we were to send him a proper contract. He was to get a percentage of the total takings, with a fixed minimum which alone was much more than his present salary.

We had absolutely no conscience about taking him from his employer, but Leonard was quite upset at the idea of doing anything to inconvenience him. He had some strange idea of his own that because the hotel-owner worked his own daughters even harder and paid them nothing at all, the staff who were paid, however little, had nothing much to complain about. We heard afterwards that Leonard used to get a bit of extra money from tips direct from the guests, as he was the only person who had any real contact with them, and that he used to share this with the wretched daughters because he was so sorry for them!

Soon after he got back to Paris we heard from him that he would accept our offer. We sent him off the contract and arranged that he should go on with his job until we let him know. We thought that if he gave a month's notice it was ample, and the chances were that he would be asked to leave at once.

Soon we were really progressing. Our publicity was in full swing and doing marvellously; we had the nucleus of our staff, and with Leonard to cope, I had no more fear of Catalan daily women; we had managed to sell most of the really rather nice modern furniture in our flat to our friends; I had bought an Edward Wolfe picture, which I was dying to see on a whitewashed wall in Tossa. It was the second picture I had ever bought; the other was the Zügel I had brought back from Tossa.

Zügel lived in Tossa and was building a house at the foot of our hill. It was his suggestion that we should have as many of his pictures as we wanted to hang in the hotel, and if anyone wanted to buy one, so much the better. I was thrilled, as the superb design and colouring of his pictures would make any room interesting.

Best of all, the house was really started. After a vigorous

exchange of letters between Marcus and me with regard to the exact situation, I finally sent a wire saying the house was to be built as high as humanly possible. I had a rather terrifying thought that Marcus might retaliate by perching it on the extreme top of the hill, but I decided his Jewish caution would prevail. We had a letter to say they had had to knock off work for a day from the excavating of the hillside because a stick of dynamite had not gone off. We often wonder it if ever did or if they ever found it. Then they had to lose another day's work because a swarm of bees interrupted them. But on the whole the construction seemed to be going on well. The weather was marvellous, which was lucky, because February and March are supposed to be the only rainy months in Tossa.

About this time we had a letter from Rovira. We had written to him to explain our intention of starting an hotel in Tossa. We were so fond of him that we hated to think that he might imagine we were in opposition to him. We tried to make it clear that we were only concerned with the foreign market, mostly English, and that any overflow from us would, of course, go to him. The chief advantage to him would be in the off seasons, as his hotel was invariably full in the summer. His letter was typically Rovira and typically Catalan. With the most charming phrases he welcomed us as fellow-hoteliers and assured us that, far from considering us as rivals, he would be delighted to lay at our feet his knowledge of hotel-keeping, his money, and his entire hotel. We knew Rovira well enough to realize that he meant every word.

The work of packing up was delayed by the constant ringing of the telephone. We had unwisely put our phone number while we were in London in our few small advertisements and also on a printed slip attached to the folder. People in town thought it would be so simple if we just came along to talk it all over with them. It was really hard to convince them that we couldn't possibly have time to see them all, even if we had nothing else to do. I did manage to see two members of the

Forum Club who asked me to tea there. They had heard about us from a colleague of Archie's. In the middle of eating delicious toast one of them made the remark that put the Casa Johnstone on velvet from the very start. 'Why,' she said, 'don't you put your folder in the *Forum Record*?'

We made enquiries, produced three thousand folders in time for the next edition of the *Forum Record* and that was that. Apart from the shoals of enquiries that descended on us the secretary of the club rang me up and asked if I could let her have some folders to keep at the club, as so many people wanted them.

We also managed to see Cyril Wyer and his friends. As his mother had predicted, Cyril was very keen to come out on his motorbike, and had persuaded to motorcyclist friends to join him. Cyril, who delivered the groceries for his father, arrived at our back door with some celery and his friends, and came into our flat for a beer while we discussed it. They were delighted with the folder and left promising to arrive at the Casa Johnstone on 21st July. Apparently the Pyrenees held no terrors for them.

I answered the phone and wrote two letters frantically while men clumped round and took away boxes. Finally they removed the one under the typewriter. 'Archie,' I said, 'the end has arrived. We must move into an hotel.'

We saw the last case out, gave away the last piece of linoleum, sold my lovely enamel gas cooker for three pounds to someone up the road, and moved to Anderton's in Fleet Street.

The *News Chronicle* kept up its reputation for generosity to the last and let Archie off the last week of his notice, but not his pay. His colleagues gave him a farewell lunch and, with an eye to even more Tossa publicity later, a really fine reflex camera. We still answered the telephone and wrote letters, but we had a little time for saying goodbye to our friends and relations.

Our last night we had a final party at the Falstaff. Some old colleagues of Archie's from Manchester managed to turn up, and Lester Wilson, Northern Editor of the *Sunday Dispatch,* spent an enthralled hour or so with a strange artist who had rung me up and said she wanted to come to Tossa. She had sounded rather nice so I invited her to the party. We had to refuse Lester's offer to come out and be our barman—he was the hundred-and-tenth on the list, anyway—so he and the artist decided to start roundabouts on the beach and a nice English tea-room. There was some dark connection between the two enterprises that no one could see. The party filled the Falstaff dive, and anyone who was there unwittingly was soon roped in. Everyone was very encouraging and determined to see us in Tossa. After closing time we all went off to the Café Royal and continued the party. Donald Calthrop came over to Archie. He had heard about the hotel idea and wanted details. I found myself at a table rather at the end of our crowd, with two strange men whose faces were very familiar. I greeted them politely, but could not place them until at last one of them mentioned *Murder in Motley,* then running at the Kingsway Theatre. They were two of the actors and they were so familiar to me because I knew the authors of the play and had often had a box for it. They were very interested and immediately joined our party. Epstein was sitting at his usual table and I should love to be able to add that he became fascinated by the Casa Johnstone and designed our bird-bath, but he did not even see us.

The next day we left by the 1 pm plane for Paris. I spent the morning walking my small black Pekinese, Beetle by name, round and round the Temple, because she could have no more exercise for twenty-four hours. Also coming with us, for his Easter holidays, was my fifteen-year-old cousin John, from Charterhouse. He had never been out of England, except to and from Ireland.

Beetle loathed the plane but adored Paris. She ate four

brioches at the Café de la Paix and had a swagger in the Champs Élysées. She did not mind the long train journey at all, but after a heavenly meal of chicken and rice, which I wheedled from the train chef, she lay flat on her back with her head in a long-suffering Frenchman's lap and snored as only Pekes can. I was so ashamed when the train stopped at stations and Beetle's snores rose above the clatter of milk-cans.

We arrived at Gerona far too excited to be tired and began the long car drive to Tossa. We were itching to catch our first glimpse of our house.

Book II — On a Winner

1

The drive from Gerona is long but fascinating. The first part, over the wide Gerona plain, goes through little villages and fields of corn and maize. Occasionally there are glimpses of the snow-topped Pyrenees in the far distance. Soon a long range of hills hides the end of the road, with the Llagostera church rising proudly in their midst. John, my cousin, was thrilled. 'Do we go over those hills?' he asked excitedly. I explained that we went through Llagostera village and climbed up a twisty road until we were at the top of the range. Then we went down and down in a series of hairpin bends until at last we came to Tossa. 'But,' I added, 'don't be surprised if you think that we will never get to the sea. The whole drive makes one think it is miles inland. I suppose it's because everything is so green and the hills are covered in cork-oak trees right to Tossa. You can see the sea just before we get to Tossa, but not the beach. And we ought to see our house as soon as we get to the straight bit of road with the plane-trees outside the village. That is, if Marcus has really built it high enough.'

We stopped the car at the top of the range to let John see the Pyrenees across the plain, shining in the April sun. Then we turned the bend and started the run down to Tossa. John yelled when he saw the sea at last, a deep-blue V beyond the rolling, tree-covered hills below us. Then we lost it again in a valley before coming to the avenue of great planes which marks the entrance to the village. By this time we were hanging out of the car. Archie saw it first. Marcus had given in nobly and the scaffolding was sticking out of a bare patch half-way up the hillside. As we got nearer we saw that the first floor was finished and the second-floor window frames were standing up in place. Dozens of men were crawling like ants up and down the new S-shaped road. For the first time I realized that the Casa Johnstone was an actual fact. However, even hotel builders must eat, and we went straight to Rovira's.

Rovira was delighted to see us and full of the new project. He took an immediate liking to John, who was thrilled by being greeted in streams of Catalan. Beetle, on the contrary, firmly made up her mind there and then that Catalan was a revolting language, the people were impossible and that never would she unbend in one degree while she had to stay in such a place. And she has not yet changed her mind. It has amused us enormously to see how the local people, who are not noted for their love of animals, try for hours to get Beetle to notice them.

Archie and I had our old room which was, and still is, known as "Our Room". John had a small room next door. Beetle slept with us. We rushed down to the patio to eat an enormous lunch before going up to the house. To our amazement the patio was crammed with people, mostly English. The year before, in April, we had been the only English people in the hotel. We asked Rovira what had happened. He shrugged his shoulders and said, 'Casa Johnstone' in a resigned voice. Then we realized that these were some of the people who had written in answer to our advertisements and who had wanted to come for the Easter holidays. I had answered that unfortunately we would not be ready, but that I could thoroughly recommend Rovira's. We expected Rovira to be delighted, but the strange little man seemed rather annoyed: he hated having to work so hard in an off season! However, later, when he calculated his takings for April, May, and June, he was reconciled to having done so much before his heaviest three months. That was the only point on which he was not quite pleased with us. He thought our idea was splendid, although he allowed himself a little quiet amusement at the idea of us running a hotel. He put every scrap of his years of knowledge at our disposal and his charming wife allowed me free run of her kitchen to learn Catalan cooking and to get an idea of catering, etc. I found out afterwards that Leonard was quite capable of doing all the catering, but I had not then realized what a treasure he was going to be. Which was just as well, as I should have sat down and done no more work at all.

We went up to the house directly after lunch and were amazed at the way it had grown. We went all over it, climbing up and down scaffolding, while Beetle sat on the ground and screamed. In our complete ignorance of building houses the place seemed nearly finished. We did not realize that it is an old Catalan custom to complete a building and then knock nearly everything down again to put in such important items as pipes. We were introduced to Jaume, the chief mason, whose father, Dionys, was building Zügel's house in the valley below. The air is so clear in Tossa that father and son used to shout easily to each other from house-top to house-top, five hundred yards away. Of course, that was helped by the Catalan voice, which is capable of more noise than a loudspeaker. Jaume is a very good-looking, huge, black-browed creature. At first sight he is rather intimidating, but on closer inspection one sees his mild brown eyes, and actually he has the sweetest nature imaginable. He tried hard to comfort Beetle, who was still shrieking at being left below with the awful foreigners, but she attacked him savagely, without the slightest effect. To this day Jaume comes over whenever he sees Beetle and tries his best blandishments, but she still attacks him.

When we had seen everything we yielded to John's silent entreaties and showed him the beaches and rocks. The coast was not so new to him, as he spent all his summer holidays on

47

the south coast of Ireland and the Costa Brava is very similar, but grander. The people fascinated him and the fishing-boats were different from Irish ones, so we left him arranging a fishing trip. We heard the fishermen talking Catalan and assumed that John was holding forth in Gaelic. However, he came back, and apparently had arranged everything to their mutual satisfaction, as later he really did go fishing.

That evening we went early to bed. We had asked the Marcuses to dinner for the following evening. Archie fell into his usual sound sleep almost immediately, but I lay awake for a while listening to Beetle's snores and trying to believe that I really was there in Rovira's huge Catalan bed with a print of San Antonio (ribaldly known as 'Toni' by the Roviras) hanging over it, and opposite an oleograph of a praying nun that was so awful we adored it and refused Rovira's offer to remove it. Next to it was a really good old French print of someone being raped.

It was not hard to convince myself that I was in Catalonia: the shouts and yells from the street outside told me two Catalans were having a quiet chat in the market-place. But I found it difficult to realize that the rush and turmoil of leaving London were over; that our baggage was on the high seas and would arrive in due course in Barcelona; that our house was actually there and I had been climbing over it. But chiefly I felt a queer feeling that things were really started and there was no backing out. For the first time I realized that we were earning no money and, despite the amazing response to the idea, it might be ages before we ever earned any more.

There is something terrifying about paying out what seems enormous sums, knowing that there is a limit to the amount that can be paid out. Horrid thoughts kept coming into my head. Suppose, after all, Archie hated this new life? He had never lived in the country before. Suppose I had made him give up his job and he regretted it? Then, what if I found I was quite incapable of running an hotel? However, at that I rallied. The one thing that made the whole project possible was my quite unreasoning faith in myself. I knew I could run a country-house party, I had done so many times in my leisured days. Little things like foreign customs and food, the fact that when people are paying for something they are not as accommodating as one's country visitors, did not deter me.

Suddenly I felt much better. I saw a vision of Archie's thin white journalist's face brown and fat; of myself looking devastating in the Tossa fashion of trousers and shirts, with what I call the blonde streaks in my hair bleached by the sun and outrivalling any peroxided curls; both of us fit as one can feel only in Tossa. I called to Beetle to shut up and went into a sound untroubled sleep. If I had realized that I would be called upon to organize the building as well as the hotel I might not have slept so soundly.

The next days flashed by. We went up to the house every day with Marcus, told him we thought he was wonderful, and went to the beach. John was perfectly happy, swimming about for hours and, as the sea is really safe, we did not worry about him. He made great friends with Rovira, who insisted on trying to teach him to wait. We made lists of things to get when we went to Barcelona for our cases. We thought we would stay a couple of days, get lots of information about electric cookers, china, glass and the thousand and one things we had to find out. I have just had to stop writing to have a good laugh. We had some very strange ideas in those days about getting things done in Barcelona.

We took things easily for a few weeks to recover from the very exhausting time we had had in London. There was still a great deal of correspondence, which I used to tackle before breakfast. It was much easier to allot rooms to people now that we could see the actual rooms, and I almost enjoyed the work. Rovira used to laugh himself tired over the way we replied to people who wrote about rooms. He utterly refused to book at all. '*Qui ve, ve!*' he said. 'Who comes, comes!'

We were already full up for August and the beginning of September. We were rather worried about the number who wanted to come for Whitsun. Would the house be ready by 8th June? We had a long conversation with Marcus and Jaume. Marcus was vague but reassuring. By all means tell everyone to come for Whitsun. The house was nearly sure to be finished, but in any case people could be put off. We realized for the first time that architects can be artists and unpractical. We explained that people could not alter their holidays at the last minute to suit us. We could put them all in Rovira's said Marcus, but the house would be practically finished. Jaume swore that at any rate one floor of rooms would be absolutely finished by 6th or 7th June. We decided that we would warn everyone that they might have to stay for the first part of their holidays in Rovira's and that we would not accept more than ten or twelve people at the most.

It was about now that I realized that the house was not so far advanced as it seemed. The hillside resounded with blows and gaping holes appeared in the walls. These were for the water pipes. It seems that to stop and measure as he goes along is repugnant to the Catalan workman; he prefers to work at lightning speed and then as swiftly undo the results of his toil. Here I must say that, whatever truth there may or may not be in the common belief that Spanish workmen are lazy, Catalans work harder than anyone I have ever seen. But they have a great deal of shrewd common sense and very little interest in money. As we found to our dismay, nothing would induce them to work overtime, although they would get nearly double their ordinary pay. And no amount of persuasion would get them to work one minute in the tiniest shower of rain.

The local plumber, a very good-looking young man exactly like Maurice Chevalier, was in charge of the cold-water system, but a German firm from Barcelona was entrusted with the hot-water and central heating arrangements. The

Tossa man was efficient enough when working with lead pipes which could be bent around unexpected obstacles or could have bits cut off here and there, but iron pipes need accurate measuring.

A man was sent from the Barcelona firm to stay in Tossa, at vast expense, to oversee this part. He was called Pedro and our one regret when the house was finally finished was that Pedro had to leave us. He knew perhaps a very little more than I about plumbing, but he made the best salad dressing I have ever tasted, and we learnt more Spanish listening to his funny stories than from years of lessons.

Juan, the Tossa man, was in a difficult state of mind. He had, unluckily for us, just met the German girl who is now his wife, and he knitted his lead pipes abstractedly, his mind far away. Most days he did not turn up at all but sent his staff, known as Juan's two and a half, to attend to the things. The two and a half consisted of a large man whose chief hobby was gardening, a surprisingly blond youth with the most heavenly voice, which rang out triumphantly above the crashings and hammerings, and the half: a small, sad-eyed boy, who seemed to spend his entire time running down the hill and toiling up again with coils of pipe.

Occasionally, the rival plumbers clashed, but on the whole there was comparative peace. Once, Pedro had to get another man from Barcelona to help with some particularly intricate bit of plumbing. The man arrived, but he had left his blow-lamp behind. We had to wait until one could be sent out from Barcelona, although Juan's two and a half had a perfectly good blow-lamp actually in the house. On another occasion only the half turned up. He had no orders, so Pedro borrowed him and he carried bundles of iron pipes up the hill for a change. The next day the full complement was at work and we heard that Juan had ordered a strike as a protest against employing Pedro, but no one had told the half. Juan forgot about it the next day, so the two thought they might as well go on working.

We at last got the news that our stuff had arrived in Barcelona. The same day Leonard, who had come over to see us once on our arrival, arrived at Rovira's to announce that he had got himself fired. We were delighted, as there were many ways in which he could help us. The Marcuses very sweetly offered to have him in their house for the time, and we found he had so many friends who were delighted to have him for meals that he added very little to our expenses. He and John became fast friends and, much to John's joy, we said we would leave him and Beetle in Tossa in Leonard's charge while we went to Barcelona. We thought we would be away at the most three days.

We went to Barcelona by the 6 am bus from Tossa. This is not nearly so simple as it sounds. The bus only goes as far as the next village, Lloret, where one must change into another bus for Blanes station. Then comes a tedious wait for the Barcelona train. It is not that the train is ever late, but Spanish people have an odd habit of being at least half an hour too early for trains and buses. It is as if they know their proverbial reputation for unpunctuality and are determined to defeat it in this one aspect.

From Blanes the railway runs almost on the beach through various little fishing villages and one or two fairly big resorts in the neighbourhood of Barcelona. The Costa Brava ends at Blanes and the rest of the coast is just a long stretch of flat sand to the suburbs of Barcelona. For the first hour it is quite amusing to see the hull of a fishing boat loom up on the platform as the train draws into a station, and to sit on the sunny side of the long compartment and look at the sea about twenty yards away. But the second hour drags rather, and by the time one starts on the third the seats are definitely too hard, the amusing country people surrounding one no longer picturesque, but frankly reeking of garlic and other things. One gets rather bitter about the absurdity of taking four hours to travel fifty miles. However, after doing the journey a few dozen times one either sleeps soundly the whole time or discusses politics lustily. Four hours of politics is a mere bagatelle for a Catalan.

We had our first surprise at the Hotel Bristol, where we intended to stay our two or three days. We had met the proprietor, Señor Albareda, at Tossa on our first holiday and he had cordially invited us to visit his hotel in Barcelona. He was delighted to see us and even more delighted when we told him we were now fellow-hoteliers. He immediately gave us one of his best rooms, with a bathroom, and refused to charge us a penny. When we protested Albareda smiled his charming Catalan smile and explained that 'wolf never ate wolf'. He was even rather hurt when we did not have all our meals in his hotel, which we felt was too much when we were getting everything free, and he asked us anxiously if we did not like his food. Not only did he expect us to make full use of his hotel for nothing, but he was immeasurably helpful over shopping and inquiries. He explained that we would no doubt find things moved rather slower in Barcelona than we were accustomed to, but what we wanted could be found and even bought if we persevered. We thought he was very amusing and went off to the first address he had given us.

Our first blow was the discovery that the magic words that had worked such wonders in London were of no use at all in Barcelona. In fact, they had a disastrous effect. When we looked rather patronizing and said in our frightful Spanish that the order would be very large, a dazed look would come into the shopman's eyes and he would say dubiously that he did not think he could do much for us. When we added, still hopeful, that it was for an hotel he looked still more shaken, but when we finally asked him to produce catalogues he brightened completely. Apparently this was decisive and there was only one prescribed way of dealing with it. He would assure us, still so politely, that he could do nothing for us, but that So-and-So's down the street had much better things than he and were so much cheaper. He even would take us to the door and point out the *Casa So-and-So*. Then, beaming with relief at having got rid of this frightful menace of a big order, he would stand at the door and watch us, waving encouragingly when we looked back for instructions as we plodded on to meet exactly the same response at So-and-So's.

After a bit we learned wisdom and the art of shopping in

Barcelona. When we wanted fruit bowls, for instance, we went into an enormous china shop full of garish tiles, hideous pottery, umbrella stands and the most frightful plaques to put on garden walls. We became entranced in rows and rows of impossible flower vases and meanwhile our eyes were furtively looking everywhere to see if we could discover a bowl. Eventually I spotted a very attractive blue and white one, a copy of an old Catalan design. Archie picked it up casually. 'Have you any more like this?' he asked cautiously.

The salesman promptly said "No"; but a Catalan saying "No" is as charming as most people saying "Yes". However, the result is the same. Archie sighed deeply. 'What a pity! My wife had set her heart on a dozen like this and I am sure she would be very happy with six. But I will put it here so that she does not see it.' This, of course, was my cue. 'What a marvellous bowl!' I exclaimed, leaving my minute examination of Japanese tea-services. 'Oh, Archie, do you think they might have some more?'

'I'm afraid not.' Archie was firm. 'This is the only one in the shop.'

The salesman was so overcome by my disappointment that he admitted that there might be another one somewhere in the back regions. Would we care to come into the other part of the shop? It was very dirty, but there might be something there we would like. We assured him we did not mind dirt at all and followed him into a dark musty room packed with bowls and plates of every shape. They were all covered with dirty brown dust. The salesman got a feather duster and we set to work to get at the lovely Catalan designs and colours. Of course, there were dozens of bowls that we wanted—big flat fruit ones with formal flower designs in oranges and blues; little brown and yellow ones for breakfast coffee; bigger ones for soup; and lovely little shiny chocolate-brown honey jars. We spent hours there and helped the salesman make out our list. Then, streaked with dust, dead tired but victorious, we reeled back to the hotel for a welcome bath and dinner. We realized now that our idea of running to Barcelona for a few days was really laughable. We would have to stay at least a week.

As a matter of fact we were still wrong, but that was our estimate before we went to get our luggage from the docks. We discovered that a Señor Puig had apparently collected our things from the boat and that all we had to do was to persuade him to part with them. He was the customs agent who had officially examined all the cases.

Eventually we found his offices. That is another difficulty in Barcelona. All the streets have two names, many of them three or four. New names are given after each revolution to honour the heroes who took part in them. And there seems to be no rule about people's addresses. Señor Puig was out this Wednesday morning, but his clerk made an appointment with us for 2.30 pm. We did just have enough sense to realize that 2.30 pm was a strange time for an appointment in Spain, where everything is shut from 1 to 3 pm, and we made the clerk repeat it. There was no doubt at all. Señor Puig would see us at 2.30 pm.

With English promptness we were there at 2.29 pm. The office was closed and the whole building appeared deserted. At last we unearthed an aged man who was presumably caretaker. He seemed very surprised to see us and still more when he heard that we had an appointment with Señor Puig. But, he protested against our insistency, did we not know that there was now a *fiesta* for three days in Barcelona?

That meant we could do absolutely nothing until the following Monday, as Saturday afternoon and Sunday are *fiestas* anyway. We did manage to learn quite a lot by shop-window-gazing and planning our campaign for when they opened again. Also, we found that the Barcelona bathing-place helped to pass the time. When the *fiesta* was over we tackled Señor Puig again, and this time found that we could

56

get our baggage at any time. He assured us with the kindest smile that there was no duty to pay at all. In England we had taken the trouble to find out as nearly as we could what we could bring into Spain free, but we were agreeably surprised to find we had been right. However, he continued, he had had the most terrible trouble arranging that there should be no duty, that if it had not been for him we should have had to pay enormous sums, and the whole business of collecting the things and opening them had been most fatiguing. Therefore he felt it was only right to append a little to his bill for all the frightful worry and trouble we had put him to. In the end he rooked us of three hundred pesetas, nearly ten pounds. That was our first experience of Spanish 'business'. Luckily, we were not often up against these methods. In Tossa we were troubled by too great a lack of business methods of any kind. There was one other occasion when we were even more badly stung, but that was by a concern with an English director. That came later.

One day I was resting in the hotel while Archie had gone plate-hunting. We wanted a service, preferably something that could be easily replaced, and something that went with our bowls. We had had the greatest difficulty over this, as unfortunately Spain does not provide the masses of ware that one can get in England. There is little except real china and the old ware, which is, of course, museum stuff. They make very good imitations of old bowls etc, but nothing that could be used as a dinner service. The ordinary hotel china was impossible thick white stuff, and really fine china was far too expensive. We had from the first decided that the keynote of our hotel must be simple, country Catalan, and the bowls that we had found were exactly what we wanted. If only we could find something to go with them!

Suddenly Archie burst into the room. He was almost speechless with excitement. 'I've got them, I've got them,' was all he could say. Then, with a sudden horrid doubt, 'Suppose you don't like them? But I had to get them at once.'

'Got what?' I managed at last to get out of him that he had bought two enormous dinner services, all to match our bowls, cream ground with formal blue, yellow and green flowers or geometric patterns on them. I was thrilled. He had found them in the usual back room, covered with dust, and the shopkeeper had almost implored him to take them away. They had been cluttering up his shelves for years; no one wanted such coarse stuff nowadays. He asked two hundred pesetas for the two sets, about six pounds. Archie said he really had no use for such a mass of stuff—over two hundred pieces—although we could really have done with more. The man explained that the plates were from Talavera (that meant nothing to us then) and it would be worth while to buy the lot and sell them separately. Archie said it was hardly his line, and why didn't the shopkeeper sell them separately himself? The man said he was sick of them and Archie could have them for a hundred and fifty pesetas. Archie said he would oblige him and take them off his hands for a hundred. The shop-keeper threw in a couple of enormous bowls to match, and that was that. I was dying to see them, but they were to be packed up and sent straight to Tossa.

We spent the rest of our stay asking about electric cookers. We were shown every other sort of cooker, but scorned them all. I was thrilled at the idea of cooking by electricity. Power was cheap, we were told by Marcus, and it would mean that I could do the cooking myself, as I had planned in England. Leonard said he would look round Tossa for two women to do the rooms and to help in the kitchen.

When at last we staggered back to Tossa we had achieved most of the things we had set out to do in two or three days. We had been away a fortnight.

3

Rovira, with his usual kindness, said we could store our packing-cases in an out-house of his. The cases arrived by lorry a few days after we got back from Barcelona. The first thing I did was to unpack my pictures and hang them in place of Toni and the praying nun. It was good to feel our things were really here.

The unfortunate result of our packing-cases arriving and the fact that we kept rushing through the patio with armfuls of our possessions was that the other English people staying at Rovira's at last realized who we were. We had kept it a dark secret because we knew that we should be bombarded with questions. Now we found how wise we had been. All the people were very nice and just the sort we wanted in our hotel, but we did not want to bother with someone else's hotel guests when we had so much to do with our own concerns. As soon as they found that there was someone there who knew Tossa and spoke English they fell on us. As the only time they saw us was at meal times our meals became a little hell.

We never sat down without someone coming over and asking us where one bought stamps; how much one put on a letter to England; what the funny building on top of the headland was; was it safe to go out alone. That seems to be a mania with travelling Englishwomen of any age. The worst were questions, terribly well meant, about the building.

'Do you think it will really be finished by Whitsun?' 'Is it quite safe perched up on that hillside?' 'Can you really get twenty people in there? It looks so small!'

We did our best and no doubt it was marvellous training, but often I could have screamed: 'No, of course it won't ever be finished!' 'It's most unsafe and we are just here waiting for it to fall! Won't it be a lovely crash?' 'Of course, it is a secret, but we can only get three guests in it really, and one of them has to sleep on the roof!'

But we let our food grow cold and answered politely: 'The post office is that place where the bus stops.' 'No, you get stamps from a tobacconist's' 'You can only post letters in the post office.' 'I'm afraid I forget what a telegram to London costs; they will tell you in the telegraph office. 'No, that is not the post office, you can only post letters there. The telegraph office is next to the carpenter's shop.' 'That building is a lighthouse.' 'A stamp for England costs fifty *céntimos*.' 'No, you can't get stamps at the post office.'

There was a family of three women, a mother and two daughters, each of whom had an adventure that sent them home to England at the end of their holidays feeling they had indeed seen life. One evening Mother, a tiny creature with white hair and an incredibly youthful spirit, got lost. I had gone up to my room directly after dinner to write some letters; John had gone to bed; Archie had gone off to Marcus's bar. Presently there was a timid tap on my door. In came the elder sister, looking very worried. Had I seen Mother? I said 'No,' and she went away. Then John came in, furious. 'They came into my room to look for Mother!' he exclaimed. I suggested we should help in the search. We looked everywhere in the hotel, but no Mother. Then the two distracted sisters roamed the streets, crying 'Mother!' in thin, birdlike voices. At last, when we were all sitting in the hall wondering what to do next, Archie came back from Marcus's with—Mother. She had slipped out after her daughters thought she had gone to bed, had met Archie, and gone off pub-crawling with him. It took some time for Archie to live it down.

The elder sister's adventure might have had an unhappy ending. We had been practising before lunch drinking out of a *cántaro*. This is a sort of bottle from which the Spaniards drink their wine—holding it high above their heads and letting a jet of wine run down their throats. While we were at lunch someone wanted a lighter filled with petrol. Rovira kept a special little bottle with a small pourer fixed in the cork. This time he sent John to fetch it and John, not quite understanding, put it on the women's table, next to the elder sister. She picked it up and there was a sudden roar from a Spaniard seated near her. We all looked up, startled. She was pouring it down her throat, convinced it was some nice new drink our kind Rovira wanted her to try! There was a moment's breathless pause to see what would happen, but apparently even Spanish petrol is harmless taken internally. Rovira gave a life-like imitation of the girl flying back to England under her own power, so to speak.

The last adventure was that of the younger daughter. She had often asked me if the sea was really quite safe even when the waves were big. I said it was absolutely safe. Of course, I meant if one used a little common sense and was able to swim. We all went down to the beach as usual, where there was a fairly rough sea. Our party, in which there was a very good swimmer, a German, was sitting in its usual place at the far end. The three women were at the other end. Suddenly a young schoolmistress who was staying at Rovira's came sprinting across the beach. She rushed up to my German friend and in a flood of breathless German asked him to rescue a girl who could not get back to the shore. Then she turned to me and said very politely, 'You don't mind, do you?' I assured her I would certainly give Hans permission to rescue damsels in distress and he set off at the double. We followed more slowly. It was the younger sister, sensibly not struggling, but foolishly bathing far too near the rocks. Even so, anyone who could swim a little would have had no difficulty in returning. Hans rushed dramatically in and ploughed through the water with noble strokes. Unfortunately some officious people had already launched a fisherman's boat which was lying on the sands and were pulling hard towards the girl who was lying quite peacefully on her back in the buoyant water.

We watched breathlessly to see who would win, those in the boat, or Hans. They almost dead-heated. Then, to Hans' fury, the girl was lifted into the boat and the enthusiastic rescuers tried to lift him in also. This was too much for German dignity and he set off for the distant rock in a flurry of white heels and swam defiantly round it. The rescued damsel was thrilled. Poor Hans even had injury added to insult. The next day a fisherman came up to him, as the only Spanish-speaking person concerned, and asked him for eight pesetas for damage to his boat.

This was such a mild adventure that it could hardly be classed among the Tossa rescue scenes, of which there are few because the coast is really so safe. I did once see two people in real difficulties who owe their lives more to the extreme buoyancy of the water than to their rescuers. It was one of the really rough days, and the huge waves were breaking over the road leading to the second beach. A few of us, who knew the sea looked much more dangerous than it in fact was, had been swimming. The only way to return was to come in on the crest of a wave, and just before it broke, dive down and swim under water up the shelving beach, clutch an upright support of one of the sun-shelters, and hang on while the sea poured back. The waves had a double break which crashed one down on the sand if one tried to surf-ride them.

Several of us had an exciting morning and were resting on the sands, rather bruised. A strange couple who, we found out afterwards, were on their honeymoon from Barcelona, had been walking on the shore in their bathing things, but had not ventured into the sea. They had climbed up the cliff and sat on the rocks watching the waves piling in. Suddenly someone shouted and we saw that they had been swept off into the boiling white mass of foam at the bottom of the rocks. The man could just be seen holding the girl up. I jumped up and ran to the edge of the waves to see if there might be any way of reaching them by the rocks.

I knew it would be useless to attempt to swim out to them, and I did not want to add to the difficulties by having to be rescued as well. However, a woman on the beach, seeing me apparently about to plunge in, seized me by the arm and held me back. I took one look to make sure she was a good hearty female, and then pulled hard, looking amazingly brave. Meanwhile some fishermen were attempting to launch a small boat. Several times it was thrown back, but at last got away clear of the breakers. Unfortunately, in their excitement, they had forgotten the oars. A Spaniard offered to swim out with an oar if someone would tie a rope around him and hold on to it. A rope was produced and tied round his waist. He plunged into the waves clutching an oar. The boat was going round and round just beyond the point where the waves broke. The Spaniard bravely struck out towards the boat, but the entire crowd on the beach hung on to the rope and forgot to pay it out. At last he lost the oar in his struggles against the rope and, miraculously, one of the two men in the boat managed to get hold of it. They paddled with the one oar towards the drowning couple, still bobbing up and down like corks in the churning water round the rocks.

Above them a coast guard watched them from a safe vantage point. He obviously could not make up his mind where his duties ended. Should a coast guard risk his life for stray visitors? He thought he should and unbuttoned his trousers. Near the last button his fingers hesitated. No, definitely not. He buttoned his trousers up again. At the top button his fingers again betrayed him. Perhaps, after all—he unbuttoned his trousers. A glance at the black rocks showing like prunes through cream made it clear that coast guards' lives are not to be risked lightly. Besides, the boat was getting nearer. He attended to his buttons firmly.

The boat at last reached the couple and both men leaned over and heaved them on board. In doing so the two men fell overboard. However, the half-drowned pair were safely lying in the bottom of the board, and the two men swam toward the shore pushing the boat in front of them. When it was nearly on the beach the crowd, which had swelled to enormous proportions by the addition of most of the villagers, and which had been waiting in a sort of stunned silence, suddenly became tremendously active. Everyone rushed into the waves to help pull the boat ashore. The coast guard's problem was solved. He whipped his buttons undone, tore off his trousers, rushed down to the shore and into the surf in a fascinating pair of striped pants and triumphantly helped to pull the boat ashore. The honeymooners were perfectly all right, although the man was terribly exhausted and his wife prostrate from salt water and shock.

Rovira was always very charming to us, but we did realize that he wasn't an easy person to live with. He was intensely moody and on occasion could fly into terrific rages. He stood no nonsense from any guest and if he did not care for one he made it so clear that the guest had to leave. He also refused to take anyone into his house if he did not like their looks.

In the market square we met some people in an enormous Rolls-Royce who were lost and wanted an hotel. We told them about Rovira's and said it was very simple but clean and with very good food, and showed them the way. Later we saw the car blocking the narrow street outside Rovira's door. We were surprised not to see the new people at dinner and asked Rovira about them. He made a gesture of throwing them out and said: 'Too rich!' We learned a great deal from Rovira, and often longed to have his ruthlessness, but we eventually developed subtler tactics with the same results.

Rovira was not popular in the village, as he was too downright in his opinions and methods to suit the cautious Catalans. Tossa people were non-committal over the church question; the women mostly went to church, the men stayed away. But on *fiestas*, when to stay away would be too

64

deliberate, or when there was an amusing procession that would be a pity to miss, the men went. Rovira simply ignored the church. On one occasion, when a procession was to pass through the streets which had been strewn with flowers by the householders, there was a noticeable gap of bare road in front of Rovira's hotel. Someone said to Rovira that he really should do something about it. He grinned, said: 'Very well,' and went into his house. Presently he came out with his dustbin and strewed the contents outside his house.

He occasionally had terrible domestic rows. I was innocently involved in one. I was drying my hair in the hotel kitchen, which is long and narrow with the big range in the middle of one side. I was allowed to sit with my head nearly in the open oven, where some chickens were roasting. Rovira started a quarrel with his mother, a queer old woman who lived in a small room near the front door and was always sitting in the open doorway chewing pieces of raw meat and mending interminable white knickers with crochet on them. Unfortunately, they were at opposite ends of the long kitchen and the streams of Catalan passed over me as I sat crouched over the oven. Then they got going in earnest and started throwing the huge earthenware bowls in which *arroz* is cooked. The bowls sailed across the kitchen: I dodged as well as I could and had visions of either being stunned or cut to pieces and served up with the chickens later. At last they stopped, after breaking five of those enormous bowls. The kitchen floor was covered with jagged pieces of earthenware. I escaped hastily.

That evening Rovira was like a thundercloud when he served our chickens. An English artist, who spoke French like most Englishmen, insisted on trying to find out what was the matter. Rovira prides himself enormously on his ten words of French. At last he unbent a little and muttered '*Mal de mère!*' furiously.

There was an Irishman and his wife staying in the hotel.

She was a clever little thing, but he was a nice, good-natured, slow-witted creature from Dublin. One day after lunch, Rovira was in his patio trying to fix some trellis that had fallen down. He was helped by his wife and a small boy who was employed as a sort of boots. The small boy was a perfect little fiend, and that particular afternoon he was being beyond everything. He was supposed to hold up the trellis while Rovira nailed it, but he always let it go at the critical moment. We watched entranced from our balcony, wondering what would happen.

At last, Rovira's never very strong patience collapsed and he seized the boy and beat him. Then, sending his wife to get the boy's wages, he pushed him out of the hotel. Rovira went back and glared at the trellis and his wife. At that moment the Dubliner appeared in the patio. He had a camera in his hand. 'Ah now!' he said happily, pointing the camera at Rovira, who was still speechless with rage, 'just look pleasant for a moment, will ye?' He took the picture and strolled out again without noticing anything. I only hope the picture did not come out.

Next door to Rovira's hotel was a library and a shop that sold things for tourists. This was run by a German, known as the Baronesa. She was one of a small group of refugees, all German, who had settled in Tossa to try to make some sort of a living. It was the first time we had come across this type of people and we found it very difficult at first to get used to their ideas. They were all charming to us and very ready to be helpful, but there was a sort of unspoken agreement among them that no one offered or expected anything for nothing. I never quite mastered that code. When I lived in the country I was used to offering people lifts, giving away surplus garden produce, having people lend horses, and in London borrowing an egg from a neighbour, offering to do her shopping for her if I went into town, or having someone give me an unwanted frock. I never realized that such articles or services involved were saleable or exchangeable value. Certainly most of the refugees observed their own peculiar rules punctiliously. If any of them came up to the hotel in the afternoon and we asked them to stay to tea they thought we were either shamelessly touting for business or being shamelessly unbusinesslike. If one of them was going to Gerona or Barcelona in his car he would ask us if we would like a lift, but we were expected to pay ten or twenty pesetas. They would stand us a drink at a café quite cheerfully, but never forgot our check in their own business.

At first I did not know that Zügel did not have these strange ideas. He was also not sure about us. Then we found that he had been wanting to give me some plants for the garden, but had thought that I might think it odd. I had been wanting to ask him for some of his carnation cuttings, but had not known how to offer him money for them. After that we found the Zügels the most delightful neighbours. Frau Zügel is one of the most charming women I know and they have two of the loveliest children. It was definitely cheering to find some people with whom one could behave naturally. The Marcuses, of course, were reasonable beings, but there has never been a house built which left the owners and the architect on speaking terms directly afterwards. Now we count Marcus and his wife among our Tossa friends, but anyone less forbearing than Marcus would never have spoken to me again after some of the things I called him before the house was finished. Later we got to know many of the Tossa villagers, whose attitude to giving and receiving favours—and life in general—is the exact opposite of the refugees, and the sanest I have yet met.

4

We found that the house had not progressed very much during our fortnight in Barcelona.

John had gone back to England to school, and Leonard had divided his time betweeen wandering round the house and helping every foreign resident in Tossa with their various concerns. The refugees swarmed over him; he ran their errands, told them how to run their businesses and, with supreme tact, kept out of the frightful feuds that sprang up between them. We found it quite hopeless to keep pace with the quarrels, and were always getting involved at the café on the beach, when we would be sitting with one faction and inadvertently ask the for-the-moment opposition to join us. The sides changed so rapidly it was bewildering.

I suddenly realized that there was something wrong with the way the house was getting on. It was obvious that it could not possibly be finished by Whitsun. Jaume still maintained that one floor of bedrooms would be finished. Marcus, when I tackled him rather indignantly about his promise that it would be more or less ready, became completely wrapped in Jewish fatalism and said what must be must be, or words to that effect. The angrier I became the more fluent my German, and I ended up with a really telling tirade about architects in general and about the necessity of doing something to hurry things. Marcus listened patiently his long face bent over me, his thick grey hair ruffling in the breeze. Then he replied: 'Look! That cactus over on the hillside is going to flower. Isn't that beautiful?' I may as well remark here that Marcus is still alive and well.

In the end, with Leonard to back me up, I insisted that more workmen be engaged. There were not enough in Tossa, so they got them from elsewhere. This sometimes led to difficulties when a man from Llagostera would not work next to a man from San Feliu, but at last I realized that a foreman was needed and took over the job myself.

I went up every day first thing and told Marcus exactly what work had to be done that day. Then I took Jaume aside and, with Leonard to translate, explained that I had already asked Marcus to give these orders, but as Marcus himself did not speak very good Spanish I was repeating them to Jaume in case there was a misunderstanding. Jaume grasped the situation at once. He was very fond of Marcus, but did not find him easy to work with. In fact, if he had not personally liked Marcus there would have been real trouble, for Marcus had little idea of how to work with these men. He had a sort of colourless irony that was completely lost on the jovial Catalans. They either thought he was in earnest and consequently were very offended or they did not get his meaning at all.

Jaume was an excellent worker, but he was a lone worker. His method was to do anything difficult himself. This was all right when there was no hurry, but for us it was impossible. The usual leisurely Catalan method of house-building was out of the question. They would have one skilled tile-setter, one staircase expert, and they would work extremely hard, but it would take months. The idea of two experts doing the same job in one house was unheard of.

I had to contend with this single-handed because Archie was lost when it came to floods of German. It was difficult enough having to interpret from Spanish and Catalan, but to have to translate all my arguments with Marcus would have been too much. Also, he is much slower at coming to decisions than I, and would ponder over what seemed to me childishly clear problems until I could have screamed. Luckily, in Leonard I had an ally. His brain works very much on the same lines as mine, and he could grasp or ignore details as quickly as I. I seemed to have Providence on my side, for I made decisions with a recklessness that appalls me to think of now, and they all turned out to be right. I must have had an obscure ancestor who was a house-builder and whose ghost watched over me.

It was terribly hard work. The worst thing about an unfinished house is that there is nowhere to sit. I stood about in the boiling sun, testing first one ankle and then the other, climbed scaffolding, leaned against walls. It would have saved much trouble if I could have given orders direct through Leonard, but I had to argue first with Marcus, who simply did not listen if he did not approve. Then Leonard would tactfully whisper my order to Jaume. Unfortunately, Leonard could not listen openly to my conversations with Marcus because I usually ended by being so rude that we felt it hardly tactful to have an outsider present. But he was usually somewhere near, and in an empty house sound carries.

Another very difficult thing to contend with was when Marcus came over all artistic. Marcus is an artist first, an architect second, and a human being a bad third. Comforts were little things that, if they happened to be there, were so much the better, but not a line must be lost for them. 'Ugly' was his invariable answer to any suggestion of mine. He did not just say brusquely 'Ugly,' he looked at me with a mixture of horror and pity and said in a sort of sigh, 'Haesslich!' Occasionally, when I wanted something almost too much, such as a small window in my own sitting-room facing west, where there is the best view of all, horror overcame pity and he said, 'Scheusslich!' in accents of such agony that I could have guessed he meant 'Hideous' even if I had not known the word. However, I got my window. I actually got everything I wanted. Marcus came to dread the word 'compromise'. I was always ready for a compromise in which I got my own way.

One of the worst moments in the building was over my sitting-room fireplace. They had built a lovely real Catalan open fire and all that was needed was some flat tiles set in round it, and no mantelpiece. I came up one day and looked in through the window to see if they had got on with the tiles. Instead I saw, to my horror, the most dreadful Victorian overmantel moulded with fluted edges and a cockleshell in the middle. I ran speechless to Marcus. For once the poor man was not to blame. Jaume, bless him, worked overtime to do this himself as a surprise for me. He had spent hours with a finger and thumb and much heavy breathing to achieve this ghastly effort. I did not know what to do. I adored Jaume and felt it was so sweet of him, and could not bear to hurt his feelings. I had wild thoughts of enduring it, but to escape from a converted Victorian flat to Spain and then find this was too much. I even thought of never using my sitting-room. Of course, it was Leonard who tactfully had it removed. I never did ask him what he said to Jaume, but probably he explained that I was slightly mad and had a phobia about mantelpieces.

Another need for a competent foreman showed itself in the weather. Usually May is completely fine, but this year there were days with occasional showers. They lasted perhaps twenty minutes to half an hour and hardly drove one indoors. But Catalans will not work one second in the rain. They do not think it is right to waste their employer's money by knocking off work until the shower is over, so they go home for the rest of the day. The fact that they are paid by the hour and so lose several hours' pay does not matter. The men working inside the house, who are not affected at all by the outside elements, decided that it is most unfair to earn money while the others have to go home, so they all knock off.

I was infuriated to find no work going on during a cloudless afternoon because there had been a slight shower in the morning. So we decided that the only thing to do was to watch the weather, and the second we saw a slight cloud to rush to the house and find jobs inside for the outside men. There were not so many outside men now, as most of the work was inside. Then it could rain all day, and they would not even go home for their lunch!

One of the loveliest things about life in Tossa is that there is no class-consciousness whatever. I am sure this would horrify our Communist friends, but we found it simply grand. The boy who serves you coffee in the café on the beach will take you out in his *patino*, a sort of raft, when he is off duty. It was the same with our workmen. When we were picnicking up at the house they would join us without any fuss and exchange their sardine sandwiches for our omelette ones. Pedro would often join us for coffee at the café after dinner not, as an English workman might, if pressed, and then rather self-consciously, but of his own accord because he liked our company and knew we liked his. At Marcus's bar, when we were not too tired to go there, I often danced tangos with the most beautiful dancers, whom I recognized the next day, shirtless, heaving bricks around.

It is a custom in Catalonia to give a dinner to all the workmen when the roof is finished. A flag is run up on the house to celebrate. The English visitors were so surprised when we did not hoist the Union Jack. We had a Spanish and Catalan flag—the Catalan one very large and the much smaller Spanish one rather hidden behind it. Zügel's house was a little ahead of ours and his roof was on first. He proudly hoisted the black and red Württemberg flag. A deathly calm seemed to descend over the village. People were seen whispering in little groups. At last someone had the courage to go to Zügel. They implored him to take the flag down immediately. After the last October revolution it was extremely dangerous to flaunt the anarchist colours.

About the middle of May our roof was finished. There were about thirty workmen altogether and we all ate in a fonda, or inn, in the village, called María Ángela's. María Ángela herself cooked the food. We started with soup, Catalan soup full of bits of chicken, bits of black sausage, odd little things like nuts, potatoes, beans and heaven knows what else. I have since watched women buying the ingredients for this, while waiting my turn in the shops, and the hours of meticulous choosing of little bits it entails is simply amazing. Then we had 'Arroz Catalan'. The simplest way is to imagine the contents of an aquarium cut up into small pieces and stewed with rice in a heavenly sauce. Each plate was piled high with this mixture and the serious eating of the evening began. Several of the men had competitions to see who could eat the most. Meanwhile every empty dish was replaced at the end of the table by a crammed one. Archie and I and Marcus were soon defeated, but the others went on and on. At last it was between Jaume and another mason. We watched, fascinated. María Ángela herself came in to see. Finally the other man gave in. Jaume finished his plate and asked for more.

This was followed by chickens. Catalan chickens are funny, skinny little things, but very tender and good. One has to eat them in one's fingers to get the best out of them. By this time conversation had revived and we listened to the floods of Catalan round us. We could not understand a word, but when anyone spoke to us Spanish was used. After the chickens huge bowls of fruit appeared and cigars. Bottles were continually being refilled, but we noticed the men drank very little in comparison with their gargantuan appetites. Chairs were pushed back and someone started to sing. Soon each man who could sing at all had to give his solo. The blond plumber was in great request and at someone's suggestion he went off to fetch another man, a friend of his, who always sang with him. The two of them sang song after song, and we could have listened to them for hours. They sang in perfect harmony old Catalan folk songs, including the famous *Four Provinces of Catalonia*, which was forbidden before the 1931 revolution. Although their mates must have heard them time after time they were enormously applauded.

We were especially struck by the atmosphere at this dinner.

We never felt for one moment we were not wanted, or that we should leave them alone so that they could really enjoy themselves. They did not take much notice of us, but they were obviously very pleased to have us there if it amused us. Later we went off to Marcus's bar and most of the men came too. The singing plumber and his mate were persuaded to sing some more, to the enjoyment of the English visitors. At lunch the next day we were, of course, bombarded with questions about the charming singers, and one good lady from Wales said it was just like home, only, of course, the language was different.

5

After the roof was on the real work seemed to begin. The staircase was a fascinating business. There is some special kind of cement in Spain that sets almost immediately and is much stronger than ordinary cement. This allows strange liberties to be taken with bricks and tiles. To make the staircase, which is a real Catalan one, it is first necessary to make a curve of thin tiles on which to build the steps. The tiles are about half an inch thick, and a man starts from the bottom and sticks them edge to edge with his cement. As he progresses upwards he sits on the ones he has just stuck together. He just puts a smear of cement on the edge of the curve, holds a tile against it for a moment, and it is as firm as a rock. The layer of tile curves from the ground to the first turn in the staircase, then flattens out for a small landing, and starts again for the second curve. Three layers of thin tiles are laid and then the steps are built on the curved surface. They are of the red tiles we used everywhere for the floor, with hardwood treads. There is a solid banister of thin bricks, plastered and white-washed like the walls, with the rounded top painted white for the hand-rail. The underside of the whole staircase is plastered and whitewashed, and looking up from below one sees a series of simple white curves curling upwards.

The ceilings everywhere in the house were of huge painted beams, plastered and whitewashed in between. All the woodwork we had painted a beech-leaf green, a colour that I persuaded the local painter to mix for me, fighting Marcus drop by drop, as he wanted a sort of blue-green which would have faded to a dirty blue immediately. This green, with the white walls and terracotta-coloured tiled floors, was the only colour in the house except for Zügel's pictures.

The house was getting on now. The men were working like Trojans and, with someone to direct things a bit, their energies were not being so wasted. We had already written to everyone to say that there was no chance of our being ready for Whitsun, and most people had agreed to come to Rovira's. This meant that for the first time we were directly responsible for any visitors. The people there before had just arrived on their own, on our recommendation, but we had had nothing to do with arranging about their rooms etc. Now we were to find how hard it is to run an hotel in someone else's hotel.

Jaume had nobly kept his promise that a floor of rooms would be ready, complete with washbasins and all pipes disentangled. Unfortunately, it is a Catalan custom to finish the top of a house first and work downwards. The top floor was ready. The fact that there was no water to run through the finished taps; no electric light; no kitchen (it was full of cement heaps and bricks); no entrance except a large gap, where there seemed to be a permanent horse and cart in what was to be the big living room; and, above all, no staircase, it did not seem to matter. We decided our guests would prefer Rovira's.

It was just before the first of our real guests arrived that we had our worst blow to date. We discovered quite in casual conversation with the local electrician that we could not have power for cooking. There are various bases of electricity charges in Catalonia, all much more expensive than we had understood when we were paying our mere fivepence a unit in England. The odd thing is that the electricity company seems to realize this and, to save one from recklessly expending one's whole earnings in a blaze of light, stringently rations the amount each house is allowed. The amount of power we were to be allowed would just about pump the water up from our well to the big cisterns above the house and run our refrigerator, but we would be allowed none for cooking.

76

I rushed to Marcus. He was abstractedly contemplating a bare heap of disintegrated rock which was to be our garden. Oh yes, he had known this for some time; he thought it really was best not to try to plant anything, but to let things grow by themselves, then the garden would match the surrounding hillside. Yes, it was a pity about the electric cooking, but after all the Catalans managed very well without. Oh, he had known before we went to Barcelona. It is true that if we had known we might not have wasted time looking at electric stoves, but one can always go again to Barcelona.

We plunged into a welter of Catalan stoves, oilstoves, anything. The chief trouble with a Catalan stove, with its odd little places for separate charcoal fires, is that there is no oven, and I had no idea how to cook on charcoal. I thought of my lovely enamel gas-cooker and sighed. Then I saw the heavenly sunshine and decided life had its compensations. In the end Leonard solved the problem. He found me a Catalan cook and an oven that worked with the charcoal stove.

Isabel was a dream of a cook. She was enormously fat and had the most good-natured expression I have ever seen. She seemed quite willing to cope with food for twenty people on four little camp fires. She had worked for a short while in a *fonda* in the village and therefore knew what she was talking about. I thought that if I could have a small petrol stove to do some cooking as well and, with Leonard's help, tone down Isabel's Catalan tendency to cooking in lukewarm oil, we would manage.

Leonard also found a devastatingly pretty little girl to do the rooms. She was called Quimeta and lived in a big farmhouse across the valley from us. We then told Isabel to find a friend to help Quimeta, someone older and more responsible. I expected we should have needed more staff, but Isabel assured me that the three would help each other and there would be no need for anyone else. This proved to be true, as there is none of that difficult *'It's not my place, mum'* business here. Quimeta and Francisca, Isabel's friend, would help in the kitchen when they were not upstairs, and they were completely indifferent as to whether they made beds or peeled potatoes. It said much for young Leonard's perspicacity that we never had to change any of our staff, who proved absolute treasures, and all we did was to get extra help when we were crammed out and had people even sleeping on the sun terraces.

I came up against Marcus in his most difficult mood over the kitchen. The kitchen is at the back and opens directly into the big living room, which runs three-quarters of the length of the front of the house. Marcus had a dream of a pantry opening into the big room and a door from the pantry into the kitchen, to avoid any chance of cooking smells coming into the room. The space for the kitchen and pantry was of necessity long and narrow, as there was not much width on the excavated ledge on which the house was built. A pantry would mean losing a lot of valuable space, and two doors to pass through from the kitchen to the big room. The chance of cooking smells penetrating through to the front of the house was very remote, as the kitchen had two large windows, a back door, and a small hatchway on to the outside terrace, where meals would generally be eaten. Marcus was unusually firm about his pantry and I had to rally Leonard openly on my side. In the end I had Isabel up as well, and she at once agreed that one large kitchen was much better. Afterwards I was thankful that I had won the battle when I found the enormous amount of space three Catalan women can take up when preparing vegetables and talking at the top of their voices.

To add to our difficulties we now realized what it meant to get things sent from Barcelona. The actual transport was no problem. There is the most efficient service in the world right here in Catalonia, the carrier service that goes from all the small villages to the big towns every day. All one has to do is to make a list and hand it in the evening to the carrier, and the next evening he brings the things back. The problem was to convince the Barcelona shops that we really wanted what we ordered. The poor carrier took the same packages backwards and forwards, but always the contents were wrong. I would delightedly say to Marcus, 'I see the fittings for the lights have arrived. We can get them fixed right away.' He invariably answered with a sigh that they had sent the wrong ones. This happened in nearly every case, and generally things went backwards and forwards several times before we got what we had ordered in the first place.

With our hot water boiler it was slightly different. The only place in Spain where they make hot water boilers is in Bilbao, so we ordered one from there. It was one of the few things that Marcus had ordered well in advance, but that did not help at all. The boiler mysteriously disappeared somewhere between Bilbao and Blanes, our nearest station on that line. We did not get very excited for two or three weeks, and then we heard that the boiler had been dispatched a fortnight before. We inquired at Blanes. No one had heard of our boiler.

After five weeks I began to agitate, but Marcus assured me that it would turn up and, anyway, we were not ready to install it. After seven weeks I was desperate, but there did not seem much that we could do. We could not order another boiler, or if we did it would not be ready for months; we had the manufacturer's word that it had left Bilbao on a certain date, and the Blanes station master's word that it had not arrived there. Short of going on a bicycle along the railway route from Blanes across Spain to Bilbao, asking if anyone had seen a boiler, it seemed there was nothing to do but wait.

After nine weeks even Marcus began to think that something should be done. Everything was ready for the hot-water system and Pedro had only to see to the fixing of the boiler and then go back to Barcelona. We hated to have him go, but it was costing us a lot of money to keep him in Tossa. The central heating was completely finished, and we knew it worked. We arrived at the house one June morning to find all the workmen pouring sweat and the heating on full blast. Only the hot water boiler was still missing.

Then at last it was found. It had been for seven weeks in its truck in a siding at Blanes station. It suddenly struck someone to see what was in that truck and there was our boiler.

By this time we had moved up to the house and were camping out in our own quarters. We had decided that even a hotelier had a right to home comforts and privacy and we had done ourselves extremely well. We had a large bedroom opening into a really lovely sitting-room facing south, with a big Catalan fireplace, and a bathroom and an office, all opening into the wide passage cut off from the rest of the house by a door at the foot of the stairs. The bedroom would eventually have huge cupboards the whole length of one side for our clothes. The whole of one wall of the passage was to be cupboards with shelves for linen. The outside boiler-house backed on to this wall, so that the cupboard was really a hot cupboard.

When we moved up there were no cupboards, and the sitting room was full of our packing cases, which we had brought up from Rovira's. I had a small petrol stove balanced on one case, and we cooked coffee for breakfast, managed something for lunch, and went down to Rovira's for a meal in the evening. I was generally too tired to go down at night, and in any case it was a relief to escape from the everlasting questions of guests at meal times. This time the poor things were justified, as they were, in effect, our guests, and Rovira himself could not speak a word of English.

Our beds and bedding were all up at the house. We had been lucky in finding a man in a small village near Gerona who made really good spring beds, and another man in Gerona who made excellent mattresses. They were fairly expensive, but worth it. We had worried in England about the bed problem. I had originally wanted to take out a type of

ViSpring bed, but the duty and transport worked out at more than the cost of the beds. So we had to trust to luck and Spanish workmanship, neither of which let us down.

We felt much fitter as soon as we moved up. Partly it was less tiring to be right on the spot and partly the air was so much fresher up the hill. I was beginning to feel the strain of my violent battles with Marcus, and even occasionally with Archie, who was so much more conservative than I and was often appalled at my rash decisions. I was also getting an odd kind of toothache occasionally. It was not just a usual twinge from a hole, but a sort of dull ache in my jaw. I did not have time to bother much about it, but it did not help matters at all.

The correspondence was a big item in the day's work, and as Archie had very wisely refused to learn to use a typewriter it all devolved on me. Leonard could type better than I, but he did not write English well enough in those days. It was a fantastic sight to see me sitting with the typewriter on one packing case and next to it, on another case, the petrol stove with something cooking on it for lunch. Every now and then Marcus would come in with some question—he had at last learnt that it was better to argue before doing something I might disapprove of than afterwards—or someone would want me at the top of the house. Leonard was an angel and did all he could, but by this time it seemed understood that I did most of the organizing, whether arranging the work in the house or trying to persuade Rovira to keep those rooms in his hotel that I had promised to people from England. That was one thing that made running our own hotel seem almost too easy when we did at last get it open. It was so good to know that room number six would still be vacant and ready when the people for it arrived, instead of finding that a room at Rovira's had been artlessly filled with a Spanish family while we were at the station, meeting our English guests.

I must hand these guests a large bouquet. They were really marvellous in appreciating our difficulties and in helping by being as untiresome as they could be. Of course, they had all been warned that Rovira's was very simple and completely Catalan, but when it came to Rovira putting them into rooms in the village because he had forgotten they were coming, or insisting on people sharing rooms when they wanted single ones, it was really good of them not to be annoyed with us. They realized that it would be useless to be annoyed with Rovira.

One delightful person, a fashion writer, was put in a room that was really no more than a barn, but she assured us that she did not mind. It was absolutely clean, but had obviously been converted into a bedroom with the aid of lathe and plaster and Rovira's imagination, and had a large window looking out on to a roof. Later she did ask us, most apologetically, if we would speak to Rovira about his chickens. She did not mind at all, she assured us, their running about the roof or even crowing on her windowsill, but she really did draw the line at having them roosting on the end rail of her bed. We had been absolutely prepared to have to cope with tiresome guests as part of our job, but I was amazed by the shoals of charming people who arrived to wait until we were ready.

They were all disappointed not to be able to come up to the Casa Johnstone, but settled down to enjoy the novelty of a Spanish inn. The weather was heavenly, and we had our first experience of the satisfaction of not having overwritten Tossa.

It was then I realized how much better it is to understate everything. People were all astonished at the attractiveness of Tossa, in spite of our folder.

6

The house was really beginning to look as if one day it might be ready for guests. The bedrooms were all finished. I went to Barcelona to get the stuff to make covers for the beds. We decided not to have curtains but to have fly-netting screens and outside sun-blinds. The screens were really only for preventing night-flying things from coming in when people were reading in bed. The beds were to be made like divans, with vallances and covers to match and covers for the pillows of the same material, so that by day the effect was of a divan with cushions.

One of the poor refugees showed me some stuff she had got in Barcelona. She could not remember the price. It had an adorable flowered pattern like Provence linen, and I wrote down the name of the shop. When I got there I found it was in the Paseo de Gracia, the Bond Street of Barcelona, and the stuff was priced to match. It was about five shillings a metre. Eventually I found some attractive, much cheaper, material in another part of Barcelona, white with tiny bunches of red and blue flowers with green leaves. This was eightpence a metre, and suited me better, as I had to get over a hundred metres.

Rovira had told me of an address where one could get special hotel rates for sheets, towels, etc. It was useful to us, as the firm sent a traveller every month to Tossa and we could see samples and order through him. We found this helpful later when we had to supplement our English linen in a hurry to contend with the extra people who refused to be turned away.

We tried to think of everything to save us going into Barcelona again. We got attractive reading lamps that clipped on to one's book. Plain round baskets for waste paper. We found some rush mats, with terrible patterns on one side but the back of them a natural colour, which were good for bedside mats. I had perpetual trouble to teach the women that we did not care for the patterned side, and for months I had to make a round of the rooms to change the mats over. After despairing of ever finding anything not hopelessly ornate, we found small green and white bathmats to go under the washbasins in the rooms. We had brought big ones out from England for the three bathrooms, and of course large bath towels.

Archie, notebook in hand, wandered around back streets, buying such things as office furniture, deck chairs and carpenter's tools. We racked our brains for other details. We had one big advantage over the general run of hoteliers in that we tackled the problem from the guest's point of view. We had stayed in hundreds of hotels and knew what we wanted in them. I loathe not being able to read in bed in comfort, Archie hates not having at least two large ashtrays. We were determined to be completely un-Spanish and have plenty of wardrobe space and coat hangers. I like a table I can write on and a chair that fits it. Also, we both like comfortable chairs in case we want to read or use our bedroom as a sitting room.

We wanted to have every essential that we could think of, but with absolute simplicity. The green beams, the woodwork and the bedcovers were the only colours, and each room had a big brown pot for flowers. We were especially keen on the simplicity idea, not only because most people prefer it anyway, but because it did mean that the Catalan women were perfectly capable of keeping such a room clean. It was useless to expect them to cope with a lot of things they knew nothing about.

When we got back to Tossa I found Leonard with a long list from Isabel of all the things she wanted for the kitchen. I thought she had better have her own way over cooking utensils, but I had won a battle over the kitchen sink. The

Catalans have a tiny shallow sink with a cold-water tap, and do their washing-up in a bowl. I insisted on having two large sinks—I had to have them specially made to my measurements—one for soapy water and one for rinsing, with a big draining board on each side and a huge plate-rack above. Of course, there was hot and cold water. Isabel was most suspicious about the hot water and said privately she would never use it.

Leonard said we could get everything on Isabel's list in Gerona. So he and I went off there in the early morning bus. We found a hardware shop and went boldly in with our list. Even Leonard, with all his knowledge of Catalan, was baffled by most of the things on the list, and all we could do was to show the man a word and watch him as he pottered slowly round the crowded shelves and eventually very carefully took down a colander, or a gravy strainer, or whatever it was. We began to have small bets together as to what each word would turn out to be. The heap on the counter was gradually growing. I was amazed at the size things had to be. We bought gargantuan frying pans, saucepans that seemed made for a regimental canteen, colossal kettles and coffee pots. Also a large collection of odd little aluminium pots like beer mugs, without which no Catalan kitchen is complete. I was rather scornful about them, but thought it best to get everything on the list.

When the list was completed I went round and, with the help of Leonard and a ladder, picked out of the mass of aluminium things, odds and ends I wanted for my own cooking. It was rather like a treasure hunt, and I was triumphant when I found the simplest thing that I recognized as having had in my English kitchen. We noticed after a while that the pile of things on the counter was diminishing instead of increasing. An officious assistant, unable to believe that anyone could be buying so much, was rapidly putting everything back on the shelves. When everything was finally restored and the shopman was starting on the laborious business of writing it all down, I remembered a mincing-machine. He produced one which had only one size of perforations. Leonard asked for other sizes, smaller, as this one was far too large. The man was very doubtful, but eventually produced a box with several spare rings, which he said were all the same size. We, by this time grown wiser in the art of shopping in Spain, looked through the box and found one with smaller holes. The man smiled and said of course he had had another one but had forgotten all about it. I handed it to him and told him to pack it up with the machine. Leonard suggested it was as well to try it. We did, and it just did not fit. We went through the box and found one in the whole lot that fitted. It was with the original sized holes, however, so we might just as well have left it alone from the beginning.

I nearly refused to buy two enormous earthenware bowls that were on the list, convinced that Isabel could only want such large things for washing up, in defiance of my orders to use my beautiful sink. Then I remembered Rovira's row with his mother, and the flying missiles. Isabel, no doubt, wanted them for their legitimate purpose—*arroz catalan*.

The house was nearly finished. There seemed to be endless small jobs to do before it would really be ready for guests, and then, of course, for months we would find out things that we needed. Whitsun was past, and our Whitsun guests had settled in Rovira's. They all wanted to come up to finish their holiday as soon as we were ready. We were able to write to the July guests that they could come straight to us.

At this time I suddenly realized that I had unwittingly offended Frau Marcus. Marcus was still as friendly and forbearing as ever, despite some of the things I had said, and Frau Marcus had no idea of them. Apparently, Marcus usually did the interior of any house he designed; I had an inkling of this by one or two things he tried to do in our house. I had very definite ideas about what I wanted. It so happened that Marcus and I agreed on most points with regard to decoration; we only differed when usefulness was sacrificed to it. Marcus had, in fact, arranged exactly where every single piece of furniture should go in a room. He had drawn little plans of each room and marked them He even put 'x' for the chairs. I caught him once moving a chair back to the imaginary 'x' mark on the floor when I had put it nearer the window to get a good view.

He knew me well enough by this time to realize that I was going to arrange my own house, but he took the same attitude as he had taken all through the building, of very quietly ignoring me and doing what he wanted. I, of course, knew this, and usually we managed to circumvent each other tactfully. Marcus has the nicest nature of any man I know and he put up with more from me than I imagined possible. By the time we got to the furniture I had learned that it was a waste of time to get really angry with Marcus. I took a leaf out of his book and ignored what he said. This wasted a certain amount of time but worked very well.

We had all the furniture made locally to Marcus's designs, and again he showed what a superb designer he was. He was again difficult over the heights of chairs and tables, as he did not care whether people were comfortable at their meals so long as the tables balanced the room. But with the cupboards he was excellent. He had made delightful little bedside tables, which we left unpainted like the cupboards.

I showed him the stuff I had bought in Barcelona, expecting him to be enthusiastic, as it was just the sort of design he liked. He was rather reserved and said something about his wife having patterns of stuff. I had noticed Frau Marcus had been around the house rather more since we had started furnishing it but I had not thought about it at all. Presently

Frau Marcus came up with some patterns, all quite nice and a little more expensive than those I had bought. I thanked her very much and explained that I had got the stuff, and that the village dressmaker was already making it up. I showed her one or two things I had done in the rooms. There was a noticeable lack of interest. I had so much to think about that the matter did not trouble me then.

Later I heard that Frau Marcus had always done the interior decoration of Marcus's houses and had thought she was going to do this one. I was sorry about it, as I had not realized at all that she was in any way supposed to be working on the house, or I should have told her firmly that I would do it myself. I would have been delighted to have her experience and advice, but unfortunately by then it was too late. Frau Marcus, although we are perfectly good friends, has never quite forgiven me.

One day our refrigerator arrived. A lorry brought it to the foot of our hill and dumped it there. It was an enormous thing, and we wondered how on earth we would get it up to the house. We decided to get another horse, try to heave the refrigerator into the cart, and get the two horses to pull it up by easy stages. There was some difficulty about another horse and I went off in different directions to find one. We came back, Leonard and I triumphant with our horse, Archie luckily without one.

When we got to the bottom of the hill, there was no refrigerator. One of the workmen saw us standing there, rather like people waiting for the hounds at a meet, and shouted that the refrigerator was up at the house. We found that four workmen had taken it up on their way back from lunch. The Catalan workmen as a rule are small but amazingly strong. We were astonished by the things they could carry and lift. They also did not worry about working overtime so long as it was voluntary and was just to help us out of friendliness. But nothing would induce them to work overtime officially.

There is one story that seems so fantastic that I hesitate to record it, but it does illustrate the oddities of the workers here. We wanted a mason's job finished by a certain time so that the men from Barcelona who came out to inspect the central heating could also see about the hot water pipes. If this job was not finished it meant the men had to stay the weekend at our expense. I went to Jaume and, as I had now found how to deal with the Catalan workmen, I let the tears well in my eyes and implored him to see if he could persuade his men to work longer for three days. He reacted suitably and said he would do his best, but he was not at all hopeful. He finally came back and said the men had agreed to work two hours longer for three days. Instead of coming at 8 am they would come at 6 am.

The next day they arrived at 6 am. Catalans are always punctual at work. They often spend the rest of the morning fetching all the things they need for their work, but they are never late. They looked at the house, looming white and ghostly in the early morning. They looked at the sea, which was not yet blue. They looked at the village down below with few chimneys smoking. It was definitely not the right hour to start work. Although they liked us very much, tradition was too strong. They all went off over the hill for a walk and came back at eight.

Yet these same men would cut short their dinner hour to help us unpack something. They often stayed long after their working hours were finished to carry things up the hill for us. They came back in the evenings to plant things in from their gardens on our slope, and always someone was to be found after sundown watering the flowers, such as they were. It was positively embarrassing for me to live in the house and try to do any work. If I tried to carry a bucket someone leapt from the top of a ladder and whisked it away from me. I never thought it would be possible for anyone to say they hated to see the last of their workmen in a house, but I was really sorry to have them go. However, we had them back at intervals for a long time.

We were nearly ready. Isabel was already up in the mornings to get things cleaned up. The water pipes were at last connected up everywhere. There had been a slight delay for two reasons. One was Juan, the plumber, who had been making the most of the last weeks of his fiancée's stay before she went back to Germany to see about her *trousseau*, and consequently was never to be found when a vital question about syphons or vents had to be answered. The other was the impossibility of getting the right fittings from Barcelona. We had been several weeks in the house and still the basin in our bathroom had no taps. I implored Pedro to do something. It was so annoying having to go upstairs to one of the first-floor bedrooms to wash.

Pedro triumphantly showed me four beautiful WCs and assured me all four plugs worked stupendously. I said that did not interest me at the moment nearly so much as my washbasin taps, and in any case one stupendous plug met my requirements. While on the subject of plugs I asked him if it were possible to make them work a little less noisily. The mixture of gurgles, groans and crashes was like miniature Niagaras. Pedro assured me that nothing was simpler. He collected the two and a half and rushed round the four WCs, then asked me with pride to try them. I did so. Gone was the noise, but now, instead of the Niagara, the tiniest rivulet came forth. Pedro seemed to think that people were never satisfied; of course it was not possible to stop the noise and have the same amount of water. I decided to put up with the noise, or rather that my guests should put up with it.

I was rearranging a bedroom after Marcus had left it when Isabel came rushing in as fast as her large form would allow. 'Señora! Señora! Water is coming down the stairs!'

I looked out and saw that a slow trickle was definitely coming from the bathroom. I opened the door and found the floor covered with water. The bath was full and slowly overflowing. I paddled in and looked. The taps were both shut off. Then I heard a gurgle and saw a bubble come out of the waste pipe. Of course the workmen were all at lunch, but Isabel showed her resource by rushing downstairs and bringing up a big cork like those used for the wine barrels. We wedged it in and it stayed. When the workmen came back they found they had connected the cold water pipe to the waste pipe of the bath.

Two days before our first guests were to come up we were working hard to get things tidy. There were still a few men around. The only thing that was worrying us was that we still had no electric light. Everything was ready and we had had the power for the water pump ever since the building started, but we could get no reply to our letters from the electricity company. We had written at intervals ever since we had arrived in Spain, and the last week or so had written more urgently and even telephoned. They assured us on the phone that everything would be perfectly all right, there was no hitch, nothing at all unusual; we would get enough current allowance for us to run the hotel perfectly.

Now we were desperate. We had managed with candles while we were by ourselves, but we could not have guests without light and we hated the idea of disappointing people again. At last Archie and Leonard went into Barcelona to see the company. They came back furious. The company would let us have our light, certainly, but owing to the smallness of Tossa and the very large amount of light we would need we would have to pay for a new transformer for the village. This would be a matter of about £130 and if we would write our cheque then and there we could have the light immediately.

Archie's Scottish blood was roused and he argued. In this account of our hotel building it has always been I who did most of the arguing. Now Archie came into his own. With Leonard, round-eyed, translating, he brought his slow, logical mind to work. The official in charge gave it up and sent for one of the directors. He was an Englishman, no doubt a lost empire-builder. Archie was at last able to roll his r's by himself. The Englishman, judged by his company's business methods, was capable of holding his own on most occasions, but he was worn down by slow Scottish persistence. Of course, Archie was in the weak position of having to have electric light immediately; otherwise we would have to put in our own plant. The company knew this and had purposely not replied to our letters. When Archie asked them about this they said, 'We never answer letters in these cases'. Which shows the sagacity of the English director.

However, all was not lost. Spaniards are much easier game than Scotsmen. Archie settled for £30. But the company played up. Having got some of their pound of flesh they sent their men out the next day, a *fiesta* day, and we had our light by the evening. We felt sore for a long time, but now we have decided to let bygones by bygones. Our electric meter has gone wrong and has not registered for four months.

BOOK III — On Velvet

1

It was just before our first guests came that we had a glimpse of Leonard working. That is not to say that he had not been working before according to our standards, but we found that his notion of work was quite different from ours.

We had lent him to the proprietor of the Buen Retiro, an attractive spot for teas, tennis, and dancing under the trees, about two kilometres out of Tossa. The proprietor was a German refugee, and he and his wife were completely new to this sort of business and completely helpless. They had been very kind to Leonard while he was waiting to come up to us, and in return Leonard had taken them in hand and managed their household affairs and their new business.

The place had been open about a week. Local people had been going out there in small numbers most afternoons and Leonard had been practising his waiting. We were too busy to go during the first few days and finally went on a Sunday. It was a glorious day and the first of the Barcelona weekend visitors had come to Tossa. We arrived at the Buen Retiro to see people streaming down the narrow road leading to the open-air tea place round the concrete dance floor.

Every table was occupied and a lorry had just arrived with more tables and chairs, which were hastily set up in every available place. We saw Leonard moving calmly but speedily about with trays and he nodded. I tried to show him by signs that there was no need to hurry about our tea, and we looked about for a table. In an incredibly short while the people before us were seated, and Leonard waved us to a table and took our order. We waited only ten minutes for our tea and yet were not served out of our turn.

I was too fascinated watching Leonard waiting to bother much about my tea. He got through the work at an amazing speed and yet never appeared to hurry at all. He was always smiling at people, even when they could not make their minds up if they wanted tea and toast or an orangeade; he calmed down gesticulating Catalans and miraculously found them tables; he went into the kitchen, organized the demoralized owner and his wife, and saw that the kettle was boiling before the tea was made. He told us afterwards that he was waiting on seventy-five people at the same time. There must have been over two hundred people there during the afternoon.

I was glad that I had seen Leonard working at full pressure because for the first four days of the Casa Johnstone's début he did not work at all. I was unversed in the Catalan temperament and tradition and did not realize that the Tossa *Fiesta Mayor* is a thing that comes before all other considerations. Leonard was now to all intents and purposes a Catalan, at least when it came to *fiestas*. The three women were worse; at least they were more frankly uninterested in everything except the revels in the village. Leonard had enough stern Prussian tradition to enable him to make some sort of show of work, and he did serve the courses in the right order and even remembered to put out the salt and pepper, although his mind was intent on the *sardanas* music that could be heard so plainly from our hill.

Our first guests were all from Rovira's, where they had been staying until we were ready. We knew them quite well, and they were very patient and kind to us. They were all interested in the *fiesta*, and were content to stay down in the village all day watching the *sardanas* dancing, the various side-shows, and the ordinary ballroom dancing which went on in a huge marquee on the front.

The marquee is a feature of all *fiestas*, and the larger it is the grander the *fiesta*. It is wonderfully but appallingly decorated with coloured lights and draped bunting, and the dance floor consists of a thick pile carpet stretched upon sand, strips and strips stitched together to cover the enormous expanse. Consequently one's heels sink in about two inches at every step and one comes out picking up one's feet like a high-stepper in a horse show. I say heels deliberately because the usual *alpargatas* and stockingless legs are forbidden in the tent; men must wear ties and keep their coats on whatever the temperature. Most of the girls wore really wonderful evening frocks, made by themselves. Every girl has a new frock for each *Fiesta Mayor* and every man a new suit.

I knew nothing about all this except from hearsay. Someone had to remain uninfected by the contagious high spirits and lack of responsibility, and I never once went down to the village during the four days of the *fiesta*. Even our most respectable guests did not escape. Canon Bedford, a charming old man with snow-white hair and merry blue eyes was found skipping, or being skipped, up and down the main street with a Tossa beauty on each arm, in company with the rest of the village, who were doing this to the blarings of the local band, as if dancing *sardanas* most of the day and ballroom dancing most of the night did not give them enough exercise. The rural dean was heard to be protesting faintly as he passed his wife, who was convulsed with laughter on the pavement. He spoke no Spanish and was saying between gasps, 'Please, how can I tell them I have varicose veins? Will someone tell them I have varicose veins?' But no one seemed to know the Spanish or Catalan for varicose veins, and he was dragged ruthlessly up and down by his lovely captors.

If I had not been so harassed I would have laughed at the spectacle of the staff legging it up our hill, trying to beat the guests to it when they came back for meals. Leonard, his Lausanne hotel school conscience awakened slightly, would be in front, followed by little Quimeta, ravishing in her *fiesta* frock, with Francisca just behind and, a bad last, fat Isabel, rolling along at full gasp, with the most nimble of the guests just behind. I had meanwhile prepared everything for the meal, and Leonard is now proud to say that never has a meal been late in the Casa Johnstone. The *fiesta* safely over, Tossa settled down to its usual routine and Leonard showed his mettle. He was even more of a treasure than we had expected. I had to leave much of the actual running of the hotel to him, as he could cope with the language and seemed to know exactly what a gramme of meat was and how many each person must have. He knew all there was to know about litres too, and Spanish pounds, which are just near enough to English pounds to confuse one, and what the fishermen meant when they said fish cost so many *reales*, which apparently means dividing something by four, a *real* being twenty-five *céntimos*, and what fifteen *duros* are, which means multiplying by something.

I am very sure of myself and extremely bossy (someone unkindly said that if I ever had twins they should be called Tossa and Bossa) but I know some of my limitations and anything to do with arithmetic is one of them. I am not just rather poor at figures, I am positively half-witted. I make remarks like: 'There are twenty people for lunch, two tables of six and one of four.' Even now I have to ask someone to make sure that that does not make twenty.

At first it was rather difficult with the women in the kitchen. Isabel was the most understanding, and soon she and I evolved a variety of Esperanto which worked very well. Quimeta always smiled adorably at anything I said, and did not attempt to understand. Francisca, who was the most suspicious of the three towards foreigners, immediately shrieked for Leonard if I approached her. Finally I had to forbid Leonard to answer, and forced her to understand that if I pointed to sheets I meant sheets and if I pointed to towels I meant towels.

Neither Francisca nor Quimeta knew anything about doing bedrooms but they were quick to learn, although they thought, and still think, the English are terribly affected about such things as dust or clean tooth tumblers. They both made beds extremely well and had a great knack for sweeping the tiled floors but, having raised all the dust from the floor on to the furniture, nothing would persuade them to flick it back on to the floor with a duster. They also persisted in their belief that I really did not mean it when I said I wanted the plain side of the bedroom mats uppermost, and I had invariably to turn the hideous green and blue patterned side downwards.

Poor Leonard must have found it difficult to translate some of the things I wanted to tell the women. I would say to him, 'Tell Isabel if she puts the coffee grains down the sink again I'll raise hell,' and Leonard would say primly, 'The señora says she will be very annoyed if you do that again,' or 'The señora is very upset because you have forgotten to cook the potatoes.' Then he would turn to me and say furiously, 'Look annoyed, won't you?' I would be standing there smiling sweetly at the women I was supposed to be scolding.

On the whole we managed very well and the women were dears. Francisca was the only one I was doubtful about because she was so suspicious of me, but later, when she got used to my peculiar ways, she proved to be the most useful of the three.

Rovira had a deep distrust of all women, especially any he employed. He occasionally had an extra one in to help for big parties for Sunday lunch and invariably she left shrieking, with Rovira shouting things after her. According to him they were all thieves, and he warned us to be careful about things being missing. We had no idea at first how much to believe Rovira, but we knew he was peculiar and were prepared to take his advice with some reserve. Leonard told us he did not know anything about this terrible dishonesty among Catalan helps, but possibly a few things might be missed from time to time.

I was prepared for a certain amount of thieving, if such a word can be used for a natural impulse to take perhaps an egg occasionally, or a few potatoes now and then. Isabel did the shopping for us on her way up in the mornings, and I was willing to allow her a margin of profit, especially as she no doubt got things more cheaply than we would. As far as I know she was scrupulously honest in her daily reckonings, and if any food was taken away occasionally I never knew it.

I did, however, get agitated when I found things which I had brought over from England, things which were hard or impossible to get in Spain, were disappearing. Some small teaspoons vanished, my red pepper could not be found, and several odds and ends that I had had in my English kitchen were no longer to be seen.

Leonard was terribly worried. I suggested making my attitude plain to the women. I did not mind their helping themselves within limits but I did mind not to be able to find things when I wanted them. Therefore, if they liked to borrow pepper, well and good, but if they told me they had taken it, it would simplify things considerably, as I should know where it was and could ask for it back. They were welcome to my teaspoons, so long as I had enough teaspoons for my guests; otherwise I wanted them back. I was delighted if they borrowed my cooking things, which were different from anything that they had seen, but it was annoying for me to find suddenly that they were not there when I wanted them. From my point of view there was no question of stealing; I did not care at all about the moral side. If I did not need certain things the women were welcome to them; they were even welcome—although I did not tell them this—to make what they could on the shopping, provided it was so little that I did not notice.

I persuaded Leonard to make it clear that the missing things must be found. My teaspoons mysteriously reappeared, the red pepper was found behind the kitchen clock, my pet potato-masher somewhere else. Occasionally after this, one or other of the women would ask me if they might take something home to show their families or might borrow one of my vegetable cutters.

I was delighted to find that Isabel was a much better cook than I had supposed. She was quite unmoved by having to produce food for twelve people or so. She had few ideas, but they were good ones, and I was able to leave many things to her while I had so much else to do supervising the running of the house generally.

Leonard was marvellous with Isabel during meals. He never flurried her when she was slow in producing a course, although by hotel school standards it was a crime to keep anyone waiting for a minute. He came cheerfully into the kitchen with his orders, '*Peix por dos*' or '*Carn por tres,*' which I found out eventually was 'Fish for two' and 'Meat for three', but which meant nothing to me at the time. He would make Isabel laugh at something in Catalan, tell me a funny story about a guest in English, take up his dish, hitch down his white Eton coat, put on his hotel school face, and whisk through the door into the dining-room.

We had definite ideas about food. We had stayed in many hotels and noted what we had appreciated and what we had missed. In Spain, *hors-d'oeuvres* are a dull affair, consisting generally of half a green tomato, a sardine, olives, anchovies and lettuce. We decided that this was good for a base, but a German potato salad, American onion-and-orange salad, and French mayonnaise over stuffed eggs would add interest. I took over the *hors-d'oeuvres*, and sometimes Leonard's lingering conservatism would be horrified at mixtures such as melons and ginger served with cream cheese, but everyone liked them.

The average English person does not like an enormous lunch. The ordinary Spanish lunch puts one out of action until dinner time. The English must have an after-lunch walk to get an appetite for tea. So we thought that plenty of salads, fish, a meat course probably cold, with potatoes baked in their skins or fried, and fruit would be sufficient. For dinner we always had a soup, for which I was generally responsible, as Isabel only made two soups, one a thin mixture like ordinary stock and the other the same mixture with slippery bits of dough called *pastas* floating about in it. I started off with polite soups like tomato and celery, but grew bolder and produced thick potato soup with onions in it, and finally threw discretion to the winds and had a lovely time with *escudella*, a Catalan soup consisting of everything the imagination can suggest in the way of bits of chicken, bits of sausage, liver, pork, every vegetable in season, and round white nuts. Isabel knew all about this soup, but had not mentioned it because it was a great deal of trouble to prepare.

In the evening we always had a vegetable course and then meat—with more vegetables, despite Leonard's protest that the meat course in Spain was meat and nothing more.

We were very Spanish, however, with our sweet course. We did not produce the inevitable crème caramel, but just gave fruit, or baked almonds, raisins and biscuits, or a sticky, sweet mixture like nougat called *turrón* and sometimes *membrillo*, which is like apple jelly and is served in slices.

Of course, at the very first the food was not up to its later standard. We had to get used to cooking for many people and it took me some time to discover what can be done with a Catalan stove. But our guests were very appreciative and we were greatly encouraged. The atmosphere of the house for the first month was exactly that of a country house party. We started with fourteen people, but two of them were definite misfits. When they were dealt with the others settled down into a very cheerful, contented party; we had to implore them not to try to help by making their own beds or by coming into the kitchen to cut up vegetables.

2

Our guests were settling down and so was the running of the hotel. A delightful couple had our best room, a big south room with its own sun terrace. They were prepared to be pleased with everything. Mrs Harvey was about twenty-five, slim and dark, with lovely clothes; and her husband, Bill, a keen-looking business man, was lost in admiration of Tossa. He could not get over the freedom and unaffected gaiety of life in the place. They had both been abroad often before, but always to large resorts, and Bill Harvey was essentially a simple creature. He revelled in Marcus's bar and dancing with the local people, and then coming out boiling hot into the fresh moonlight, or even better, the starlight, which is almost as clear as the young moon in England.

On the way home one had to pass the beach, and it was impossible to resist the soft shish of the waves on the shore. The whole party would run down to the water's edge, take off what few clothes they wore, and rush into the phosphorescent water. As drying with one's shirt rather takes the edge off romance, the practical ones would have left their bathing wraps round the corner of our wall, which was right at the edge of the beach, so that they could climb the hill in warm comfort and linger to admire the night view.

We had another young couple at this time, who were the antithesis of the quiet Harveys. They were a journalist from London, Frank Jellinek, and his wife Marguerite. Frank never stopped talking, neither did Marguerite, and as they both talked at the same time and both of them spoke extremely indistinctly, it was difficult to understand a word. But it was worth the effort of listening carefully, because they were both extraordinarily amusing and Frank was really witty. We always were utterly exhausted after an evening with them in Marcus's because we had laughed so much. Later we got to know them better and could understand them without effort and then we laughed still more. Oddly enough, although they gave the impression of being clever nitwits, they were both extremely efficient in their own fields. Frank was a very clever journalist and Marguerite painted assiduously.

This painting was difficult because Marguerite had a habit of painting anything within reach as well as her canvas, and because when she was out in the country busy with a landscape she forgot all about meals. Frank would come in about half an hour late, which is punctual for a journalist, find his *hors-d'oeuvres* put out on his table, and eat it. Later, Marguerite would arrive, and we would find Frank had eaten the *hors-d'oeuvres* meant for them both.

The Storr-Bests were lovely people. They were a middle-aged couple who were devoted to each other, and who were invariably arguing as if they were not. Mrs Storr-Best was tall, with a lovely slim figure and curly grey hair. He looked short because of his enormous deep chest and colossal breadth of shoulder.

Poor Mrs Storr-Best had the bad luck to slip on the shore and break a bone in her wrist. It was while she was at Rovira's, and she was carried almost unconscious into the hotel. The local doctor arrived. Rovira took her hand, the doctor her elbow. After a great deal of pushing and pulling they seemed satisfied that the broken bits were set and the doctor strapped her wrist up in a very tight plaster. Two of the women from Rovira's kitchen fainted. Mrs Storr-Best was marvellous. She must have suffered agony, but she managed to pull round with the aid of Rovira's special sherry, which he kept for favourite visitors or, presumably, accidents. She even appeared at dinner, her arm swathed in a sling.

It was in the plaster for several weeks, and both the Storr-Bests began to wonder if the wrist really was properly set. The plaster was immovable. At last the day came when the doctor yielded to their insistence that the plaster be removed. It was a *fiesta* in the Hotel Rovira. The doctor appeared, with a small sharp knife. Rovira came to help. All the women of the household stood round. Several guests joined the audience. The knife was useless against the plaster, which was by this time like cast iron.

Luckily, the wrist no longer hurt and Mrs Storr-Best was able to sit back with her usual amiable smile and enjoy the proceedings. At last Rovira produced an enormous butcher's knife from his kitchen. It was rusty and rather chipped, but wielded by him and the doctor alternately it did break through the plaster. I was terrified it might break through the wrist, too. However, all was well. The wrist, although so weak that it was still almost useless, was healed and seemed beautifully set.

By the time they came up to the Casa Johnstone the wrist was almost well. They had still another three weeks of their holiday and Mrs Storr-Best was able to join her husband in his swimming. He was a tremendous swimmer. He gave me some very good advice which was extremely helpful. Mrs Storr-Best did not pretend to be in his class, but she would go for miles with a hand on his shoulder, and he was more proud of her three-hundred yard swim from one end of the beach to the other than of his own twice-round-the-island, a big rock which is more than half a mile from the shore.

They were both good mixers, and had so many interests that conversation with them was always a delight. Professor Storr-Best was a first-class chess player, as well as being an authority on philology and Russian literature, and Mrs Storr-Best, nearly as well read and multilingual as her husband, ran him close.

The rest of the party consisted of Mrs Gustav Holst, a completely cheerful semi-invalid; Miss Macnamara, the novelist, a charming Irish person with the greatest sympathy and understanding of our difficulties; and Sigmund Pollitzer, with a collection of delightful water-colours he had done in Italy on his way to Spain. He did not find anything in Tossa to compare with his brilliant sweeps of light and shade, and his favourite terracotta was nowhere to be found. He had not left himself enough time to get the atmosphere of Tossa, which is soft and insidious, and has to be wooed by slow degrees by artists. He was keen to get back to England to exhibit his water-colours, and had no time to coax colour and form from a coy Spanish village.

We also had a dark and sinister-looking Czechoslovakian, who spent most of the day in his room drawing lurid surrealist pictures, with charcoal, on pieces of three-ply. He was really quite harmless and, we discovered later, terribly henpecked by his wife, a vivid blonde lady living at Rovira's. We did not discover for some time that she was his wife; we only noticed that on the rare occasions we had persuaded him to join us for a drink at the café she invariably swept by, blonde head high, bosom out-thrust. He would wait a moment, and then get up hastily with some muttered excuse, and disappear in the direction of the lady's progress. Why he stayed in one hotel and his wife in another we never discovered.

Almost as difficult for us was a party of four from Paris. They came in the same car, and seemed to consist of two married couples. They then gave us their passports (there are no secrets from hotel-keepers abroad), and it appeared that there was a Herr and Frau Blanck, a Fräulein Zander and an Austrian called Adamek. We then discovered that Herr Blanck was here with his girlfriend Fräulein Zander, and Frau Blanck was here with her boyfriend, Herr Adamek. They all lived in Paris, and it was simpler for them all to come together in Herr Blanck's car. They were so occupied that they hardly came into the party at all. They were known as the Blanck ménage.

The last of the party at this time was a tall thin girl we had known at the London Ice Club. Ray Blomfield, the well-known dress designer, 'Amethyst'. She was very quiet, never missed anything, and was intensely entertaining. She was immediately caught up in the daily round of the Harveys and the Storr-Bests.

The peaceful atmosphere was rudely shattered by the Blanck ménage, who were getting mixed up among themselves. The Austrian and Herr Blanck's girlfriend suddenly discovered they were affinities. That left Herr Blanck to Frau Blanck, which was obviously not right. After much arguing, shouting, and tears the party decided to go back to Paris. The exit was rather ruined by the fact that they had perforce all to go in the same car.

However, our party was not long depleted. On 21st of July a motorcycle appeared round the sharp corner at the end of our drive. It was followed by another and yet another. All three took our hill in their stride, and with exhaust roaring and clouds of blue smoke arrived bang on to our terrace. I rushed out to see the first motor vehicles that had ever come up our hill, and out of the haze of vapour emerged the dirty but smiling face of Cyril Wyer, arrived as per schedule.

'Ullo!' he said. I was amazed, but delighted to see them. I had never really believed in this motorcycle trip across the Pyrenees by three Cockney lads who had never been abroad. However, here they were and no doubt hungry.

'What would you like in the way of food?' I asked, after I had shown them their room. They were all three sharing one of our big double rooms.

'What time do yer eat nights?' asked Cyril, rather anxiously. It was then six o'clock.

'Oh, about eight. But I mean now. You must all be starving.'

All three brightened visibly.

'I guess we could do with a bite,' said Ernest.

'What will you like?' I asked.

They looked at each other helplessly. Then Cyril spoke up.

'Aw, you know what three 'ungry English lads'd like. Whatever's going and a bit more!'

'In five minutes,' I promised and sped downstairs. In five minutes a high tea was ready on a large table in the sunshine. A huge earthenware teapot stood at one end. A dish of cold meat, salad, and tomatoes, butter, and a large loaf were in the middle, and an enormous dish of potatoes baked in their skins that were intended for the evening and which Isabel had for once put in the oven well in time.

The boys were a tremendous success in the party. They were utterly unselfconscious and out to enjoy themselves. Everyone liked them. They came down to the bars with us and immediately fraternized with the villagers. Cockney or Catalan, it was all the same when it came to standing each other drinks. The boys learned some Spanish, but taught the village lads plenty of English. At least their influence was apparent when a Catalan would say to us, " 'ere's 'oping" or "Cheeriow!"

Of course all three got terribly sunburnt. We did our best to stop them but they went straight on to the beach each day after breakfast and came back for lunch red and sore. Cyril and Ernest were harder, but poor Cecil was in agony. All the other guests were very sympathetic, and everyone had their own special remedy. Someone mentioned that the best thing of all was to rub vinegar on one's skin, instead of oil, which was what most people used to prevent sunburn. Some time later everyone in the big room heard a strange sound as of clumping feet overhead. The feet grew frantic, they seemed to rush backwards and forwards, stop suddenly, leap in the air and come down with a crash, then start all over again. I went upstairs. The noise was coming from the boys' room. It was poor Cecil. He had rubbed vinegar on his sunburn.

' 'Eavens, it didn't 'arf smart,' he said afterwards.

While everything was going so well with the hotel, things were not so good as far as I was concerned. The tooth trouble that had been worrying me on and off since the Rovira days became acute. The only thing was to go to Barcelona and see about it.

We left Leonard in command. I refused to go near Spanish dentists by myself. The fact that I spoke poor Spanish did not matter as the amount of talking that can be done at a dentist's is slight, but I insisted on having Archie as a referee. Leonard was supremely capable of taking over the hotel, and I left him with knitted brows looking up *hors-d'oeuvres* recipes.

We discovered in Barcelona that I was cutting wisdom teeth. Or at least I was not cutting them, and they were getting restive about it. The dentist had a lovely time, and all that happened was that I was nearly dead with starvation and anaesthetics, but the wisdom teeth were grand. Finally the dentist gave it up. Archie looked at what was left of me and rushed for help to some friends of ours, who found us a real doctor who knew his job. He immediately decided that the only thing to do was to have a proper operation and cut out the teeth, and I was sent with Archie to the nursing home to which the doctor was attached. It was a large house in its own grounds and, downstairs, an atmosphere of Sabbath calm. All the nurses were nuns, and we were received by the Mother Superior, or whatever she was, and shown an attractive room with a big window. It had two beds. I feebly protested that I must have a room to myself. Archie translated sternly, feeling very self-conscious at having apparently landed himself in a convent. The nun looked surprised.

'But surely the señor would be staying too?' she asked. It was the bravest thing my husband has ever done. He did it nobly too, and never complained, even when he set out on a terrifying quest for the bathroom.

The actual business of removing teeth was priceless. The hospital had a new operating theatre, of which they were extremely proud. I think it could not have been used much, because they fell on me as a gift from heaven. The house surgeon arrived, his assistant was called to see the fun, and for some unknown reason the whole business had to take place at about two in the morning. I suppose my doctor, who was a famous person, could not get away until then. Anyway, they decided to do things in style. They produced a beautiful white theatre trolley on which they insisted on laying me like a corpse. I protested I was able to walk, but I was not allowed to spoil their fun. To Archie's horror I was laid flat and wheeled away.

My last recollection in the theatre was of seeing a nun, aged about fifteen, with a large lump of cotton wool, shaking chloroform carelessly on to it out of a bottle. Then she plonked it on my face.

I came to as they were lifting me on to the trolley again, preparatory to wheeling me back to my room and Archie. I sat up and protested vigorously. I knew Archie would have a heart-attack if he saw me wheeled in stretched flat. They pushed me sternly down and covered my face carefully with a white cloth. Just as we got inside the room I managed to push the cloth aside and wink at Archie.

If anyone talks about the cloistered calm of a nunnery, or soft-fingered nuns, pale and quiet, it is all nonsense. These were red-faced, hearty females, who clattered about day and night. They were so excited about their 'case' that they came all day into my room to see me. The ones on night duty peeped in at intervals all night to look at Archie asleep.

The doctor had left orders that I was to have no solid food. This was before the 'big operation'. Unfortunately he forgot to rescind this order afterwards, and nothing would induce the nuns to disobey. For two days the doctor did not bother to come to see me, as I was perfectly well again; all I needed was something to eat. We could get nothing out of the nuns. They agreed to let Archie have his meals sent up to my room. So I ate them and he went out to get food outside.

While he was out at lunch they came in again with the

trolley. Everything was all set for another operation. I used every bit of Spanish I had ever heard and at last convinced them that I was not the appendicitis case next door.

By this time I felt that I must get back to Tossa at once. The doctor said three more days. He was most unfair, because he was a very handsome young man, with long curly eyelashes, and when he seized my wrist in an impassioned grip of course my pulse beat much faster. However, I was so insistent that Archie got a car and we drove back to Tossa. When we arrived I found I could not walk up our hill.

The next day I was up in a long chair in the sunshine. In a week I was swimming again.

3

The workmen were still lingering around the house. There was no more work inside, but they were making another terrace in front of the house. There was a constant procession of incredibly graceful figures, balancing baskets of earth on their heads, past the terrace where our guests sat. The workmen seemed unconscious of the blazing sun that drove our guests into the shade, and strode by with swift springy steps in their alpargatas, with bare mahogany backs glistening in the strong light.

The 'garden' was beginning to take shape a little. The local people were so kind with their offers of plants, and Tonet, the handyman, owner of a wine shop, boss of the Tossa gang of quarrymen, smuggler in his spare time, had planned a surprise for us. He had sent his gang off collecting agavas, the spiky blue-green cactuses that grow everywhere here, and had planted them all over our hillside. The hillside was the earth that had been excavated for the house foundations and flung down, making a bare, sandy slope. We woke up one morning to find it studded with equidistant bunches of blue-green spikes in straight rows.

There was nothing to be done about it, and Tonet was right in a way, as agavas are the best things for binding the loose earth together. But how we disliked those agavas. An enormous one, magnificently growing out of an apparently bare rock, can be decorative, and most English visitors take photographs of them: 'So like Mexico, my dear.' But rows of small, peevish-looking spikes were not inspiring; also they were a constant danger to the person of whoever was trying to plant geraniums in between, which was generally me. To have to garden with one foot on a level with one's ear is bad enough without being unable to bend without two inches of murderous spike running into one.

Our chief difficulty with the garden was the fact that none of us knew anything at all about gardening. Archie was willing and was really an incipient gardener, only he had always lived in a town. I had either lived with people who were crazy about gardening and consequently I had firmly refused to spend my time weeding the rockery, or else in the real country, where flowering shrubs are the only things rabbits do not eat and are confined to a walled garden and a short-tempered gardener. Leonard frankly asserted he knew nothing at all about plants in any language, and was determined to have one subject about which he retained his ignorance. Our guests always asked us embarrassing questions about the local flora, and it was Leonard who found the right answer. I heard him saying one day, with his usual winning smile and innate politeness, to a persistent guest who insisted on knowing if *jubjullas* grew well here, 'I am sorry, I don't know. You see, I am not a keen gardener myself.'

This ignorance of gardening proved a definite advantage in Spain. If we had known the rules we would have given up trying. The only maxim in Spain is that everything grows. It does not matter when it is planted, whether the book says it will only thrive in damp woods, plant it any time on a sandy slope in Spain and it will flourish. Our only real difficulty was to disentangle our young trees and bushes from their stakes, which brought forth greenery in such abundance that the real plant was overshadowed.

Our specialty was what Archie called 'non-flowering stocks' which happened to be cosmos. I grew them tenderly from seed and planted them out in a border of good earth round one of the terraces. They grew and they grew; one side of the terrace was sheltered by them from light, wind, or rain. When they were about five feet high and we could no longer see any view at all, I said I was tired of a mass of green with no signs of any buds. I rooted them up and threw them away. Archie, his repressed gardening instincts becoming active, replanted them on a waste bit of rock and sand. Leonard and I were kind, but scornful. I felt I must give Archie some real flowers for his birthday, poor lamb. The non-flowering stocks wilted a little, rallied, and burst into the most magnificent show of bloom. They were the sight of the countryside. Archie threw out his chest and said he was not surprised.

Another peculiarity about plants in Spain is that they have two springs, as it were. Naturally, in spring one expects things to grow, except that the Spanish spring starts in February. But in October everything starts again, plants that have been flowering since the last spring send up a lot of new shoots, the old leaves and flowers die down, and with a new lease of life they gaily flower again all the winter.

We lost a lot of time our first year because we did not know about all this and listened to keen English gardeners, who told me when and what to plant. Now I rush out when I feel like it and throw some seeds about, or break a bit off a geranium and stick it in the ground and the result is startling. The real English gardener is always a little surprised to see wall-flowers, scabious, zinnias, heliotrope, morning glory, marigolds, petunias, begonias, antirrhinums, narcissi, dahl-ias, chrysanthemums and carnations growing haphazardly everywhere at the same time. Begonia, bougainvillea and wistaria are almost weeds in Spain, and geraniums and carnations have to be uprooted and thrown away. We have not yet got to the stage of wholesale uprooting, but I have got my eye on a battle between eschscholtzias and mesembry-anthemum on what was a bare slope. And I have secretly removed, at great personal risk, some of Tonet's agavas.

The running of the hotel was getting easier every day. The women were more used to me and I was picking up a mixture of Catalan and Spanish which worked very well in the kitchen but probably would have been startling in a Madrid drawing room. Leonard was a tower of strength and I was leaving him pretty much to it. Archie was a perfect maître d'hôtel and had the marvellous faculty of being able to talk to guests by the hour without being completely exhausted. He actually liked it. He escorted them round the Tossa night life, kept everyone amused, and was invaluable as a general mixer.

It was very important in a small hotel that people should be friendly and Archie was a genius at seeing that some lone female, who might have been too shy to join in the bar parties, was included. I found that an occasional evening with the guests, chatting to them on the beach or telling them some of our comic experiences, was all I could manage. Leonard was quite occupied with the running of the hotel, but he always had time to be charming to the guests.

'Isn't he a nice boy?' was a constant chorus.

'What nationality is he?'

'Where did you find him?'

I always said I would have a little placard made with 'Yes, isn't he? . . . German . . . Yes, he does look much more like a Spaniard . . . In the bulrushes,' written in large capitals, which I could produce when required. The other startling metamorphosis Archie underwent was to become an expert waiter. Under Leonard's tuition, and consequently that of the hotel school, he learnt to tuck the knives under the forks when he cleared the plates, and a great many strange ways of carrying several plates at once, but he developed a different technique from Leonard. Instead of the quiet, charming efficiency that the latter radiated as he expertly whisked plates away or laid a dish down, Archie utilized his gift of wise-cracking, coupled with great speed and skill, so that the guests never noticed how much of the actual work they did themselves as they collected their plates together with shouts of laughter.

Almost our only difficulty with Leonard was to persuade him that one could live without working from morning till night. He had worked hard at school, slaved at the hotel school, and was nearly worked to death at the jobs he had had after that. I found him tiring me out because he had to be doing something all the time. Also, he was not used to working with anyone else. Neither was I. We used to get furious with each other in the kitchen. I have a mania for organizing everything so that the least amount of work is necessary. Leonard had an equally strong mania that to get things done one must work and work. After a bit he began to see that my idea of arranging things so that we each had a part of the day free had its advantages. I forbade him to do any work after lunch until it was time to lay the tables for dinner.

Archie took over the tea making. He found no difficulty at all in producing eight or nine teas in a few minutes. But nothing would induce him to cope with breakfasts. Leonard insisted on doing the breakfasts entirely alone. My efforts at organizing them infuriated him, and with his ears laid back and a Prussian gleam in his eye he would take the coffee off the fire where I had put it, put it on the fire where I had put the milk, and put the milk on the fire where I had put the coffee. Nothing gave me greater pleasure than when a guest sent down to say his coffee was not hot enough, although it was probably because the guest had fallen asleep again after the breakfast had been taken up.

With Archie to help with the waiting, do the teas and entertain the guests, especially lonely females; with me to organize, chase round after the women upstairs, do some of the cooking and get in Leonard's way, occasionally help to entertain the guests, especially lonely young men; with Leonard to do the catering, the breakfasts and, most important, the bills, we got through the work very comfortably, each sticking to his own particular duties. Leonard was prepared to be charming to everyone, but he drew the line at entertaining guests, at least individually.

114

Adele had other ideas. Adele descended on us out of the blue. She was with a party of people who were motoring through Tossa on their way to Barcelona and stopped for lunch. Adele decided to stop for ever. She was an American who had landed in London three weeks before, and was determined to see Europe. She went from London to Paris and met these friends who were motoring to Barcelona. She got as far as Tossa. There she stayed until it was time for her to get her boat back to New York.

Adele watched her friends drive on to Barcelona, her deep blue eyes peering short-sightedly through her enormous horn-rimmed spectacles. The highly magnified blueness grew misty and she rushed upstairs and shut herself in her room. I went up later to see if she had everything she wanted and found her prostrate on her bed, almost buried in a swirl of frilly garments which she had unpacked.

'I'm so lo-onely!' she sobbed. I cheered her up and presently persuaded her to come down to dinner.

'I caan't eat all alo-one!' she exclaimed.

'I'll come and sit with you,' I promised.

'I don't want much. Just a little salad, a few vegetables, some fruit.'

I sat at her table and talked to her while she ate soup, fish, vegetables and meat. It was while she was at the fruit course that she noticed Leonard.

'Isn't he a darling?' she exclaimed. 'Where has he been all my life. Look at his eyelashes!' She turned to the scarlet Leonard. 'What's your name, honey?' she asked.

'He is Leonard. He really *is* the Casa Johnstone,' I hastily interposed. 'He does all the work.'

'Le-on! What a cute name. Oh, Leon. Do you really do all the work around the house?'

Adele's eyes were excellent at everything except seeing. She was using them now.

'Not quite everything,' said Leonard coldly, and moved to

another table.

'I think he's just swell,' said Adele, now completely happy and at ease. I felt I could leave her with perfect safety and get my own dinner. When I looked into the big room after dinner Adele was entertaining the entire houseful with stories of her stay in London. 'I was so lo-onely!'

Adele settled down in the Casa Johnstone. She insisted on having her breakfast downstairs on the terrace, and would appear in the most amazing pink confection consisting of thousands of petals of georgette, in which she would sit on the stones on the terrace, her small dark head and vivid little face looking up from a mass of foamy pink. The men working on the terrace were fascinated and the work progressed slowly. She would sit there gazing up at the unmoved Leon, as he was now universally called, as he stalked to and fro with coffee. She would often appeal to me.

'Le-on, he's so shy. Caan't you tell him not to be so shy?'

I often laughed at Leon about his conquest, but he was adamant. 'My mother always told me I should never work in a hotel,' he would say fiercely.

I told him his attitude was most unfair to 'poor lo-onely visitors'.

He was extremely clever with Adele, as he managed to be the nearest thing to an iceberg and yet scrupulously polite. She could have everything the hotel school decreed as reasonable for guests to expect, but nothing more.

Ray Blomfield, besides taking a professional interest in Adele's marvellous clothes, was enormously entertained by her. She would listen by the hour to Adele's tales about how she overcame her 'lo-onliness'. No one could help liking Adele: she was kind-hearted and not nearly such a silly little thing as she made out. Underneath the frills and fluff there was a shrewd business sense that had made the lady come out

116

very much to the good in any adventures she may have had.

Poor Ray was stricken with sudden frightful internal pains, which she thought must be from some fruit she had eaten. She lay in bed in agony, while we did everything we could to help. Finally she thought only drastic measures would be any use and Leon went rushing off to the village for castor oil. Adele was very upset and insisted on sitting by Ray's bed, complete in pink *negligée*, rocking herself to and fro, saying, 'It's pto-maine, that's what. It's pto-maine.' At last Ray managed to sign to me to remove her at all costs.

The castor oil was magical and Ray recovered almost immediately.

Luckily for Adele she made a real conquest. An American painter staying in the village was enraptured. She gave up flopping about in pink *negligées* for Leon and instead unpacked all her Paris evening frocks and appeared every night at dinner in a different one. She tottered down the hill in heels three inches high to meet her painter at the café, and as she decided horn-rims did not go with evening frocks and love, she insisted on leaving off her spectacles. The effect was entrancing, her enormous blue eyes with thick black lashes gazed raptly at everyone, without, of course, seeing anything. The only difficulty was she was quite unable to find her painter among the crowds at the café, and would teeter up and down between the tables, peering at each, until the painter would have had his laugh and would claim her.

She looked wistfully at Leon, but told me he was too young anyway.

4

We now had to prepare ourselves for the summer invasion. We had let ourselves in for a party of people under the wing of a school inspector, one Mr Brooke. Mr Brooke had telephoned me in London and I had refused to consider a party of twenty. But he had persisted, and in a personal interview with us had persuaded us to arrange for those who could not be fitted into the hotel to be given rooms in the village. He also said no one minded sleeping out on the upstairs terraces, and three to a big room would be quite all right. He was so eloquent, and so full of assurances that they were a party of young people who wanted to camp out and enjoy life that we had at last yielded, and had regretted it ever since. We were refusing people daily for August, and individuals were of much more value as contacts than a party from one source, school-teaching.

We had managed to push most of our guests away on their right dates, but the Jellineks refused to leave. We told them we had to have their room by July 26th. They said they would be packed and ready by lunch time. We were expecting the new arrivals in a large bus for a late lunch. At twelve-thirty I rushed up and helped Marguerite throw in the rest of their things, and piled all their luggage in our office. The women cleaned the room, and it was ready just as the bus was sighted.

The Jellineks, who had refused to leave Tossa and were removing to Rovira's, had implored to be allowed to see the party arrive, so they were lingering on the terrace as the bus stopped at the bottom of our hill. Leonard and Archie were there, Leon to take the ones in the village to their rooms, Archie to escort the others up the hill. Twenty people look an amazing number climbing out of a bus. They were all women except three: Mr Brooke, a youth everyone called George, and a furious-looking little man loaded with cameras. They streamed up the hill, very English and drab, with the usual English nondescript summer hats, so cautiously designed that they do not look ridiculous on a cold wet day. From my vantage point on the front terrace I could see Zügel standing in his garden, watching them all coming up the hill, more slowly now.

'My dear, what a climb!'

'I declare there ought to be a funicular.'

'Isn't it hot? I never thought there'd be such a difference.'

'Let's stop for a breather. You look worn out, Gladys.'

'Isn't the view just all right?'

'Look, Mabel, there's the sea, ever so near.'

'I can hardly wait to get into it.'

'Fancy doing this climb every day!'

'Good for your figure, Miss Wills. You won't know yourself in a month!'

On they came, and at last arrived breathless and panting at the house. I was quite used to greeting four, or even six, guests at a time, and offering them chairs right away while they got their breath again, but this engulfing mass staggered me. They seemed to fill up every chair and overflow on to the terrace. Marguerite giggled behind me. Spots where there were no people were littered with small handbags, raffia baskets, striped canvas holdalls. I was bewildered to think I had to sort out all these people and find their rooms. I had an elaborate list, compiled by Mr Brooke and myself by post, about who was sharing a room with who, and I produced this. There was no difficulty at all. They answered to their names like schoolchildren and were shortly all established in their rooms with their right bags. I rushed downstairs to find Frank and Marguerite having drinks with Ray Blomfield. They said nothing, but poured me out a stiff brandy. I saw Zügel signalling to me from his garden.

'I must go down and hear what he thinks about this,' I said. 'They have all decided to bathe at once and have lunch afterwards, so I have plenty of time.'

Zügel pulled my leg unmercifully about the influx of English youth and beauty. We were laughing in his garden when a noise of shrieks and whoops made us both stare up at Casa Johnstone. Trooping down the hill, girlish spirits having their fling, was the party. In front was Mr Brooke, immaculate in white flannels, pure white shirt-sleeves rolled above his bronzed arms, with a resplendent figure on each side. They were all resplendent. Huge cartwheel sun-hats of every conceivable impossible colour; striped, checked, spotted bathing wraps, twinkling white legs and feet in Marks and Spencer's latest in beach sandals. Everyone carried a shiny American cloth bag (every girl must have one of these damp-resisting beach bags this year for her waterproof make-up or her knitting) and those without sun hats had paper sun-shades.

Zügel was thrilled. We both fell into the nearest chairs and laughed and laughed. Frau Zügel came out in time to get the last glimpse of the cavalcade as it rounded the corner. The last of the party was an angry-looking man, looking almost human in a pair of old flannels.

Isabel found the name for the party. She asked me when they all went down to bathe what time *la gente* wanted their lunch. *Gente*, pronounced 'henty', means 'people'. From that moment they were known as the 'Twenty Henty.'

The Henty came up from their bathe very enthusiastic and very hungry. Leon told them lunch would be at two o'clock. We put them at four tables inside the big room. They changed, came down, and sat outside in the sun. Leon came to me and said: 'It is after two and I have put their *hors-d'oeuvres* out, but they do not seem to be coming in for lunch'.

Ray Blomfield interrupted. 'Don't you see? They are waiting for the bell!'

They were. As soon as Leon announced lunch they all got up and trooped in, in a body. After lunch I asked if anyone wanted tea in the afternoon, and if so at what time. They did not answer but looked at Mr Brooke. He looked around his flock and said: 'I would like my tea at five o'clock. Who else wants tea at five?' Half the party put up their hands.

'Splendid. Now, anyone earlier?'

No hands.

'Later?'

A few wavering hands. The rest wished to sleep.

I fled to the kitchen.

I owe most of the detailed knowledge of the Henty to Ray, who studied them with serious interest. She was fascinated by them. I found the changing over of guests more than occupied me. Ray was the last survivor of the house party.

August brought new types, new difficulties. We had thirty-five people now to contend with. It took Archie and Leonard all their time to wait on them. I am proud to say that Archie waited on twenty and Leonard coped with fifteen. It is a pity to qualify this by explaining that Archie tackled the Henty, who came and went in a mass with the precision of a regiment. The fifteen were known as the 'People', and they straggled up from the beach at different times and were more difficult to wait upon.

It was not long before Mr Brooke became known as the 'Führer'. Why he had ever explained to us that the party was got together simply because of the cheaper railway fare and after they arrived they would all separate, we could not think. They had done this year after year. The angry young man, who was engaged to a nice sensible creature in the party, seemed to have a little spirit left, and they were both inclined to take a left turn if the others all turned right after the Führer. We guessed this was their first holiday with him, and we were right. Ray made friends with the engaged couple. They were charming when one got to know them, and only too anxious to get away from the school atmosphere.

One night we were mystified by a request from the Henty. After much giggling and whisperings they asked for some candles, some biscuits, and a bottle of wine. We knew by this time that it is not an hotel-keeper's business to inquire into anything, and Leonard produced the things.

We were walking from the café to Marcus's bar, when someone looked up at the Casa Johnstone. For a moment we thought it was on fire. Then we saw a soft glow from the roof terrace. Ray, who had an uncanny insight into the ways of Henty, said at once, 'A midnight feast'. It was.

Our chief complaint about the Henty was the noise they made. As Ray put it, they were always either whispering or shouting. It was difficult for them, because they were cramped for space and no one grudged them a relaxation of the control they presumably must have exercised at school. But it was trying for some of the People, who had every right to expect occasional peace in the house.

By this time we knew the faults of the house, and also its advantages. The chief fault, which had nothing to do with the much cursed-at Marcus, was the typical Spanish one of the whole house being one huge sounding board. Hollow walls and hollow ceilings make for coolness in summer and warmth in winter, and noise at all times. Spaniards are indifferent to noise. Any Spanish hotel is pandemonium. If there is a wireless blaring outside, so much the better.

In most ways the house was a pleasant surprise. Most astonishing was the plumbing. It worked. The hot water was always hot. The plugs plugged. True, nervous guests jumped when the waste pipe in their basin suddenly emitted a noise like someone in agony for no apparent reason, and the cisterns triumphantly made their clarion cry at all hours of day or night. But as Pedro had patiently explained to me, one can't have everything.

All the guests were delighted with the design of the house.

It really was a triumph for Marcus. I quickly forgot how angry I had often been with him, although he had never realized that I was angry. There were minor difficulties we still had to contend with. Frequently we needed a small alteration to a door or a window, or perhaps a cupboard refixed. We then discovered we had had four carpenters working on the house. We always found the last one we tried was the one whose door or window it was needed fixing.

There was also the small matter of my cupboards. It was not until the hotel had been running over a month that I was able to put the household linen away; it was lying in piles covered with newspapers in my sitting-room.

We still had not got rid of the Jellineks. The day they were almost forcibly removed to Rovira's was the day the Henty arrived, and Marguerite was back for tea. The Henty clattered their spoons and sipped their tea ('I can do without most things but I do like my cup of tea in the afternoons') and eyed Marguerite sitting hunched up in a corner in her favourite attitude, with her knee under her chin. She was wearing an old black and white check frock smeared with paint, and her hair was curling wildly over her head. I came in with some hot water.

'My God, that woman again. Leon, throw her out.' I had completely forgotten the Henty. They eyed me over their cups. They never felt quite at ease with me after that.

The Henty were priceless when they went to tea at the Buen Retiro. Ray was there having tea with the engaged couple when the Henty arrived with the Führer. The engaged couple had openly mutinied and were not spoken to by the rest of the Henty. The Führer chose a spot near the dance floor and had four tables moved there. They all sat round in a semi-circle facing the dancing. The Führer and George were the only men. The new Spanish waiter came over. The Führer looked round the ring of expectant faces turned to him.

'Let me see,' he said. 'Tea, who wants tea?'

He counted the hands.

'Lemonades? *Piñas*?'

The amazed waiter dodged back at the first outthrust hands, seemed to realize they meant him no harm, and watched fascinated. Obviously some new political party.

There was the terrible night George was locked out of his room. The engaged couple, of course, were chastely separated, and the man shared a room with George. One night George was out late at the bars and most of the party was in bed when he came back. The Führer was awakened by a whimpering George. He could not get into his room. The Führer tried the door and called, but there was no reply. With a glint in his eye the Führer sent one of the girls who was awake to see if the rest of the engaged couple was in her own bed. She was, sound asleep. There was nothing for it but George to shake down in the Führer's own room. In the morning the engaged couple appeared at breakfast, and a tired and cross George demanded to know why the door had been locked. He was assured that the door had not been locked at all, but it had stuck a little and there had been some difficulty about opening it in the morning. Ray, who had heard the whole proceeding, enlightened them about the Führer's evil thoughts. They looked at each other and laughed.

The Jellineks came up to say goodbye. They really were leaving Tossa that day and going farther south. We wished them luck, and saw them the next day on the beach.

The Henty had their uses. They helped us get rid of some unwelcome guests. A family came who were at first tremendously enthusiastic about everything. We learned later to distrust too much enthusiasm too early. However, we were very pleased, and the fact that they were more nuisance than the whole of the rest of the guests together did not seem to matter. They consisted of father, mother, and four children. The younger children were nice kids, a boy and two girls; the boy was about twelve and the girls were twins, aged nine. The elder son was about nineteen, and seemed a little peculiar, as he was always pretending to be a boy Scout and pinned up strange death's head signs over his bedroom door. However, he was perfectly harmless. The father was a nice business man, the head of a big concern, but frankly envious of Archie for having found such apparently congenial occupation as running an hotel.

The mother was very strange. She was charming and full of gratitude for the hundred and one jobs we did for her, but she had odd ideas about her children. The girls, perfectly healthy children, were sent to bed at six-thirty every evening and had to have a special supper in their room. As Isabel and the other women came up later to get the dinner I attended to this myself. The children liked an omelette, lemonade, fruit, and bread and butter and biscuits. The lemonade had to be specially made with boiled water that was kept in a large bottle given to me by the mother. The children were not allowed to touch a drop of water that had not been boiled (and presumably out of this bottle). Everyone else drank the ordinary water out of the tap.

The boy had to have his supper at seven on the balcony of his room. He did not undress, and he always came down and sat with his parents and elder brother while they had their dinner, at eight o'clock. Their great troubles were the Henty and the flies. I do not know which finally caused the departure, aided tactfully by us, of this nuisance of a family. If the mother was not rushing after the Henty, telling them to make less noise, she was flapping at the flies. They were bad, the flies, but not nearly so bad as at most southern resorts, and most people did not bother about them. We fought them all we could and there were no flies inside the house, but our first year we had not learnt the gentle art of dealing with the Mediterranean fly. Now we have. With the aid of 'Flit', swatting, and flypapers we have downed them, without waiting for the aid of Saint Narcissus, who is supposed to eat up all the flies on the 29th October.

However, the poor mother of the family suffered agonies. She feared the beach was too shelving, the sea not safe, the rocks perilous. Everywhere lurked danger. We thought it was amazing that she had ever thought of bringing her precious children abroad.

The children were quite dears. One day the parents went on an excursion and actually dared leave the younger boy with us, as he was always car-sick. I brought him some lemonade, made as usual with his boiled water. He reached without thinking for some ice blocks which were near. I stopped him. 'Sorry old chap,' I said, '"but this ice is made with ordinary water.' He looked disappointed for a moment. Then he grinned and picked up a bit of ice. 'Take this away and boil it for me, will you?'

The mother was the type that all hotels must dread. She seemed to think that profuse thanks would cover any amount of trouble. She was positively lyrical about how obliging I was and how lovely we all were. I longed to tell her I did not want thanks, only some common sense. However, the hour of deliverance was at hand.

Oddly enough, it did not look like deliverance, it seemed like making things worse. Mama and 'My Dear Boy' arrived.

Mama had written to say she would be coming by car from Barcelona with her son. The son was a painter. We exchanged many letters all about the climate, the landscape, the way from Barcelona. I took my usual precaution of advising her to do the journey by daylight. She arrived after dark. The first we knew about it was an hysterical shrieking from the front room. I rushed in to find an apparently mad woman dancing about.

'How dare you call this an hotel!' she screamed. 'How can it be an hotel! There isn't even a path up to it, let alone a road.'

'I beg your pardon.' I was very much surprised but kept telling myself an hotel-keeper must never be surprised at anything. 'There is a perfectly good road. It is rather rough.'

'Rough! I should think so. My stockings are in ribbons. It is a wonder I have not broken my leg. It's the most disgraceful—'

'Look here,' I said firmly, 'there seems to be some mistake. Who are you, anyway?'

That did quieten her a little, and she explained she was Mama. My Dear Boy was waiting down below in the car.

'And I am thankful the Dear Boy did not come up. He would have been ill for weeks. It is the most unheard of thing to build a hotel and have no road—'

'Would you like me to take you down the road to the car?' I asked. 'I am so sorry if you have come the wrong way, but that really is hardly my fault. I can't do more than ask you to come by daylight or at any rate to show a little sense in the dark.' I marched out through the fascinated guests, followed by the woman, a little quietened. As I went out I winked at Leon.

'Leave it to me,' I whispered. 'She'll come back eating out of my hand.'

She did. She realized she had made a fool of herself, and was quite nice about it. The car was up a side turning near our turning, and she had got out and walked straight across country without attempting to look for our notice or find a reasonable path.

My Dear Boy was very strange. He was evidently desperately ill and had a high-pitched querulous voice. He brought more canvases with him than I should have thought anyone could use in a year. They were all shapes and sizes. I asked him about them when we were in his room. He said, 'Of course I have to have so many sizes. Suppose I find something to paint and I haven't a canvas that suits it?'

I could not find any reply to that. We saw very soon that Mama and My Dear Boy were not going to like it here. My Dear Boy wandered dejectedly round trailing his painting things, saying 'It's all too, too obvious.' Mama wanted a man. There were plenty of men, but none of them wanted Mama.

She was a thin, nervous wreck of a woman, who had been very good-looking in a hard way, and she wanted a gay resort with plenty of men who were interested in nervous wrecks, but where she could live as cheaply as possible. She and her son were simply terrible at meals. They sat at their table rather away from the others and talked in loud, well-bred voices about all the lovely hotels they had stayed in and all the lovely food they had eaten.

'My Dear Boy, do you remember the heavenly *bouillabaisse* we had at the attractive little hotel near Marseilles?'

'Mama, do you think we shall ever taste anything again like the *chabichou* at Poitiers? Or, at Rouen, Mama, the *andouillettes?*'

'The *langoustes* at Saint-Malo were perfection. And, My Dear Boy, at that quaint little inn, quite near Saint-Malo, so cheap and so pleasant, do you remember how we drank Calvados together?'

Such fun for our other guests. We asked Mama one day why she stayed in Tossa. She admitted she did not like the village, so dirty and smelly. Archie was furious. One may say anything about the Casa Johnstone but nothing against Tossa. He was extremely rude. Mama was quite shaken and suddenly remembered she had stayed at a resort near Barcelona once before. Such a charming place, the hotel was so clean and friendly. The proprietor was a great friend of hers and would do anything for her. My Dear Boy had so enjoyed painting the flat beach and the main Barcelona road. She really thought she would go there. We thought so too. We saw Mama having a long talk with the Mother of the Family. We spent a long time telling Father what a lovely place Mama was going to.

At last they all went. Mama and My Dear Boy absent-mindedly said goodbye. We felt quite sure we should not be added to the list—'My Dear Boy, you remember that charming little English-run hotel in Tossa?' The family departed more emotionally. The younger children were in tears, poor kids;

Mother was positively overcome with gratitude for all we had done; Father was gruffly uncomfortable because we refused to let him pay for the rest of his stay. But the peculiar elder boy walked away to the car whistling and pretending to be a boy scout.

5

We were now realizing that we could pick and choose our guests. The fact that when we heartily disliked guests they did not seem to care for us and, more important, all the guests that we did like were of our opinion, encouraged us. Without having to be so drastic as Rovira, we could arrange so that the household consisted of people who were congenial and happy. We found, thanks to our folder and general advertising matter, that we seldom got people who were really quite unsuited to our perhaps unusual methods of running an hotel. However, when they did come and when we saw that the friendly, easy atmosphere of the hotel was getting spoiled, we managed to edge them out, gently but firmly.

We were very lucky in that our publicity was on too large a scale for such a small place, so we had a choice of guests. At first I was not at all clever at reading people's characters by their letters. Of course, some were so obvious that I could see at once that it was definitely expedient to write and say we were full up. When anyone wrote that they were not at all fussy but they did like a room facing south-west and wanted the early morning sun; were vegetarian but could eat anything except meat, eggs, fish, green vegetables and potatoes; was it safe to come to Spain alone? And they did not know when they might come but could I advise them about clothes?—I did realize that we would be quite full at whatever date they finally decided on.

It was extraordinary how persistent people were if we did not much like the sound of them and wrote trying to put them off. One painter wrote to me in the winter and explained that he liked the sound of our hotel but he must know whether I could absolutely honestly say the house was warm. I replied that we had very little accommodation for the dates he mentioned, which was true, and that I could only let him have a south room for the first half of his stay and then would have to move him to a west room. But I assured him that although the house was typically Spanish, with tiled floor and no carpets, the central heating worked well and the tiles and walls were thoroughly warmed through.

He wrote again, still insisting on this point. I replied as before that the house was absolutely warm, but I added that the Costa Brava was not tropical and the winter was comparatively cold. I said he would be warm indoors, with the heating and the big fire in the hall, but outside it was, after all, winter. I added that I would like to know soon if he was coming, as other people wanted the room, and I said that perhaps if he felt the cold so much it might be better to choose some warmer place where he could get exactly the room he required. Of course, he answered booking the south room, prepared to move to the west room later.

He arrived with his wife. She was a little meek person who waited on her husband hand and foot. He was a thin, anaemic individual, with a cold, pointed nose, slightly red at the tip. He went upstairs and before he took off his coat or hat he felt the blankets on his bed.

'Those aren't very thick,' he said, in his high-pitched voice. 'Is it possible to have thick woollen blankets on my bed?' I gathered that his wife could manage with the ordinary Spanish blankets which we used, with a thick English blanket, to each bed. The cold painter must have all English blankets. I said I would see how many I could find and left him, still in his hat and overcoat, taking the woollen blanket off his wife's bed.

He came down to dinner and asked to have his table moved nearer the fire. Someone had opened a window at the far end of the room and he went over to shut it. The heating was on full and several people complained about the heat. Halfway

131

through dinner his wife went upstairs and came down with his overcoat.

He seemed all right the next morning and sat outside in the sun, painting. In the afternoon he and his wife went up to their room and asked to have their tea sent up. Archie took it up and came down shrieking with laughter. He insisted that I should take up some hot water. It was a wonderful sight. The two were sitting side by side in two armchairs. He had his hat and overcoat on and they both had rugs over their knees. In front of them was a table with the tea things and a thermometer on a leather stand. I looked at the temperature. It was sixty-nine.

He came down to dinner that night with his hat and overcoat. His wife looked rather warm. I put his table as near the fire as possible and made a roaring blaze. His wife was white with the heat. He actually removed his hat, but only to mop his brow.

The next day he complained to some of the other guests that it was ridiculous putting his table so near the fire.

He asked for more blankets. With grim determination I put nine woollen blankets on his bed. He did not even remark on them. By this time I was beginning to wonder if the house really was hot. I asked other guests and they all said, 'Much too hot.' We had been stoking up the central heating and keeping up such enormous fires that everyone was nearly dead with heat.

Archie, Leon and I had a *conferencia*. We decided that the man must be ill and that it was absurd to make everyone else uncomfortable for him. We put the heating back to normal and had our usual good-sized fire. We thought perhaps the sudden change to arctic conditions might persuade him to move. Not at all. He wore a muffler as well as the usual coat and hat, and shivered. Everyone began to get goose-flesh whenever he came into the room. His querulous voice could be heard all day telling some victim about his sufferings. As a sort of Greek chorus his poor little wife would chime in: 'Poor man, he has terribly poor circulation.'

We tried everything we could think of, but he would not go. We told him how one could get so easily from Barcelona to Valencia, and from Valencia boats went daily to Oran—Oran, darkest and hottest Africa, or at any rate well on the way. He knew Oran ('nasty, dirty place, full of smells'). We left colourful travel literature everywhere. We talked about lovely Tangiers. He knew Tangiers, he could not paint there. He liked Tossa. Then I had a brainwave. I would tell him he had to change his nice sunny room to the west room sooner than he had expected. He complained bitterly, but moved into the west room. He asked for more blankets.

He left the day he had arranged to leave. By this time the whole house was shivering. The day he left we rushed round, flung open all the windows and let the fire out. All the guests stopped shivering, took off their extra pullovers and life was back to normal. He wrote to us later to thank us for the pleasant holiday. He wrote from an address in the high Pyrenees. Archie swore he saw the snow on the envelope.

We got some strange letters. The type of letter that gladdened my heart when I opened it was a typewritten one, with the queries tabulated. These were very few and far between. It surprised me how few women were able to write a concise letter. Of course, I let myself in for a good deal of trouble by the rather unofficial tone of my own letters, but some of the results were unexpected.

I wrote a friendly but factual letter to a woman who had seen our folder and wrote for particulars. I received the following reply:

Dear Madam,
Thank you for your very kind letter, which makes everything sound just the place I was looking for. I think the nice big south room you mention sounds lovely but, of

133

course, the east one would get the morning sun, wouldn't it? I feel sure you will do the best for me, but I think the south room really does sound very nice indeed, especially as one is apt to be in one's room more in the afternoons perhaps than in the mornings, but of course one's breakfast in the sun is always a treat, isn't it? I feel sure you will do whatever is the best.

I hope I shall not be lonely in Tossa. I am a widow but I like bridge. Can one buy a watch in Tossa? Mine is just broken and if you think I can get a good one in Tossa I will not get it mended, but perhaps Tossa is rather a small place. What do you think? This is the first time I have been abroad alone, as my husband only died this winter, and I think I shall enjoy my stay with you very much if there is some bridge. I do not walk much.'

Another woman wrote to me as follows:

'Thank you for your letter. I think my sister and I will be very happy at your hotel. We would like to come for three months. In that case could you see your way to making a reduction. We do not eat much, as we are vegetarians and really are not at all fussy. I hope you do not use oil at all, as we are not allowed to eat oil or fat of any kind. My sister must have a jug of barley water every morning. We do not care for green vegetables, but we are very fond of potatoes and like an egg every day in some form or other. And how is the butter, for eating, I mean?'

'Will you tell me what voltage you have in your hotel? We shall bring our electric iron with us; we never travel without it. We shall bring our own tea. Perhaps you could provide the boiling water without extra charge?

Is the water really safe? If not, perhaps you can have boiled water for us. Are the local people friendly or do they spit at one and the children throw stones when one is sketching? We had some very unpleasant experiences in other places abroad. Is it safe to walk about alone? I mean, the two of us, of course.'

'The room you suggest sounds very nice. You say it is near the bath and lavatory, but I hope that does not mean too near. We are very poor sleepers and lie down every afternoon until tea time, so I hope that we shall not be disturbed by other guests.

Thank you very much for your exhaustive answers to our questions in our first letter.'

As a rule men wrote short letters, but some of them rivalled the women in vagueness. One man wrote that he wanted a room for a certain date, but he did not quite know whether he would be able to arrive then or not. He wrote on thin paper with mauve ink and finished in pencil:

'I still cannot decide whether to come now or wait for a month or two. It depends on whether I want to come by ship or by train. As you say you are so full up perhaps I had better definitely book for the first date I mentioned, but that will be rather awkward if I still find I wish to go by ship. Suppose we say I let you know by postcard as soon as I get to Paris, which will mean I am coming by train, and you can see if you have a room or not.

I am so sorry to be so uncertain, but you see how it is.'

The prize booking was from a London solicitor. He rang up from London, spoke slowly and clearly and said exactly what he wanted, asked me to confirm it by letter, and wrote a short letter himself with all the facts set out and numbered.

The letters we liked best began: 'I have heard from a friend in Fleet Street—' I had no doubt about those at all.

Later I developed quite a talent for sorting out people by their correspondence. But it is one of the most difficult things about hotel-keeping.

Of course, we had colossal cheek to attempt to run an hotel on the lines that we would only have guests we liked. But we found it was worth it. We found that we did like the majority of our guests, and in a year we only pushed out about eight. We never got rid of any guest unless we saw that all the others were dying for them to go. Occasionally we even tamed people, and they stayed and liked it. A couple came unexpectedly; they were passing in a car and had liked the look of Tossa. We had a room free for a week. The couple were quite nice, but very refined. He was a retired business man, insignificant, out to be pleasant. She was a large lady in a spotted foulard, and she kept up a monologue about how she did not like Spanish hotels; she was used to the best of everything—in her own home they had nothing but the best and she was not going to do without it just because she was on holiday. My heart sank. I foresaw someone who wanted bell-hops, obsequious servants. The poor woman had not even seen the folder, so she was totally unprepared.

We decided the next morning when we found their shoes outside their door that it was no use breaking it to them gently. I went in.

'I have cleaned your shoes,' I said, 'but I thought I would just let you know that you do not get your shoes cleaned in hotels in Spain. In towns they clean them in the streets and in the country you send your shoes to the laundry.'

'To the laundry?'

'Yes. Everyone wears these rope-soled alpargatas. They are much more comfortable and much safer for these slippery hills.'

As they went down the hill slipping on their leather soles they called up to me, 'Where does one buy these—er—alpa—rope-soled things?'

A few days later the lady announced that she 'had never been so comfortable in her feet' for years. In a week she asked if it would be possible for them to stay on.

'This place seems to grow on you, somehow,' she remarked, as she put down the breakfast tray she had kindly brought down from her room. We managed to fit them in, and they stayed three weeks. As we escorted them down the hill, sliding in their leather travelling shoes, she laughed.

'I *was* silly to think of getting my shoes cleaned,' she said.

6

The Henty were getting ready to leave. When we could get any of them separately we found them pleasant. It was only in a body that we found them overpowering. The engaged couple were dears and promised to come back on their own.

Their last great fling was a day in Barcelona to see a bull-fight. There was a tremendous discussion.

'Well, you go if you like, but I wouldn't, not for the world.'

'I never could bear the sight of blood—turns me all cold.'

'Listen to Doris! You wait till you get there, Doris, then you'll laugh on the other side of your face.'

'I'd like to see it, though, just once.'

'Oh, I'd like to say I'd been, but I don't know—'

'You can always come out if you don't feel well.'

'After all, it's once in a lifetime, I say.'

In the end they all went except George and the engaged couple. We were rather disconcerted because they insisted on taking their lunch. We were longing for them to come back, to hear what they thought of the bull-fight. Most of the guests were in the big room just before dinner, when there was a noise outside. The Henty had returned. The string curtains at the big door parted and one of the youngest of the Henty stood there. She was a dear little thing who would not hurt a fly. She looked at us, her face flushed, and struck an attitude. We could see the rest of the Henty pushing behind her.

'Well?' we chorused.

'Four bulls and a horse!' she exclaimed victoriously.

With the exit of the Henty we had a moment's breathing space, and then the hotel filled up rapidly. I swore never again to have more than twenty people.

The Jellineks came up to say goodbye.

Again they were bathing as usual the next day. A car arrived one lunch time at the bottom of our hill. In it were six Fleet Street toughs. We knew four of them and had told them in London they were not going to be admitted to the Casa Johnstone. They came up for lunch and tried to talk us round. Luckily we had no room, but in any case we would have been firm. Barcelona, we felt, was definitely the place for them. The other two did not look tough at all. They were a man from the Star and his wife. They took us aside and implored us with tears in their eyes to let them stay. They were finding the others a bit too hilarious. We said the only thing we could offer them was the roof terrace, and they could use my sitting-room and bathroom. They jumped at the offer. We saw the others off to Barcelona.

The Star-man and his wife adored Tossa. He was a big Yorkshire man and she was small, with pretty, fair hair. We took them down to Marcus's. In the bar were several of the Civil Guard whose shiny black hats always fascinated visitors. Mrs Star-man immediately remarked on them, and a very beautiful young *guardia* lieutenant from Barcelona was visibly impressed. Blondes are at a premium in Spain, real blondes, that is; there are plenty of synthetic ones in Barcelona, looking most peculiar with their black eyes and olive skins. The *guardia* kept sending impassioned glances at our table; Mrs Star-man was a nice little thing and was slightly embarrassed.

As the evening wore on the party became more and more cheerful, and the effects of a long motor run and Tossa brandy began to be noticeable in the Star-man. He sat smiling before him and his wavering glance fell on one of the *guardia*'s rifles lying against his chair.

'Want ter see t'goon,' he said thickly.

His wife pulled him back into his seat.

'I wanna see t'goon,' explained her husband patiently.

We tried to distract him. We told him funny stories, we

gave him black coffee. We did everything to keep his mind off the *guardia*'s gun. Meanwhile the young lieutenant was thrilled at having apparently caused a sensation, and he redoubled his efforts to attract Mrs Star-man's attention. Our efforts to attend to the Star-man were liable to fail while we were continually getting up to dance. Suddenly we missed him, and found that he had joined the party of *guardias*. He was earnestly explaining that he wanted to see 't'goon.' We felt the only thing to do to avoid having the poor man shot or at least landed in prison was to join the party too. Mrs Star-man was not at all sure she would not prefer her husband shot. Now the young lieutenant could have a lovely time, leaning across the table and gazing right into her eyes. She became more and more embarrassed and kept telling me to do something. I could not resist whispering: 'If your husband is willing to barter you for a look at a *guardia's* gun I can't do anything.' But I saw that she was really upset. So I suggested we all go bathing.

Everyone thought the beach was a splendid idea; so did the *guardias*. Not to bathe, at least not at night. But they did bathe in the daytime. They would march across the beach in full uniform, rifles slung across their backs, disappear behind the rocks, and presently emerge in bathing suits, their hats on, carrying their clothes and trailing their rifles in the sand.

At night bathing was simply a game of the mad foreigners, but it would be fun to watch. The whole party, including the ardent young lieutenant, went down to the beach. Mrs Star-man was frantic. 'I won't bathe, not with these horrible Spaniards there. I can't stay on the beach alone with them. You must stay too.'

'But I want to bathe,' I objected. 'Why don't you go back to the house if you really are worried by the young man. But I assure you it is only *costumbre* to behave like that. He is only showing his admiration. He really doesn't want to rape you.'

'I don't care; I think he's horrid. But I can't go and leave my husband; he is sure to get drowned or something.'

'All right, I'll stay on the beach with you. But it is awkward for me to have to chaperone you. The young lieutenant will probably have me shot.'

We sat on the beach side by side. The *guardias* grouped themselves around, and the lieutenant sat as near to Mrs Starman as he could. She kept moving nearer to me and I kept moving away. The others ran down to the water's edge and took off their clothes. All one could see was occasional glimpses in the beam of the lighthouse which flashed over the beach at intervals. It showed up odd-looking dark figures dressed apparently in white pants, the white pants being the un-sunburnt parts of their bodies.

The whole picture was weird, with the towers of the old town standing out against the clear starry sky, the dark water flickering with occasional flashes of phosphorescence as someone swam. Every now and then the whole scene would be lit up and for a split second one could see plainly the beach, the fishing boats, the old walls beyond and the little group of *guardias*. Behind us, alone but determined to preserve the good morals of the town as well as he could, sat the Tossa mayor.

I was now beginning to learn that an hotel-keeper, especially in a place of our size, was expected to perform a number of duties which are never imagined by the average hotel guest, never taught by the pundits of the hotel schools, and, unfortunately, never figure as an item on an hotel bill.

A family from Wales had booked rooms and wrote to say they were arriving from Barcelona by the bus. Archie went down to meet them. It was simply amazing the way he could carry enormous trunks up the hill. This time he was defeated. He arrived with the family, a charming elderly lady with white hair, the most wonderful-looking elderly man with iron grey hair and bright blue eyes, a very pretty daughter who looked about twenty-five but was seventeen, and a good-looking son of fifteen. Archie introduced them and said Tonet would bring up the luggage.

By this time Tonet had added to his numerous occupations by adopting the Casa Johnstone. He did all the odd jobs, and we bought our English cigarettes from him cheaply. When he occasionally disappeared for a few weeks and was asked on his return what he had been doing he would answer dryly: 'Proving an alibi.' He was as useful a handyman as he was a smuggler. When Archie said Tonet would bring up the luggage it meant a cart and much baggage. I showed the family their rooms and said their things would be up shortly. In the meantime it was dinner time, and no doubt they would like to eat at once.

We were eating as usual on the terrace, under a shelter of leafy bamboos with lights slung along them. We were halfway through dinner when the luggage arrived and was dumped at the end of the terrace. Everyone stared at it. There was nothing larger than a big suitcase, but there were twenty-five pieces, bags and cases of various shapes and sizes.

The old people were dears but they were so silly about their children. The boy was a nice lad and spent his entire time on the beach, either bathing or poking round the rocks. He was sweet to his parents. The daughter was a little fiend. It was not all her fault; her parents did not attempt to control her at all. When she arrived she decided to attract attention by pretending she could not eat anything. Her mother told me: 'You know, Susette has been rather difficult lately. Her father and I hope this holiday will do her good. I do wish she would eat a little more. Perhaps you could persuade her.'

It appeared Susette could only eat omelettes. She had an omelette for every meal. She would arrive at meals after her parents. She would scowl at them, tell her brother he had not washed his hands, and shout for Leonard to bring her omelette. Leon was marvellous. She ordered him about, never dreamed of saying 'please' or 'thank you', but he was always exactly as pleasant to her as to everyone else. Only if one knew him could one notice that his ears were laid back and that there was a glint in his eye. Leon has elf ears, pointed at the tips, and I swear they flatten against his head when he is being mulish. I regret to add that almost invariably he turns out to be right on these occasions.

We could not understand the situation with Susette and her parents. She was simply abominable to them. There was evidently something more than just modern thoughtlessness of children to parents. After a few days her mother took me aside and explained.

'I am afraid you will find Susette a little strange,' she told me in her soft Welsh voice. 'The truth is she is very angry with us. She was very much attached to a man at home, a well-known singer, as a matter of fact, and she did not want to come away at all. So she is determined not to enjoy herself. I do hope she is not being rude to you.'

'Please don't bother about that,' I said. 'As a matter of fact she avoids me because I think she has realized that she won't get any change out of me at all. I'm so sorry that your holiday is being spoilt. Perhaps she will settle down later.'

'I do hope so,' sighed the poor lady, and smiled away.

Susette soon found that not eating was a waste of time, because no one noticed it. So she ate her food normally. Several of the young men in the house were only too anxious to give her a good time but she treated them all with contempt.

I was exasperated with her parents, but they were so charming that I felt I would like to help. I tried to get the child to take some interest in her holiday and persuaded her people to let her come down to the bars with us at night. They demurred, but she overruled them.

'They think I am such a sweet little innocent,' she said

contemptuously to me. 'Silly old fools. What did they think I did all those years at school in France?'

I declined the obvious opening, but asked with a show of interest, 'Well, what did you do?'

'You wouldn't believe me. There isn't much I don't know, let me tell you.'

I was afraid she might, so I escaped.

The business of taking the child dancing at night was complicated. The parents were pleased that she wanted to come with us, but were terrified of what might happen. For several nights the poor old things went with us, having extracted a promise from Susette that she would come back with them at one o'clock. She never once kept her promise, but made such a scene that the parents went home without her. Once they asked me to look after her. I was firm.

'Nothing can possibly happen to the child. All the people in our party are perfectly safe. I will try to persuade her to come up when we leave, but I do refuse to be responsible in any way. Why on earth don't you insist that she comes with you now?'

They shrugged their shoulders helplessly and left.

Help was at hand. A charming French boy suddenly arrived and insisted on staying with us. We had no room, but sent him to Rovira's with the promise that he could come up whenever he liked and could join our party at night. Raoul spoke the most delightful broken English and we all caught it from him. New arrivals were mildly astonished to find apparently sane English people saying 'Ex-cus, pleece,' or that something was the 'more better in whole Tossa'.

Raoul took in the Susette situation in one shrewd glance, decided she was pretty enough to make up for everything, and took her in hand. She was thrilled. Raoul made friends with the parents, and promised to look after the dear child while she was dancing in the evenings, and that she would be brought back at one o'clock. And she was. He punctiliously took her home every night and then came back to the bars. Susette lost her sulky look, became even prettier, and was almost civil to her parents. She still treated Leon like something lower than a very under-footman, but he bore up bravely. Susette meant very little in his young life.

Raoul solved nearly all our problems with regard to Susette, but one night he failed us. It was not his fault. He had to go to Barcelona for a few days on business. Some of the lads staying with us thought they would hire a car and make a day and night of it in Barcelona. Susette heard about it and decided to go too. None of the boys wanted her at all, especially as the parents were against it. That settled it. Susette would go. The parents went to the poor young men and made them swear to look after little Susette. Little Susette herself told her parents that the party would be back in Tossa by midnight. They went off about ten in the morning.

After dinner I noticed the parents were fussing about, and persuaded them to come down to Marcus's for a drink. They went home early and I went with them. It was about a quarter to twelve and I noticed they kept looking towards the Barcelona road.

'She won't be back yet,' I said cheerfully.

'She promised she would be back at twelve,' said her father, but rather doubtfully.

'Oh! There must be a mistake. I know the boys are not coming back until about five in the morning. No one ever does.'

The poor mother looked as if she had been struck. 'How terrible,' she kept moaning.

I rushed and got her a drink. Then with some difficulty I persuaded them to go to bed. I told the old man to convince his wife that the party could not possibly be back before morning.

I had just got to sleep when someone tapped on my door. It was the old man. 'It is two o'clock and there is no sign of them.'

I got up and came out. 'Please make it clear to your wife that they will *not* be here until five o'clock at the earliest. I heard them give the orders to the driver. There is no chance that they have had an accident.'

At three-thirty he was back again. Could I please come up, because his wife was in a dreadful state. I was annoyed, but terribly sorry for the two silly old things. I went upstairs. The mother was sitting by the window with streaming white hair, looking like an illustration for *Where is my Wandering Boy Tonight?* She was almost hysterical. It was useless to repeat the time of the car's probable arrival. I wracked my brains. Then I had an inspiration. Tea. Of Course! The refuge of the British in any circumstances.

I rushed downstairs, made tea and brought it up with some sandwiches and biscuits. I insisted on them both eating and drinking. They revived a little. I managed to persuade the old lady to get back into bed and made her promise that she would not stir out again until five o'clock. I told him that he could wake me again at five if the car hadn't come. Mercifully, nothing disturbed me again until the usual time for getting up.

Those parents suffered agonies that night. I do not think they said a word to their daughter. The only outcome was that the mother retired to bed for the rest of the day with a bad cold and suffering from nerves, and her husband wandered miserably around trying not to worry about both his female relatives. The boy was quite happy and dear little Susette completely unconcerned. How I longed to beat that child. When they left, her mother thanked me profoundly for all I had done, and said that Susette had said that she so enjoyed her stay and wanted to come back alone in the winter. I smiled grimly.

146

7

The *Fiesta Mayor* at San Feliu was held much later than the Tossa one, and by that time the hotel was running smoothly, so we all went. Several of the guests wanted to come too, and we ended by chartering the village bus. Leon was in charge of the party. He had insisted on our wearing evening frocks and stockings, because at San Feliu, which is quite a large town with a big harbour, the *fiesta* is graded according to clothes. There are three dancing tents, a very grand one which can only be entered by immaculate young ladies in stockings and floating skirts and young men in tight leather shoes and ties, and even then one must know someone on the dance committee; a smaller one in which a silk afternoon frock passes muster and the young men may take off their ties after the interval; and a frankly low-class affair of *alpargatas* and cotton frocks where anyone wearing a tie or being clean shaven is definitely sissy. Tossa has none of these distinctions at its *fiesta*. After the hair-raising drive we stopped in San Feliu at the first bar and called for drinks. I asked for a brandy and forgot to name a brand. There are several well-known makes, but the *corriente* or house brandy is served unless one specifies otherwise. The drinks were brought and I gulped mine down. I have never learned to like the taste of brandy, least of all the fiery *corriente* kind. For a moment after swallowing it I just kept my mouth open and made faint wheezing sounds, then I managed a feeble cough: I could only whisper for the rest of the night.

When we arrived at the grand tent, self-consciously holding up our trailing skirts to show that we had stockings on, we found that we needed vouchers. Shades of Hurlingham! A very smart little man recognized Leon and handed him his own pass. The little man was on the dance committee and had the freedom of San Feliu for the *fiesta*. He said we could give the pass back to him any day; he would see us in Tossa. We swept into the tent and I had my first experience of dancing on a carpet laid over sand.

In the middle of the dance someone said they were playing *sardanas* outside, so we rushed out, and found two *sardanas* bands, one at each end of the long front. As soon as one stopped playing the other started, and everyone streamed up and down the front rushing from one band to the other.

Sardanas is the traditional Catalan dance. Men and women join hands in a circle and make skipping movements with their feet in time to peculiar music. *Sardanas* bands are rare, and the half a dozen really first class ones are in great demand for the big *fiestas*. The music is unlike any other kind of national music. Strange shrill instruments are used, and there is a steady tom-tom motive running through the time like a pulse. The whole dance, lighted by lamps hidden in the rustling plane-trees, is reminiscent of tribal rites under flickering torches in the jungle.

However, one glance at the band dispels instantly any idea of Darkest Africa. A *sardanas* band invariably looks like a collection of Methodist ministers. They sit on stiff wooden chairs on a little wooden platform. They are dressed in black suits and black felt hats. Their faces are solemn. One gets the feeling that a member of a *sardanas* band never relaxes, even in the home. It is extraordinary that music which wails of throwing off inhibitions and throbs with savage intensity can possibly come from such a repressed-looking group.

Catalans do not learn *sardanas* dancing. When they are just about able to stand without their mothers they stagger about in time to the music while their elders are dancing. By the time they are able to walk properly they join in the circle. Foreigners who have lived for years in Catalonia have told us that no outsider can learn *sardanas*. It is certainly impossible to learn it properly by watching it. Everyone has variations of the steps, but all seem to get certain movements absolutely synchronized. I bought records and tried at home. The schoolmaster, a beautiful dancer, offered to teach me. He showed me the fundamental rules of *sardanas*; the rest is just practice. A good sense of rhythm is essential and the more one has done any form of dancing the better.

We used to make a ring in Marcus's bar to a *sardanas* record. At first I felt the Catalans might not like a foreigner butting in on their special dance, but the schoolmaster and Francisco, a waiter at one of the other hotels, who was a born dancer, were insistent, and everyone seemed delighted that a foreigner had taken the trouble to learn the dance properly.

There is a complicated system of etiquette about dancing. They join the circle in couples, a man and a girl, and a girl never joins in between two couples by herself. Generally a small circle starts, after the band has played a long introduction which is listened to solemnly like an overture. Then the circle gets larger and larger, and soon another one starts inside the first. As this gets larger, yet another starts, and when the circles move round in different directions the effect is beautiful.

The music is in sections and certain steps have to be done to certain parts of the tune. There is generally someone in each circle who is watching for this and counting the complicated time, and he gives a signal for changing to another phase. Occasionally there are arguments between two self-appointed leaders and they yell good-natured abuse at each other, dancing perfectly the while. Then the whole circle pushes round suddenly and bumps into the two arguers and settles the matter.

Sometimes, when the *sardanas* get really warmed up, the signaller will pretend he is going to change in one direction and the circle will sway away to the right as, with shouts of laugher, he swings it back to the left. I found at later Tossa *fiestas,* when everyone knew I danced *sardanas,* that someone always invited me into the ring, and the schoolmaster and Francisco showed me off with tremendous pride. From the moment I learned *sardanas* I became a complete *fiesta* fan, much to the amusement of Leon, who remembered my scornful remarks about him at the opening of the Casa Johnstone.

At San Feliu we found the *sardanas* lovely but exhausting. One needs to be in strict training to dance seven or eight *sardanas* straight off. The way all the men keep it up without getting in the least tired is amazing. We wandered along the brilliantly lit streets looking at the side shows. We rode on the roundabouts, our best evening frocks tucked up to the knees. The streets were packed with San Feliu youth and beauty in their evening clothes.

It was surprising how well turned out the girls were. They have little money and mostly make their own clothes, but, besides being natural dancers, Catalans seem to be natural dressmakers. Their long frocks were beautifully cut and fitted marvellously. Their hair was permanently waved, and they were all made up skilfully and attractively. They went about in colourful groups or singly, with mother in anxious attendance. Mother was invariably an old country woman, with screwed-back grey hair and no attempt at adornment. If one peered close it was sometimes possible to get a fleeting glimpse of the radiant young daughter in her mother's wrinkled, careworn face. It was often possible, too, to see a shadow of mother's stout hips around the daughter's still comparatively slender ones.

The cafés were packed. Flashy young women with bedraggled hair sat at tables in little groups, and at nearby tables young men from neighbouring villages talked loudly and sent them covert glances. San Feliu had its own brothel, a very elegant affair, and the high spot of the evening to the lads from the less fortunate surrounding villages was a visit there, or at least a date with one of the young women at the cafés. Generally parties of men would come over in motor-buses for the *fiesta*. The only stipulations were they must all pay their share of the bus and must be prepared to wait until the last one wanted to come home. Consequently the outside of the San Feliu brothel was a pathetic sight about six in the morning. Several dead-tired small boys of under fourteen who had persuaded the grown-ups to take them to the *fiesta*, could be seen propped up against the wall waiting for their elders and betters to come out—reminiscent of English pubs with wretched children trying to keep awake until their parents finished their beer.

We wandered into the other tents. I was sad because no one asked to see our stockings. We danced as well as we could in the crowd. Catalans love noise and company. To make it a party they must have two bands and be surrounded by humanity so that they can hardly move or breathe. Eventually we decided to go home. We collected our party, including our little Quimeta who was tired and wanted to come with us instead of waiting for the rest of the Tossa crowd. We watched the sunrise as we drove along the cliff road.

We stopped at Quimeta's house and let the car go on into the village while we cut across the vines to the Casa Johnstone. It was daylight and the sun was beginning to appear over the hill. We took off our stockings and rolled up our long frocks, sprinted across the vines, and crept into the house. In a few minutes we came out again in our bathing suits. It was heavenly bathing, with the sea still golden-pink with the sunrise. A few fishermen stared at us. We felt it was the only way to end a *fiesta*.

At breakfast I noticed an unshaven, weary-looking workman, stripped to the waist, fixing some stakes in the garden. It was the elegant little man who had lent us his pass to get into the San Feliu dance tent.

We found visitors rather trying about *sardanas*. They

always wanted to learn it and could not realize that they had to practise the slow steps for hours before they could attempt the fast ones. They also could not see that the music was so peculiar that it was useless trying to dance at all until they knew the music well and had heard and watched people do it many times. As soon as they knew I could do it they always asked me to give them just an idea how it went.

It is extraordinary how perfectly normal people, holding very often jobs that show they must be intelligent at times, seem very stupid when they are on holiday. It is as if their minds take a rest as well. We were probably luckier than most hotels with our average of really clever, sometimes even brilliant, men and women. We had well-known writers, painters, journalists, business men, yet a rough list which we kept of inane remarks and questions was added to daily. There was so little variety that after we had twenty or so we just had to add a tick as they were repeated.

The inevitable question, 'Why don't you have a funicular?' topped the list. We began to give credit marks to people who did not say that.

'What is the English name of this fish?' In vain we suggested that Catalans, when they named their fish, had carelessly omitted any thought for English visitors. We were quite unable to invent English names on the spur of the moment for lovely pale-grey fish with purple stripes shading into bright orange, or odd green fish with long-way stripes of yellow, or tiny bright-red creatures with sky-blue gills.

'Are those real oranges on that tree?'

'Yes, it's a real tree too.'

'Isn't Leonard English? I could have sworn he was English.'

'Isn't Leonard Spanish? I could have sworn he was Spanish.'

'Would Leonard mind if we tipped him? He has been so good to us.'

Or as a variation: 'What shall I get Leonard? I don't like to tip him.' We assure them that no one in the house is at all proud.

'Is it *pimienta* or *pimiento*?'—'Both, but they mean different things.'

'Are there really no tides? It seems extraordinary.'

Wearily we try to explain that the tides have something or other to do with the gravitational pull of the moon, which does not seem to work in the Mediterranean. We are rather hazy about this; all we know is that there is no appreciable tide, and that it seems to be quite obvious.

'Why do they let the onions and lettuces go to seed like that?'—'For the seed.'

'What are those tall plants with bushy tops like bamboos?'—'Bamboos.'

'Catalan is really only a dialect of Spanish, isn't it?' We get eloquent about the independence and racial purity of Catalonia and the derivation of Catalan direct from Latin like French or Italian. 'Really? That is interesting. I never could do Latin at school.'

'How do the people look so well fed and clean and well dressed?' The only reply seems to be that they are well fed and clean and dress well.

'These people seem so kind to their animals. How can they enjoy bull-fights?' We get out of that one by saying we have never seen a bull-fight. 'Why haven't you seen a bull-fight?' That one is easy. 'We haven't wanted to see a bull-fight.' A glint in our eye warns them not to persevere.

'It must have taken ages to build this house. Did you find the Spaniards very lazy?' The answer to this depended on the amount of time at my disposal. I could praise the Catalan workman *ad lib*.

'What would be the thing like a Mason's apron that I saw a goat wearing?' Usually a dear old lady asked this. We hesitate to go into details about the contraceptive methods among goats, so I find it difficult to explain. When the large Fleet

Street party came out they promptly christened the poor old Billy the Baffled Goat.

'What made you think of coming out here and starting an hotel?'

Not one guest failed to ask this question. People wanted details. So I wrote a book.

Some of comments overheard at meal times or in the café were illuminating.

'Real Bohemian, isn't it?'

'Well, sub-tropical, anyway.'

'Yes, but it's in their blood, the tango is!'

'No, "cactuses" is the plural. I looked it up.'

'So I took out my little phrase book and tried to look while we were dancing, but I couldn't see anything like the word he used.'

'They do look Spanish, they do really.'

'He said "*me cuesta mucho.*" I suppose that means "I love you."'

'Oh, you never know, not in these Latin countries.'

'I suppose they have these big lights on the fishing boats so that they can see what fish they are getting.'

'I don't know where I'd be without my little book. Is yours a Hugo's too?'

Phrase-book Spanish can lead to amusing situations. We took a very pretty girl with us to one of the village Sunday dances. She had a great success, and in the interval an ardent young Catalan attached himself to our party and proceeded to carry on a long conversation in Spanish with Diana. She could not understand a word, but she had brought a phrase book to Spain and had memorized whole chunks of it. When the young man asked passionately, 'Shall I see you tomorrow?' she replied in faultless Spanish, 'Show me the way to the railroad station.' When he grew bolder and suggested seeing her home after the dance she answered severely, 'Have you taken my umbrella?' Surprised but still hopeful the young man offered to show her his house the following day. 'You have charged far too much for this laundry,' she said coldly. 'I only sent three shirts, two pairs of drawers, some silk stockings of my mother's—' But the young man had fled.

Diana's pet phrase was *'Que perro tan feo,'* which means 'What an ugly dog!' She would say it indiscriminately, looking very lovely with a bewitching smile. As long as people did not have a dog it was all right, but it was disconcerting for anyone who was rightly proud of his magnificent Alsatian to have a beautiful young woman come and say charmingly, *'Que perro tan feo!'*

Diana was a dear. She painted—really painted, not the usual English woman's effort at water-colours. She made friends with Zügel, and the pair of them would argue for hours about whether Soviet Russia was really discouraging art. Zügel gloomily thought so; Diana hotly denied it. Neither of them had ever been to Russia.

Diana suffered from an ambitious mother. Her mother had definite ideas about her daughter; Diana had definite ideas about herself. She adored Tossa, was perfectly happy wandering about in an old pair of trousers and a paint-covered smock, scraped her lovely fair curls back off her face with an old piece of ribbon, and did not care if her nails needed manicuring. Her mother, who oozed Debrett, almost wept in her despair.

'And do you know, Mrs Johnstone,' she would tell me, 'the chances that girl has missed. Tony Wilding was crazy about her—you know, Lord Webster's son; Arthur Clarence, who after all will have the title and Clarence Place some time—his father can't go on much longer, even if the family do all live till about a hundred—would marry her tomorrow if she would only make an effort, but you can't expect anyone to want to marry a girl who takes no interest in her appearance.'

'But after all, she is only nineteen!' I protested.

'I was married at seventeen,' said the lady severely. 'That admittedly was a mistake. But I married again at twenty, and I was twenty-three when my last husband came into the title. Of course, *here* Diana can do as she likes, there is no one in this tiny place of the slightest interest matrimonially. In fact we wouldn't stay here except that it is so cheap.'

'I am sorry that you are not enjoying your stay,' I said.

'Oh, I am all right. I never mind an occasional rest in a one-horse place, and it does one good to be bored to tears occasionally. How you stand it, I don't know, having to be polite to people all the time.'

'Sometimes it is difficult,' I admitted.

'You must get very tiresome people at times. But after all, I suppose it doesn't matter to you so long as their cheques are honoured.'

'Oh, we have no bother about cheques,' I said.

She was one of the rudest women I have ever met, but I liked her. She had a wicked tongue, but was sometimes so amusing that one forgave the sting in the remark. She would say biting things about you behind your back, worse things to your face, and even worse things about herself. Actually I am sure she was an extremely lonely person who simply could not help putting everyone's back up. Her bitter worldliness was a sort of defence against herself. She was always pleasant to me, as pleasant as she knew how to be. I did not mind her barbed retorts, and I think she liked people who stood up to her. She bullied Diana and nagged her unmercifully in front of other people, but Diana would retire behind a misty absent-mindedness that almost drove her mother frantic. We used to argue occasionally about ballet-dancing; she was a keen ballet fan, of course only first nights. Some months after she had left she sent me two books, both illustrating her point in our argument, it is true, but I thought it was extremely nice of her.

Luckily, I liked most of our guests. Archie is much more

tolerant than I and is often annoyed with me because I find it impossible to be pleasant to people I can't bear. These were mercifully very few.

Both as hotel-keepers and as private individuals we loved genuine people. We found the real Cockney fitted in as easily as the real top-shelfer. Tossa's lack of class distinctions and the polyglot nature of all conversation in Marcus's bar had a very levelling effect. It is difficult to be affected in a foreign language.

Occasionally we struck something really "refained", but generally they meant so well that one put up with them and got considerable amusement out of them. Lady Twickenham was ever so genteel. She was not called Lady Twickenham, but she was so grand and talked so much about her 'flaht' near Richmond, that the name just happened. Lady Twickenham was unbelievable. As a character in a play one would say she was hopelessly overdrawn. She used every cliché and every refined intonation that has ever been spelt out laboriously by tired authors trying to characterize a genteel lady. She even said 'Eow' before every sentence.

'Eow, Mrs Johnstone, I do think Mr Johnstone is just tew, tew wonderful. The way he has adapted himself to this new life, I mean.'

'It is lucky that he likes it so much,' I said brightly.

'Eow, I think he is wonderful. The way he waits . . . just like a waiter. It is wonderful of him, right out of his class, tew.'

I was very controlled. 'Do you think he has gone up or down?' I asked earnestly.

Lady Twickenham loved to sit in the sunshine and reminisce over the good old days. She was quite a young woman, about thirty-five or forty, but looked as if constantly living up to the standards of Richmond had aged her. She would always preface any remark with a deep sigh. 'Eow, dear old Monty,' she started one day. We thought at last the sad story of her life was at hand. But we were wrong. 'Such a gay old place. I love the Riviera. Cannes—ah! Cannes.' We waited. What about Cannes? Lady Twickenham sighed still more deeply. 'Dear old Monty,' she repeated sadly. We never got any further. We always found ourselves sitting and sighing in unison. One day she left us. She was going to meet some friends in Barcelona and go back to England with them.

'Good-bay, good-bay!' she cried from the car. 'So sad to leave. But dear old Barcy, you know, dear old Barcy—'

8

Fleet Street descended on us in a body. We had been getting very restive about them. They all swore they were coming but they would not fix their dates. We were getting more and more full and still they would not book. However, some of the more steady, and, incidentally, the more comfort-loving ones, did book their rooms in advance. At the very last moment, when the house was completely full, I got a wire from Owen Lookyou and Jimmy Foster saying they wanted to come and please could we fit them in somewhere? I wired back 'Room in office for two half-wits.' They sent a comforting wire signed 'Wit.'

It was good to be back in the Bloomsbury pub atmosphere. It was grand to hear Archie calling the guests a bunch of bastards when he felt like it. The only questions we were asked were, 'How much is brandy?' and 'What time are meals?' We did not have to show them the bars or even give them directions.

The day the half-wits arrived most of the household, including them, disappeared after lunch. We went into the village on some errands and heard strange dismal sounds coming from behind the closed windows of one of the bars. We listened and heard strains of *The Red Flag*. We rushed in, to find most of our guests in a heaven of delight at being able to sit in a bar all afternoon. They had a definite routine. They managed to get down to breakfast in time to allow them a bath and a sunbathe before moving over to the café for beer. They came up for lunch any time between 1.30 and 2.30. They were very considerate about not being too late when we explained what a lot of extra work it meant for us.

After lunch they would lay about in the sun until it dawned

on them that it was time to eat or drink again. They went out to the Buen Retiro and wallowed in tea, cocoa, and sweet cakes. Fleet Street toughs will be boys. They danced there, had a quick drink before leaving and strolled home through the woods. At the bottom of our hill, specially sent from heaven for our guests, was a long low building that had been converted into a bar.

Dinner was from eight o'clock.

At 8.15 Archie would go down to the bar to collect the crowd. At 8.45 I would go down and succeed in whipping them all in, including Archie. I had a secret arrangement with the bartender to close the bar at 8.30; he was as anxious for his dinner as I was. Fleet Street insisted on teaching him to say, 'Time, gentlemen, please!' and 'Last orders, please!' It usually took him about half an hour to close his bar and say his piece to the approval of his teachers. He was a charming German boy called Adam, and at night he would push everyone out of his bar about 12.30 because he wanted to go along to Marcus's, which stayed open until morning, and enjoy himself with the crowd.

I found for the first time that running an hotel could be tiring. At least trying to run an hotel and live like one of the guests was tiring. I had to go down in the evenings with my friends and we never got to bed before three or four in the morning. They could lie in bed all the morning but I had to get some work done so that I could go out with them to the Buen Retiro in the afternoons. Owen and Jimmy were so used to having me round in London that they could not understand if I said I could not come dancing or bathing or drinking with them. In any case it was such fun having them again that I wanted to be with them as much as possible.

They slept in our office, originally converted into a bedroom for a honeymoon couple who cried when we said we had no room for them. They had been staying elsewhere on the coast and had not liked it very much and came to Tossa and us by accident. We liked them so much we said we would put them up in the office. They stayed for five weeks and we loved them. From then on we never had a chance to change the room back into an office again, and had to build on an extra office outside the kitchen.

We found ourselves inevitably reacting kindly to honeymoon couples. They generally gave themselves away to us at once and we instinctively laid our hotel at their feet. They got the best available room, the most sympathetic service, their secret was carefully guarded if they wished. The next time Archie and I spend a holiday in an hotel we have decided to pretend we are on our honeymoon. It seems to pay.

We had a large percentage of people honeymooning. We loved them all. One of them was the man who tried to sell me a vacuum cleaner in London and to whom I had sold Tossa instead. He arrived proudly with his new wife. The first of our friends to come with his bride was Norman Clark, of the *News Chronicle*. He visited us early in our first year, before he was married, and became immediately an unpaid member of the staff. He did all the odd jobs in England for us when he went back, and whenever we wanted anything sent out or some message safely delivered we always said at once, 'Write to Norman'. He came again the next year with Bae, his wife. We tried to pull out a little extra for them, even above our usual for newly married couples.

With the half-wits in the office, we were full-up. An aunt of mine from London was put in my sitting-room. She was adopted by the entire household and was known universally as 'Me-Ant'. She was a tremendous success and a great help to us. She giggled with the toughs and they adored her; she chatted to the few non-Fleet Street and rather bewildered strangers, who were not sure at first if it was a hotel or an asylum they had struck, and immediately put them at their ease. She helped me in the kitchen and made the kitchen staff shriek with laughter, although they were quite unable to understand a word she said and she was equally unable to understand them. To watch her explaining something to Isabel was a lesson in the art of pantomime. In a very short while she knew most of the villagers intimately and knew the names of their children and all about their expected children.

Geoffrey Edwards and his wife arrived unexpectedly one day. He is the wireless editor of the *News Chronicle*. We simply could not refuse them so we put them on the roof terrace and they used our bedroom for a dressing room. Percy Rudd, *News Chronicle* sports editor, had had the foresight to book well in advance, and he and his wife had the 'Royal Suite', as they called it. It was simply a large room with a big sun terrace. 'La Rudd', as Mrs Rudd was immediately called, somehow suited the best room in the house. She was definitely the uncrowned queen of the Casa Johnstone. She held court over the toughs and was the envy of the very young girls who looked tousled after bathing, or hot and shiny-faced after long hours dancing in the bars. La Rudd always looked exactly as if she had just stepped out of a bandbox. She lay in the sun and swam in the sea for hours, but her perfect pink and white complexion remained the same and her lovely black shiny waves exactly in place. She danced heartily in the atmosphere of Marcus's bar and would stay up until three in the morning without a hair out of place or a spot of powder disarranged. She wore the loveliest clothes but never looked overdressed. As the entire Casa Johnstone at this time went about in a body like a school, we always needed several tables at the café or in the bars, and generally made a huge circle. With La Rudd presiding over half the circle and Me-Ant over the other half, Archie and I sat blissfully somewhere in between, listening to them both doing our stuff.

Leon was not very interested in coming down to the bars with us. He worked harder than we did and needed more rest; also the journalist jargon was uninteresting for him. He did not know half the references to limericks or funny stories, and on the whole he thought the wit of Fleet Street just about as silly as it probably is. When every other word is an expletive, which is senseless enough taken at its face value anyhow, it makes a sentence idiotic to a foreigner. It is just as illuminating for a German to hear something called 'bloody' as for an Englishman to get all worked up because a German says 'thunder weather'. Leon does not drink because he dislikes the taste of alcohol; he does not smoke because he dislikes the taste of tobacco; and there really wasn't much else for him to do in a bar.

I admit bar conversations are not exactly brilliant. There were moments in Marcus's bar when pearls of wisdom were flung around; when, for instance, one found oneself sitting with Zügel, Masson, Petersen and Matisse, and one could follow the rapid south German of Zügel and the Düsseldorf of Petersen or, when Masson started to speak, a flood of French from him and Matisse. A table with Ralph Bates or A J Cronin would no doubt produce something of moment. But on the whole, especially towards the small hours of the morning, the brilliance would be definitely lacking.

'Have you heard the one—?'

'Come on! Just one for the road.'

'Old Johnny got sacked at last. His chief got tired of doing his feature for him.'

'. . . and he brought the girl back with him from Paris to his London flat and found his wife had cleared out with every stick of furniture, so they had to sleep on the floor.'

'Pity he drinks.'

'So long as he keeps off whisky—'

'They haven't a bean, but she makes rugs out of his pictures and they sell quite well.'

'He's all right, but I can't bear his woman.'

'They had to divorce because they were both so busy working for Peace.'

'Oh! Was there a child? They must have got rid of it

somewhere.'

'And when I answered it was someone phoning me from my flat. "Where do you keep your food and drink?" they asked. I answered, "In the cupboard near the fireplace. Who the hell are you, anyway?"'

'So in one week he was sick in every capital in Europe.'

'Then Buck House butted in and we had to kill the whole story.'

'The wretched girl was waiting hours at the registry office and we all sat about dying for a drink. Suddenly he came in, supported by Bill and Henry. He drew himself up with dignity and said to the registrar, "Hail to thee, blythe spirit, bird thou never wert."'

Owen took a great liking for the schoolmaster, and they would sit for hours together with Owen trying to teach Moreno English.

'You drink brandy,' Owen would say clearly and distinctly, 'I drink beer.'

'You drink brandy,' Moreno would say obediently.

'No, no. *You* drink brandy, I drink beer.'

'I drink beer—' the schoolmaster would try.

'No you don't, you drink brandy. Look here, listen, damn it. *You* drink brandy, *I* drink beer.'

The bewildered Moreno would try again. '*You* drink brandy, *I* drink beer.'

'No, no, blast it all. Look at that, can't you? That's beer, isn't it. I'm drinking it, aren't I? Try again. '*I* drink beer—'

'*I* drink nothing,' said the schoolmaster, unexpectedly and firmly.

Owen was rather attached to a German girl staying with us. They would carry on long conversations in English, he speaking with a hearty German accent, she speaking quite good English. At the end he would turn to her: '*I* had no idea I spoke such good German.'

One of the charming things about Marcus's bar was that so many Tossa people came as well as visitors. There were always some of the best Tossa dancers there, and a group or two of fishermen, unshaven-looking toughs with delightful manners and flashing smiles. They came to look at the comic foreigners. The foreigners came to see the funny natives. Moreno and Francisco sometimes organized a *sardanas* to one of Marcus's records. It was not nearly so effective in the tiny room, but the visitors loved watching it. Moreno was a handsome creature, with curly black hair and twinkling brown eyes with long lashes. He danced *sardanas* and *tangos* equally well. Francisco was a lightly built wiry man with the Catalan's natural grace. He danced *sardanas* beautifully. One got the impression of suppressed power in Francisco and felt that, with his knowledge of people and the fact that he had travelled and spoke several languages, he would make a shrewd hotel manager. The *sardanas* in Marcus's bar became almost an institution, the Tossa lads would join in, and always from some dark corner a black and beery-looking old man would emerge and proceed to dance better than anyone.

The schoolmaster was deeply in love with Mattie Pritchard, the lovely blonde wife of Caradog Pritchard, the well-known Welsh bard. Caradog was amused, and used to sit in a poetic trance watching the black-haired schoolmaster and the primrose-haired Mattie tangoing. Mattie spoke fluent French, which Moreno could manage, and the schoolmaster was entirely overcome at last to find a foreigner who was both beautiful and conversational. He has never forgotten her, and now one only has to say to him, 'Do you remember a very lovely blonde with blue eyes,' and he interrupts with a rapt, 'Ah, Mattie!'

Norman Cliff, the *News Chronicle* foreign editor, was one of the sober members of the party, although there is a libellous story, spread by the riotous ones, that he was found sitting in a puddle at the bottom of our hill trying to swim up to the house. He has never denied the story, no doubt thinking his quiet smile sufficient to discount any such rumours. Also the fact that there was no rain during his stay may account for his disregarding the story.

Peter Hall, *Herald* chief sub, was here with his wife. They had the wisdom to realize that they had enough of Fleet Street in Fleet Street or Long Acre and occasionally broke away and went off on their own. We liked them enormously, and of course had to nickname them 'Albert and Queenie'.

9

We were very excited about the visit of Lotte Leonard. Leon's mother had never been to Tossa and we had never met her. We had heard so much about Leon's mother that we had rather forgotten that Lotte Leonard was a very famous person. The excitement among the German colony brought it home to us. Various refugees ran up and down our hill with flowers; inquiries about Frau Leonard's arrival poured in.

Before Leon's mother came, his brother Wolfgang arrived from Berlin. We adored Wolfgang at sight. He was the antithesis of Leon but had a charm of his own that was almost as strong. It is hard to imagine two brothers more different. Wolfgang, solid, slow, with round, horn-rimmed glasses, was so exactly the Englishman's idea of a German that one almost thought it could not be true. With Leon one felt there was a hope of persuading him to do something he did not want to do; with Wolfgang one knew it was useless to try. While Leon would chat away happily in six languages, Wolfgang would be silent in probably as many. No one ever knew how many languages Wolfgang spoke. He and Leon had in common the fact that they never missed anything anyone else said or did.

I used to be chaffed about the number of bathing suits I had. It was said I wore a different one each day. After Wolfgang had been staying with us for just over a week I was running down to the beach in a pair of bathing pants with a handkerchief top. Wolfgang surveyed me from the top terrace. 'Eight and a half,' he counted solemnly.

The two boys went to Gerona to meet their mother. Leon was almost as speechless from excitement as Wolfgang was from habit. We were thrilled, too, and Isabel kept running from the terrace to see if the car was back yet. Leon had so endeared himself to everyone that we all shared the excitement of his mother's visit.

The moment we saw Lotte Leonard we knew exactly why Leon and Wolfgang were so nice. She was the loveliest person. Without knowing anything about her singing voice, one could see that she had the personality of someone used to being successful at a job. She had a delightful mixture of shyness and shrewd humour. Me-Ant and La Rudd both loved her at sight; Archie and I wanted to adopt her and have her permanently part of the Casa Johnstone. Leon was simply adorable about his mother and went about with his grey eyes positively sparkling behind their black lashes. He bore it bravely when she gave a shriek of horror and attacked his clothes, turning out boxes and shelves, and having a real field-day among shirts and socks.

Leon had a tiny bedroom, which he insisted he preferred because he could get at everything more easily when there was no room for anything to get mislaid. However, he had a passion for hoarding old *alpargatas*, and it was usually impossible to get into his room at all except by some method known only to Leon and the women who bravely tried to clean his room. His mother triumphed over this and spent ecstatic days sorting and airing and cleaning, and finally she packed away all the things she thought he would not need in Tossa, including two suits of tails, relics of the days when he really was a waiter, and a hat which she wrapped up in paper and labelled Hut, just in case. Leon was hysterical with laughter when he saw everything was so carefully labelled, and thought it really rather absurd to put everything away, but his mother was firm, much to my admiration. I have never been able to be firm with Leon.

One of the refugees, with rare organizing ability, arranged for Lotte Leonard to give a concert. There were several large halls in Tossa and plenty of chairs, in fact everything necessary for a concert except a piano and an accompanist.

168

Miraculously both were found. Fräulein Magnus, a visitor to Tossa, came to the rescue, and a piano, tuned to concert pitch, was discovered in a rambling farmhouse perched on a hill just outside the village.

The house was about six hundred years old, with a roomy entrance hall festooned with bunches of orange-coloured corn-cobs, strings of scarlet tomatoes, and glistening onions hanging from the old beamed ceiling. An enormous Catalan kitchen could just be seen through a wrought-iron grill, out of which four sleepy chickens peered in amazement. The piano was in an inner room, which opened out of the hall through a big archway, under which Lotte Leonard stood with the glow of candles lighting up an old carved shrine in the corner behind her.

The hall was packed. Everyone was asked to bring their own chairs, but many people preferred to use the sacks of nuts and beans which made the pit-stalls. We realized as soon as she started to sing that here was Lotte Leonard, until the Nazi régime leading oratorio and Lieder soprano in Germany, soloist with Furtwängler, Bruno Walter, Mengelberg; heard from all German radio stations: now known to listeners of Geneva, Lausanne, Zurich, Vienna, Amsterdam, Luxembourg, and London stations. Under the orange and scarlet ceiling flickering in the light of two candles, everyone was under a spell. Even the hens behind the grill were silent. Outside, crowded people who could not pack into the barn-like entrance hall, children, old women, fishermen, famous painters, writers, journalists. Oddly enough, in that queer old house in this small fishing village, Lotte Leonard probably had as many distinguished people in her audience as at the Wigmore Hall. Most famous singers would be horrified at being asked to sing under these conditions, with an untried piano and an unknown but, as it proved, very efficient accompanist. Lotte Leonard is no ordinary singer.

It was during the visit of Leon's family that some of the

Fleet Street lads decided to make a day and night of it in Barcelona. The idea was to hire a car, and, if one got the right driver, one might leave Tossa after breakfast and return in time for breakfast the following day, all for the ordinary charge for a trip to Barcelona plus a substantial tip for the accommodating driver. Chico was the lad to get, as he liked a night out himself and had no objection to staying in Barcelona until five or six o'clock in the morning.

This particular bunch invited me to go with them and I insisted on taking Wolfgang as well. He was rather dubious about the company and the fact that we would not guarantee at what hour we might return, but he decided that it was his only chance of seeing Barcelona. He was most unwilling to wear shoes again and I told him to wear his *alpargatas* if he wanted to. He looked at me seriously through his glasses and put on his shoes.

We started off hilariously, singing songs and telling stories. Wolfgang sat in front with Chico. He occasionally looked back to make sure I was all right. He was rather doubtful about the wisdom of me being the only woman in the party. We rocked round the twisty road to Lloret and settled down for a comparatively straight run to Barcelona. We passed through a village and the road bent round a group of bamboos and straight up a hill, with a corner at the top. Round the corner swayed a large lorry. It swerved across the road, gathered speed down the hill. To our horror we realized it was out of control. The driver was helplessly tugging at the wheel. I do not think anyone spoke a word as the clumsy monster lurched towards us.

Chico, driving as he always did, well on his own side, did not change his course by a fraction. The lorry ran across in front of us, straightened out with the camber of the road, and was past. It scraped so close to us that I could have sworn it scratched the paint. Chico continued, quite unconcerned. Wolfgang looked back to see if I was all right. Someone in the back seat shouted that the lorry had ended up in the clump of bamboos. That broke the still stupefied silence of the others. Everyone started talking at once. Owen, who was sitting behind me, kept saying, 'I might have been killed.'

'I should have been killed first,' I said, rather tersely.

We decided that a drink at the next village was definitely called for. Of a bad collection I spoke the best Spanish and I tried to tell Chico what we all thought of him. He smiled quietly to himself and drank his vermouth.

When we got to Barcelona we were held up in the usual traffic jam on entering the town. In Barcelona the lights are worked by a policeman on a crossing, who steps off his safe perch on the pavement, blows a little whistle, and walks up to the lights and switches them to red or green, or whatever it is. As we waited for the signals to do something, or have something done to them, a *guardia* walked up to the car. He wanted to see our passports. There was a state of war in Catalonia. There always is a state of war, because the last one is never over before the next one begins. No one takes any notice, but *guardias* wander about with nothing much to do, and pass the time by asking people for their identity papers.

This *guardia* tried the window where Wolfgang was. He did not know Wolfgang. Getting no response he tried at the next window where Jimmy was sitting. Jimmy offered him a drink in English. I had whispered to Chico to keep quiet and was prepared to know even less Spanish than I did. The *guardia*, rather hot under the collar by this time, had one more try at my window—then saw the lights were going to be changed. He could not admit defeat, so he decided that after all he had only wanted to have a look at our nice car. He ran an appreciative finger along the mudguard, humming softly under his breath, and, with an absent-minded pat or two on the window ledge, he wandered off, carelessly shifting his weight from one foot to the other.

We let Chico garage the car and arranged to meet him at

five o'clock in the morning. We then went off to see Barcelona. That to Fleet Street meant only to find the nearest pub. It was a matter of complete indifference to them what the pub was called or the name of the street where it was. But not to Wolfgang. Before he would touch his beer he whipped out a map of Barcelona and stood on the pavement opposite our table turning solemnly round and round, deep in the intricacies of the Barcelona maze. When he found where we were he was greatly relieved and was able to drink his beer. When we penetrated, by devious and delayed routes, to the Plaza Cataluña and fell exhausted into the Baviera at the top of the Ramblas, we lost Wolfgang. We found him taking photographs of the Plaza Cataluña.

At the Baviera we collected some friends of mine who had an appointment with us. One was a Frenchman, the other an Englishman and both had jobs in Barcelona. Consequently I had arranged so that we arrived an hour later than the appointment, and we had only half an hour to wait. I had learned quite early that in Barcelona it was impossible to get to a play and difficult to get to a cinema unless one went alone. Even if one arranges to have dinner with people before going to a play with them it is the same. They arrive an hour late, they stay at least an hour over drinks before dinner, not drinking so much as watching the people passing on the Ramblas and talking, and are then always having just one more when one tries to move. Dinner takes two hours in any restaurant, and then the Spanish waiter feels he has been hurried.

On this occasion there was some hurry as the Frenchman had to catch the Paris express which left punctually, like all Spanish trains, from a terminus at 2.30. We started lunch at one o'clock, knowing that gave us very little time. The usual delay, the usual charming but deliberate waiter, the usual excellent food that seems to have been gathered by the cook in person at a distant market while you wait—I realized there would be a rush for that train. We all got our food eventually, except Wolfgang who had ordered something that sounded as if it might be a *Wiener Schnitzel*, and anyway had plenty of potatoes. I looked at the time and realized we had a quarter of an hour to make the train. There was no question of leaving the Frenchman to catch his own train; we had promised to see him off and anyway he would never have got it alone. I asked for the bill and told everyone to eat as fast as they could. Wolfgang looked tragic. The waiter brought the *Wiener Schnitzel* but no bill. I asked again and we all got up. All except Wolfgang who was determined to save something from the wreck.

Finally I told two of the party to go out and get a taxi. I asked again for the bill. The waiter smiled sweetly and went away. I wrenched Wolfgang away from his *Schnitzel* and we all went downstairs, where the others had a taxi outside. A protesting waiter followed us out.

'If you don't bring the bill now you just won't get paid,' I said with one foot on the step of the taxi. The bill appeared at once. We arrived at the station as the train doors were being slammed. We crashed the barrier and flung the Frenchman into the train. He owes us a vote of thanks. He went to Paris to get a job at a thousand a year.

Wolfgang protested. He had had no lunch and he was not enjoying himself at all. We all went across to a tiny pub opposite the station and had our shoes cleaned. Wolfgang did not want his cleaned, but the man did them by mistake. We offered Wolfgang beer; Wolfgang wanted his *Schnitzel*. Finally we forgot him because the bootblack turned out to be a boxing fan; he borrowed a paper from a nearby stand and we heard all about Joe Louis in Catalan. We all read the paper and when we left we solemnly gave it back to the owner of the stand. It never occurred to any of us to buy it.

After this Wolfgang struck. He said he had some business at a bank and would meet us at 7.30, in time for dinner. We were all certain that he spent the afternoon visiting museums. I decided to get my hair cut, and the boys went off to see a *pelota* match. I was certain they never got further than the café at the door of the *frontón*. We all arranged to meet at 7.30 and to spend a leisurely evening seeing the night life of Barcelona.

Of course, I was much longer getting my hair done than anyone, especially the hairdresser, thought. By the time I managed to get to the rendez-vous even my other Barcelona friends, who had offered to show me around, had arrived. The boys were most amused at something and I discovered that poor Wolfgang had been positive that I had been kidnapped at least. He was shocked by the levity with which this suggestion was treated, and every time he put forward the idea that I was probably by now almost beyond reach of help, all he got was, 'She's all right. Who cares anyway? Waiter, another beer!' The boys thought this very entertaining, but I was grateful for a few kind thoughts and saw that Wolfgang had a real meal at dinner.

Barcelona night life is quite the dreariest form of entertainment one can find. There are streets and streets of cabarets where one goes into a place rather like an aged provincial cinema, only with shelves on the backs of the seats. One buys an extremely bad cognac or even worse coffee, puts it on the shelf in front and may then stay until the end of the performance if one can bear it.

A typical Barcelona cabaret show is terrible. The people who go because they hope to see—well, the sort of thing you can't see at home, dear—are disappointed, because it is not even particularly shocking. The whole show is obscene only because it is bad. There is left no single excuse for any of these women to stand up on a stage and take off their clothes. One feels they are definitely in a wrong setting, but even in the dark they must be pretty dreadful.

The whole show is just a crude form of prostitution, and

anyone who can bear it can make dates with the performers and retire with them to little curtained boxes in the gallery. After watching the women trying to sing and dance no doubt people think they must be able to do something. Occasionally there is a turn which has obviously nothing to do with the business of the cabaret. This is inevitably the manager's wife or near relation. Probably she once worked in a cabaret, but now comes on as an amateur. She is dressed in the usual Spanish skirt, flowing from a tight band round the hips, and with various crossed straps and bands round her waist and bosom. In between the straining bands her rolls of fat bulge and shake, and she waves her stout little arms, tightly encased in bracelets. She has done this dance so often that she really need not think at all, and her mind is obviously on the *bacalao* which is doubtless steaming at home. She has the blank expression of all Spanish dancers, but her movements are blank also. She sometimes comes to in the middle of a step and stops as if surprised to find herself there at all, then she shakes her still neat little head, heaves round her enormous bulk and, on oddly slim ankles, trips off XL according to original stage directions.

The desperate visitor stands about an hour of this and then moves to another cabaret, which is exactly the same. We went off to the 'Creolla'. This is a so-called tough joint, and people warned us to watch our pockets and look after our handbags. The whole show is run by what Victorians politely called 'female impersonators'. We all went into the usual small enclosure, which is 'safer' than being let loose among the audience. In front were seats with tables, and in the middle a dance floor. I looked round for some toughs. There were several large parties, obviously families, consisting of father, mother, a few small boys usually asleep, grandmother, very much awake, and generally a tiny baby. Several newly married or engaged couples entirely occupied with each other, a few English sailors trying hard to get enthusiastic about the well-

175

worn females with them, a few tourists rather thrilled at being in the underworld but puzzled by its respectability, seemed to make up the rest of the audience.

A band started the usual tango and a few couples danced in an uninterested way. Then a spot-light shone on the floor and the performance started.

The first turn was a series of impersonations of well-known actresses, all Spanish and unknown to us. The boys taking the parts were marvellously made up and wore really wonderful clothes. All the turns were practically the same; the boys sang and danced, all dressed as women and looking exactly like women. That was the trouble. Everyone always talked of 'Creolla' under their breath as being a haunt of vice and homosexuals, but it seemed to me that to disguise a homosexual so perfectly that, unless one knew it was impossible to tell he was not a woman, rather defeated any object of it being a sinister performance. Most people would think they were just another bunch of women performers, who sang and danced even worse than the lot in the last cabaret.

Wolfgang flatly refused to believe they were not women. He looked at us kindly but pityingly when we assured him that they were really sweet little boys. This evidently weighed on his mind, because afterwards when we were having supper in 'Hollywood', where one can dance on a really good floor, he broke his habitual silence at intervals to mutter, 'Of course they were women.'

We found dancing on a real floor in leather shoes after months of dancing on tiles in alpargatas was perilous. The Barcelona members of our party were all right but the rest of us risked our necks at every step. Wolfgang was getting very bored with us. He wanted some proper food, he wanted to go to bed and, to make things worse, a very lurid lady at the next table had her eyes on him. Wolfgang glared at her over his glasses but it needed far more than that to discourage her. When we saw that he was really hating it we moved off. I was ready to go back to Tossa, but there is nothing harder than to collect a bunch of Fleet Street people to go home. As soon as they all seem to be under way someone says, 'What about one for the road?' and they all disappear into the nearest bar. Every time someone said, 'Well, what about home?' Wolfgang's whole face brightened. Then someone would add, 'Just another cognac,' and it would all fall again.

At last we all collected in the car. I sat at the back with Owen and Jimmy on each side. Wolfgang sat by Chico but with a firm eye on me to see if I was all right. Jimmy fell asleep immediately, with his head in my lap and his feet round Chico's ears. Owen was rather cross because the rest of us had insisted on eating fish soup with garlic and he had not had any. We settled down for a peaceful run back to Tossa.

Presently we heard a whistle. Jimmy woke up and said 'Goal!' and went to sleep again. Chico did not take any notice. We had passed a car a few minutes before. Suddenly a big car came alongside us and tried to run us off the road. We could just see that there were two men in front. Chico shouted at them and accelerated. The car then drew alongside and the man not driving opened his door and banged it against our car. Chico swore at them and tried to get away. Then they came up and pushed us on to the grass verge between the road and a field. We stopped with a jerk and sat in the car, too surprised to do anything. The back door of the other car opened and out climbed eight *guardias*. We almost went to sleep counting them. They all had rifles and made a circle round our car and waited, rifles levelled. Our headlights glinted on the barrels. Jimmy woke up again, gave one look and roared with laughter. We immediately silenced him. A *guardia* will not stand being laughed at, and he is allowed by law to shoot first and inquire afterwards.

Chico was meanwhile arguing with the two men in the front

of the car. They were not in uniform and Chico had had no idea it was an official car. I tried to follow the extremely rapid exchange of comments and, as they were speaking Castilian, I gathered that we had offended against some law about dipping our headlights. Chico showed the same coolness as when the lorry came at us. The moment he realized he was dealing with officials he did not lose his temper or shout, but appeared to be reasonably explaining something. The other men were shrieking and screaming with rage. Wolfgang suddenly realized he was no longer in Germany. He became extremely fluent and cursed the officials heartily—mercifully in German. They took not the slightest notice but continued to scream at Chico. At last Chico succeeded in persuading them that we were just a bunch of foreigners who really meant no harm, and the men seized Chico by the hand and they all made nearly as much noise assuring each other that everything was all right. The armed guard was called off and we continued on our way to Tossa, Wolfgang still muttering maledictions in between asking me if I was sure I was all right.

The next day Wolfgang was very thoughtful. In the evening we were in Marcus's bar with the Leonard family. Me-Ant and La Rudd were each trying to persuade Lotte Leonard to stay with them when she went to London for concerts. Suddenly Wolfgang said firmly, 'Of course they were really women.' At that moment Tonet came in with his gang. Tonet's gang look rather like a chain gang. They are all husky louts with bristling black chins. They filed past our table, grinning and greeting us in their deep Catalan voices.

'Wolfgang,' I whispered, 'these really *are* women.'

10

The Jellineks came up to say goodbye. They were leaving that afternoon by the Lloret bus. In the evening we met them in Marcus's bar.

Archie was working hard at our publicity for the winter. He had been extremely successful in getting the Casa Johnstone known and talked about during the summer, and had managed to get pseudo-news paragraphs almost every week in pages dealing with resorts. References to Tossa kept creeping into such unexpected places as wireless notes, theatre notes, educational notes and other features run by our guests, and into talks on the radio about bird life in Spain and autonomy in Catalonia.

Some serious advertising was needed for the winter. We hoped to get a few guests the first year and then have a full winter when Tossa became known as a winter resort. Until we built our hotel with central heating and fires people did not think of coming after October. Archie hit on what proved to be the most successful of our advertisements: 'We live at Casa Johnstone, Tossa de Mar, Gerona, Spain, because we like it.' That, with our names, was the whole ad. We found the people who responded were exactly the people we wanted. We were getting wiser in framing our letters and advertising so as to attract congenial guests and scare off the others.

Archie considered doing the publicity was work. He would say it was the only work he did. He did not count waiting as work—one colleague said, 'As a waiter you're a bloody good sub'—or keeping the back premises tidy, or seeing that the rubbish bins were emptied, or digging the garden between the agavas. He was also in charge of the finance, at least with regard to any money in England. Once the money arrived in

Spain it was handed over to Leonard. Archie considered escorting guests round the bars as part of his own entertainment. Someone said to him, 'Archie has three big jobs—finding the money, finding the guests and getting rid of the rubbish.'

Archie's greatest triumph was over our plates. His Barcelona find of two large dinner services in what we thought resembled Talavera ware was enormously admired by all the guests. Several people said we should hang the plates on the wall instead of using them all the time. We laughed. A Catalan guest was especially interested. He said he had a beautiful collection of Catalan antiques, and as we were obviously interested he invited us to see them if we were in Barcelona. I said how much I would like to have some real old stuff, but that we were doing our best to keep things at least in the old tradition with our plates. He assured us that our 'Talavera' was really Talavera ware, and now extremely valuable.

Our Fleet Street party began to think of getting back to their jobs. Betty Margetson and Margaret Fuller, Roger Fuller's wife, who arrived one day in Betty's sporting Singer, had added to the newspaper atmosphere. Betty's reaction on waking for a late breakfast in bed after her first night in Marcus's bar was to clutch her head and say in an amazed voice, 'I can't understand it, I only spent half-a-crown.'

Betty and Margaret were a riot among the Catalans. All the lads lined up to dance with them, after asking Archie's permission to do so. All Catalans do this. They always ask Archie if they may dance with me, and if Archie is not there Leonard graciously gives them permission. The lads of the village still ask us to send messages to Betty and Margaret to assure them they are not forgotten in Tossa. Betty almost lost one friend. Chico, the car driver, took complete charge of the Singer and washed it and oiled it with loving care. He was devoted to Betty and danced rapturous tangos with her. When

Betty was leaving she felt she must give Chico something for all the trouble he had taken over the car. After much thought she gave him a very beautiful note-case with a twenty-five peseta note inside. He threw the case back at Betty and stalked away. It took all our powers of persuasion to induce him to realize that Betty meant it for the best and to prevail upon him to keep the case. He has now forgotten the pesetas and is intensely proud of the notecase.

We found it was another of our strange jobs as hotel-keepers to see that people got back to their jobs at the right time. Owen and Jimmy refused to go. In the end I packed for them and we put them in a car, took them to Gerona and put them on the Paris train. Even then they went astray in Paris, but that was none of our business. We found we often had to do this. When we did not know the people or their jobs it was all right by us, but when we knew what being a few days late might mean we were firm.

Just before we got rid of the last of Fleet Street our two lovely pansies arrived. They came by car and were travelling through Spain studying art. One was tall, slim and graceful, with the blondest hair and the loveliest curling eyelashes. The other was small and dark, and had long curly hair and plucked eyebrows and a nervous giggle. They both wore grey flannels and gay tweed jackets. The fair one had a blue and yellow checked shirt open at the neck, the dark one a purple and red striped shirt with a square neck. They had high affected voices and impeccable English accents. They wished to stay three nights and had a rather querulous argument about unloading the car.

'But John, I must have my book about Nijinsky.'

'David, my dear, I simply could not live without the gramophone.'

They must have been rather shaken to find themselves in quite such a collection of nasty rough he-men. Later they were quite happy. They met the two little German boys who lived in the village. They gravitated towards each other with squeals of joy, bought themselves big sun hats and raffia sandals, and lay on the beach in a picturesque group with their new friends. One or two others, not so obviously labelled, gave themselves away by joining the group, and that corner of the beach was almost a herbaceous border.

Early winter seemed to be the time for painters. We had eight at one time. Peter Janssen, of Düsseldorf, was working hard for an exhibition and was doing a series of pastels. He gave us one when he left and we added it to the Zügels in the big room. We also had a number of architects among winter guests. They were all most enthusiastic about the house and congratulated Marcus on his work. They were especially struck by the clever way Marcus has designed a modern house to fit in with the general antique atmosphere of Tossa. It is never an easy job to put a house down suddenly in the middle of an unbuilt-over hillside, but it is more difficult when the opposite hill is covered with medieval towers and the houses in between are straggling white and grey cottages. Marcus had not attempted to be anything but modern, but he had achieved a purity of line that would never be out of place anywhere.

Besides the painters we had our share of eager water-colourists who plodded over the hills with little camp-stools and much hope. Two friends were very enthusiastic. One of them was stout with red hair, the other tiny and dark. The large one had reduced the younger almost to idiocy by never allowing her to think or act for herself at all. She was told where and what to paint, what to wear, if the day was fine or rather cool, whether she preferred tea or coffee. The pair of them were very concerned about walking far alone. Was I sure it was perfectly safe? That is one of the hardest of our many questions to answer. One can hardly look at the inquirer and say heartily, 'Good heavens, yes! You'll be all right anywhere.' In any case an assurance of safety, which truth compels one to give, is disappointing.

The friends went off every day and systematically recorded the lovely oranges and purples of the Catalonian autumn in pale washes in their sketch books. One day they came back in great excitement. A man had spoken to them. The large one said she had noticed him for several days; he was always waiting in the same place. They were sketching a certain view and the man had spied on them. The commanding friend told him in English to go away. She was voluble about it. The little one was unable to speak, as she was almost prostrate with a severe attack of hiccoughs. 'Poor child,' said her friend, looking sternly at me. 'You see how upset she is. She always gets like this after a bad shock.'

'What do you do about it?' I asked with interest. I was torn between amusement and concern. The poor woman was exhausted and seemed unable to stop.

'She must go straight to bed.' The commanding lady pushed the hiccoughing figure, now looking about half its size, out of the room. Later I insisted on sending for the Tossa doctor. He was an excellent doctor when the diagnosis was in no doubt. He gave her some medicine and went away. As he left he said to me, 'The best cure for hiccoughs is a good fright.'

We investigated the story and found the man. He wanted to ask them not to sit in that particular spot because he had to drive his goats that way every day and the goats did not care for people sitting on camp-stools on the only passable bit on the hill-top. For several days he had tried to pluck up courage to speak to them.

We had many plans for the winter. I was going to learn Catalan; Archie was going to learn Spanish; we were going to Do Things About the House. Archie's idea of a house of his own was definitely to do things about it. We have never found out what these things are. We thought four or five guests would give us enough work to keep us amused and the rest of the time we could get some of the jobs done for which we had never had time since becoming hotel-keepers. The first thing about the house was to remove all the furniture out of our ex-office bedroom and have the wall between it and the big room removed so as to make enough space for all our winter guests.

To our surprise the first winter season in Tossa was a success. We had every room occupied throughout the winter. That did not mean we worked to summer capacity, because most people came for several months and had single rooms, or double rooms as single rooms. The big downstairs room, ample for summer guests who were out all day and who had all their meals outside on the terraces, was too small for the winter. I went to Jaume, our mason, and told him that the wall must be removed as quickly as possible and at times that did not interfere with the guests. He did a really good job. I warned the guests and the men started banging at 8 am. By half-past eight the wall was down. We put a screen across the end of the room and carried on as usual while the workmen tidied up behind. The next day we had a room nearly half as large again.

Our winter guests were older than the summer ones and mostly retired people or people who had never had jobs. One reads about terrible retired colonels and frightful old maids inflicting themselves on hotels on the Continent, but we escaped them. We had our share of the aristocracy who are just managing to pig along on five or six thousand a year, and really Spain is such a cheap place just now and so restful after the Riviera. We had our share of spinsters, but none of them could be called typical of the hibernating spinster of fiction.

Two of the nicest people who ever visited us were two spinster sisters from New Zealand. One was very deaf but consoled herself by painting and writing. She did not pretend to paint very well, but her sketches gave her enormous pleasure to do, and made up in some measure for being deprived of conversation. Her sister was a quiet little person with a plain face which had such an attractive expression that one thought afterwards she must be really good-looking. She wore odd old ladies' frocks of serge with tight bodices, and did her hair in two coils on the top of her head. The whole effect, instead of being frumpish and unattractive, was of a kindly, simple soul who was completely unaffected and completely unselfconscious. She took Tossa and the Tossa people to her heart and they adored her. She spoke no Spanish when she arrived, but took lessons every day and soon could talk a little with the shop people. She walked for miles with her sister over the hills, collecting fir cones and sprays of eucalyptus flowers for the big room. Arbutus berries made lovely Christmas decorations instead of holly, and huge pinecones with coloured candles and great branches of eucalyptus with silvery blue-green leaves and delicately traced white flowers like frosting made the big room look beautiful. Everyone put their Christmas cards along the cowling of the big Catalan chimney-place, in which we always burned pine logs, although we had the heating on. We found people liked the heating turned low in the hall, and to have a big log fire.

Christmas was a problem. Spaniards do not celebrate Christmas Day but have their *fiesta* on *Tres Reyes*, the Three Kings. This is Epiphany in England, I believe. The *Tres Reyes* bring presents for the children as they pass.

Instead of a Christmas tree the Spanish child has a little cardboard model of a stable and puts into it various tiny religious figures that are sold everywhere on stalls lining the streets of the towns, or in the villages in the usual village shop, which sells everything. In Catalonia the religious aspect is not very important and all kinds of figures can be bought for a model stable, which is very often far more like a farmhouse. A typical model will have figures of old women plucking hens, a fisherman or two, every kind of farmyard animal, three Eastern-looking gentlemen who are probably the Three Kings, an old woman mending fishing nets, some fir-trees, the Virgin in a blue mantle, a boy with a donkey, some miniature cocks with real feathers in their tails, a baby in a crib, and an old man squatting on a chamber pot.

We combined a Spanish and an English Christmas. We had a Spanish lunch, with strawberries and cream, on the terrace in the sunshine. Small strawberries are in season from January until March. In the evening we had our Christmas dinner, with turkey and, instead of pudding, an invention of my own consisting mostly of beaten egg and rum. We decorated the tables with tiny Christmas trees, made out of branches from the fir trees that grow here, as there were no proper Christmas trees to be found in Barcelona, and hung them with tiny presents and silver tinsel. I discovered marvellous miniature pale-blue angels with silver wings and the most cynical expression, and put one on the top of each tree. The trees were too small for candles, so on the other side of each table we put a model farm with gay candles on the roof and all the farmyard animals in the yard. With these candles and a row of them stuck in big fir-cones among the Christmas cards in the cowl of the fireplace, we had enough light without having to use the ordinary electric light.

A few older people had wanted a service on Christmas morning. There was a parson staying in the house who suggested he might do something about it. I said he could do whatever they liked, but it must be done upstairs so as not to disturb the other guests, and they must tell me exactly what they wanted. The parson said he wanted a chalice and a paten. I knew what a chalice was. For the first time Archie and I regretted having given our skating cups away before we left England. The only thing large enough was a silver beer mug, but it was obviously a beer mug. Suddenly my eye fell on the cocktail-shaker. We whipped off the top, gave the bottom a polish, and there was the chalice. The paten would have defeated me if someone had not said an ordinary plate would do. So in a bedroom we had cleared of most of its secular equipment, we fixed up an ordinary table with a white cloth, left a bottle of Tossa wine by the chalice, put some Tossa bread on an ordinary plate, and everyone was happy.

11

The Jellineks left. They forgot to come up to say goodbye again. They wrote to us from Altea, a small village between Valencia and Alicante. They were going to stay a few weeks before going back to England. We were amused by the re-fraternizing of the refugees for the winter. By the end of the summer practically no one was speaking to anyone else, but as winter approached there was a noticeable tendency to make friends. The prospect of months of isolation without the buffer of visitors was enough to make even deadly enemies decide that until next season, when rivalry would of course begin all over again, they might as well have someone to talk to. The refugees clung together only in times of stress and had no interests in common except in thinking that the others were trying to do them down. They made no friends in the village and had to settle down to a winter of each other's company.

They were a most unsuitable collection of people for a country life. There was not one of the women among them who was interested enough or even able to look after a house or do the cooking. They left all their domestic arrangements to Catalan women. They could not sew or knit. They had no interests at all outside their particular little businesses, which were shut all the winter. They had nothing to do outside the summer season, except to collect in little groups and gossip about each other.

Leonard went off to visit his parents in Paris. We missed him terribly. By this time he was in the Casa Johnstone as a partner. Archie and I could never get over our luck in having found him. It was obvious that three people in such a small business would of necessity always be together. We had our own sitting-room to escape from our guests and any third person would share it with us; we could hardly leave them in the kitchen. I used to look at Leon curled up in a chair in front of our fire, his black head bent over a book, and think how frightful it would have been to have had a Spanish waiter who would probably have disliked being with us as much as we disliked having him around. Leon's only drawback was that he laughed out loud when he was reading, but a cushion skilfully thrown would stop him for a little.

After Leon's holidays Archie and I went off to the mountains for some skiing, leaving Leon in charge. The skiing in the Pyrenees is fun, but perilous. The best way to tackle it is to forget you were ever in Switzerland and imagine yourself a pioneer in some undiscovered region. I was told to go on a run to a place called New Cross. I went off with a Catalan who was a 'stranger in those parts' and we climbed and climbed (it is considered very sissy in the Pyrenees to wear skins for climbing, but I noticed several people surreptitiously took coils of rope in their pockets, which they tied round their skis when no one was looking), and found the higher we got the harder the snow until at last we were walking on solid ice, carrying our skis.

There was a thick mist and we could see only a few yards ahead. When the ground began definitely to go down again we decided that something was wrong and we had better go home. The run down was a valley between two mountains and we found these mountains were a godsend. We skated down one side of the valley, our skis slipping and skidding on the frozen snow, and shot up the mountains on the other side. Then we did the same thing again, landing halfway up the other mountain. So we reached home. When we complained that we had seen nothing looking in the least like a cross we were told there was no cross; it was only the name of what used to be a monastery, but of course it is gone now and there is nothing but snow.

While we were in the mountains the election results came out. Everyone was wild with joy. All the Tossa old men had told us there would be a swing to the left, but we had smiled and sadly disbelieved them. We decided to go back to Barcelona at once to hear more news. Barcelona was perfectly calm but everyone was looking very pleased, and the people we knew were delighted. When the results had been announced, we were told, everyone had cheered and rushed round the streets, and the cafés were packed with people celebrating. The stigma of the disastrous 1934 rebellion was wiped out.

We stayed several days in Barcelona. On the third day Leon, to whom we had telephoned from the mountains that we were going to Barcelona, rang us up. He sounded agitated. 'Are you all right?' he asked.

'Perfectly. Why on earth—'

'I've just seen the English papers. They are full of the frightful riots in Barcelona.'

We were amazed. We had seen absolutely nothing, not even a bunch of thugs beating each other up, which one often sees in the back alleys of London, and certainly nothing approaching a Mosley meeting.

When we got back to Tossa everything was running beautifully in the hotel. The guests were full of praises for Leon. He had only one complaint about the guests. 'It was the laundry,' he said. 'I could sort out most of the things, but I wish everyone didn't wear pink knickers. I couldn't put them all in a heap in the dining room and say, "Ladies, please take your knickers!" '

The laundry book was almost a collection of short stories. Leon had written laborious descriptions: 'Petticoat, with sort of brown lace'; 'Night-dress, with sewing round top, blue with bits of pink'. The most pathetic entry was 'Bodice, sort of grey'.

The Tossa people were thrilled by the election results. They elected a new mayor, but otherwise seemed to carry on their lives exactly as before.

Companys came out of prison, with all the other prisoners of that particular revolution, and the extreme Rights who had not managed to get across the frontiers went into the prisons instead. Everyone was delighted to think that for once a political upheaval had been managed without any bloodshed. A few hardened revolutionaries were not quite convinced that such a big change from Right to Left would be really valid, as it were, without a few battles. Companys, once again president, addressed the people in Barcelona. Every lorry in every village in Catalonia was requisitioned and people streamed into the capital. We were unfortunately very busy and could not get away, but Isabel and Francisca went. It must have been a wonderful sight. The interesting part about the whole business was that every single *guardia* and traffic policeman was withdrawn from Barcelona. Companys made a speech in the Plaza Cataluña, which was black with people, and the big streets and *ramblas* radiating from it were crammed. Isabel wept when she told me about it. Even the English newspapers did not report any disorders.

We noticed one result of living under a Left regime. People started adding to their letters: 'I suppose all the stories in the papers about Spain being so unsafe are just newspaper stories. It really is perfectly safe to come to Spain just now?' Two months after the elections, a friend of mine wrote to know if we were all right after the recent revolution. I answered that we had not noticed any revolution, but that we were very well, thank you. It became rather annoying. We were lucky in that our hotel was small and therefore easily filled, but big hotels dependent on the tourist, which really meant the English, were suffering. Everywhere we heard fellow hotel-keepers complaining that trade was falling off.

People were scared to come to Spain; the Foreign Right Press was producing all sorts of stories about trouble for tourists. The papers which did not go so far as to report a trifling street row as signs of the Red Terror suggested that the regulations at the frontier were now so impossible and the customs officials so uncouth that it was really better to go to some other country. We had dozens of letters asking us about this. We had no single case of anyone being delayed or discourteously treated at the frontier. We wrote to everyone and said that there was no reason at all why they should not come to Spain and told them not to believe newspaper nonsense. I added that I was not qualified to speak about the south of Spain or Madrid but, judging from the reports about Barcelona, which I knew to be untrue, I should imagine that one could take other reports at the same valuation.

We heard from the Jellineks, who still had not succeeded in leaving Spain and were at Altea. They had not observed any trouble. A report that the gutters of Alicante were running with blood was discounted by Frank, who said that the streets of Alicante had no gutters.

One lovely story was traced to its source by some Americans, who read in a well-known American paper that the Mayor of Barcelona, Señor Calasparra, had been shot. The Mayor of Barcelona was not called Calasparra, and furthermore was alive and well. The Americans investigated the story, and at last found that in a small town called Calasparra in the south a man had been shot in the main street, the Calle Mayor.

Despite the scare stories we had no trouble in filling the house for the spring. We actually rather scored, because the people who were willing to brave the unknown terrors of a mildly Left Spain were the sort of people we wanted.

We were now becoming known among the foreign residents of Barcelona. This was a mixed blessing. It was useful to have weekend guests to fill in the odd days between people coming and going, but Barcelona residents soon become very Spanish. They just turn up, usually late on Saturday night, and hope for the best.

The worst offenders were a couple who came every weekend for months. They were a Russian and a Greek, both working for a film company in Barcelona. The Russian was incapable of telephoning to let us know if he was coming on Friday or Saturday and, once here, could never decide if he would leave on Sunday night before dinner, after dinner, or wait and leave at seven o'clock the next morning. His friend, the Greek, a handsome young man with spaniel eyes and a large nose which saved him from a too "collar-ad" appearance, could do nothing without the Russian's approval, so he was no help in making any decision. They were such nice creatures that we could never really get angry with them, although they caused an enormous amount of work. The Greek was most helpful about giving Leon a hand to lay the tables, at least when he was not an hour or so late for meals. There were few things Leon hated more than being helped with the tables.

The Russian and his friend came out from Barcelona in a large car belonging to the Russian. He drove it like a fiend, with the wireless on full blast, and singing Russian songs to himself as he swirled round the corners of the cliff road. Oddly enough, he seldom had accidents, but I was definitely a sort of hoodoo. Whenever I went in the car something happened. The least trouble was scraping the wings against a mule cart with one of our wheels almost over the edge of a sheer drop of about three hundred feet to the sea. The worst was when we hit a tree and I cut my face on the windscreen. I then refused to go in the car again, much to Archie's relief.

We had just got used to the pair and their weekends when things became complicated by a third member of the party. She was called Margot and was very strange. She was German, and one never knew which film star she was being at which particular moment. Generally it was a sort of cross between Marlene Dietrich and Garbo. She belonged, I think, to the Russian, but whichever one she was not with at the moment would come to me and tell me how he disliked the woman, and that he could not understand what his friend saw in her. The situation was beyond me, and really only interested me because the general vagueness of the pair was much worse when Margot was with them. She probably had some scheme or reason for her odd behaviour, but it was not apparent to me.

The first weekend she came she spent the first day lying in a deckchair covered with rugs, a thermometer in her mouth, while the Greek played her portable gramophone to her. The Russian apparently did not care for women in deckchairs with thermometers. He told me she was impossible.

In the evening the Russian and Margot sat side by side in Marcus's bar, while the Greek told me she was ruining his friend's life. There was the usual argument about going back to Barcelona, made more complicated by Margot, who disagreed with whatever conclusion was reached. I had all their beds made in case they stayed and all I wanted to know was if they wanted an early breakfast. As they had not decided by one o'clock in the morning I went to bed, telling them they would get no breakfast before eight. The next morning we found they had left for Barcelona at 3 am.

One weekend was priceless. There was some great trouble with Margot, who was being more difficult than usual. She came into lunch alone, very early, and sat gazing before her tragically. Archie was waiting on her table and every few minutes she would cry in a Garbo voice: 'Mis-ter John-stone, please take this away. I am not hun-gry.'

A charming elderly couple, who were very concerned about this strange young woman, asked me what was the matter. I said it was beyond me.

In the afternoon both the men told me their troubles at once. I did not get quite all the facts, as the Russian was speaking German and the Greek French, but I gathered that

Margot was refusing to go with them when they went back to Barcelona. Could they leave her in my charge? I said, 'No' in four languages. The Russian had given up his flat in order to get rid of Margot and wished to send her to a *pensión* in Barcelona, but she refused to go. I said it was none of my business, but they were both perfectly idiotic not to be able to control a silly little ass like Margot, and would they be leaving tonight or tomorrow morning?

In the middle of the discussion Margot suddenly came out on to the terrace and stalked by us, crossing the terrace and going off up the side of the hill. At last the men decided to have a very punctual dinner and to leave immediately afterwards for Barcelona. At dinner there was no sign of Margot. The two men ate as quickly as possible in order to get off to Barcelona without having to argue with her, hoping, no doubt, that I would cope with her after they had gone. Before they finished she came in, looking very much more like a sulky child than Greta Garbo. She sat down at the table with the two men and refused to speak a word. Everyone in the room was watching her with concealed amusement. The nice elderly couple called me over to their table as I was passing and asked anxiously, 'Do you think she is ill, poor girl?'

The Russian and the Greek went up to pack their cases and Leon took them down to the car. Margo sat at her table glaring in front of her. The elderly man thought he should say something. He had a bushy moustache and muttered his words behind it, so that it was difficult even for English people to understand him, and Margot's knowledge of English was slight. He lent towards her table and said pleasantly, 'It's a nice night for your drive to Barcelona.'

Margot slowly moved her head towards him and lifted her intense gaze. 'Pardon?' she said.

The old man was still full of hope. 'It said it is a nice night for a drive,' he mumbled.

The rest of the guests listened breathlessly.

Margo languidly inclined her head in his direction. 'Pardon?

The old man was on his mettle. He cleared his throat, but was interrupted by the sight of the Russian and the Greek, their arms piled with Margot's clothes, going out to their car. She ignored them utterly. They dumped the things anyhow in the back of the car and went upstairs for more. The old man tried again. 'Nice night. Car. Barcelona.' Margot stared at him and rose. She had decided it was better to go to Barcelona than to stay trying to understand this silly old man. We thought he was a brilliantly clever old man to have achieved the exit of Margot.

12

Our second summer season promised to be good. We were well filled up for May and June, and the July and August bookings were rolling in. I checked up with the previous year's bookings and found that we had been full for August at a much earlier date the year before. On the whole we were not affected by the scare stories; in fact, we should have been overwhelmed with requests for rooms if it had not been for them. Later bookings showed that the scare stories had evidently died down, for none of the July or August people asked 'Is it safe?'

One thought about bathing again. Hardy ones had bathed all the winter, but by February and March the water is cold. Tossa girls were already whispering about the *Fiesta Mayor*. The two big winter *fiestas* were past—Carnival, when the whole village parades the streets in amazing costumes, the girls in groups representing the same characters, Cleopatras, Marie Antoinettes, shepherdesses, flowers; and the loveliest of all Tossa *fiestas*, the January *Fiesta* of the Pilgrim.

The story of the pilgrim has been published by the retired Tossa priest, who is a charming old man, living happily among his collection of wild flowers, birds' eggs and Tossa legends. Hundreds of years ago Tossa was afflicted by plague. Prayers to the patron saint, San Vicens, were unanswered, and the villagers found the Wickedest Man in Tossa and sent him on a pilgrimage over the mountains to Santa Coloma, a village about twenty-five miles away, which had a shrine dedicated to San Sebastián. The man had to travel barefoot and fasting and pray at the shrine for deliverance. Immediately the plague was lifted and the triumphant pilgrim returned to be welcomed by the villagers of Tossa.

Every year someone is chosen to be the pilgrim and to go barefoot to Santa Coloma. I thought at first it was always the wickedest man who was chosen, and was thrilled because the first year we were in Tossa the local doctor was the pilgrim, but apparently anyone who has some special reason for wanting his prayers answered can be a candidate. The Tossa priest makes the decision after hearing all the claimants, and no one knows who the pilgrim will be until he actually starts from the church at five in the morning for his walk over the hills. It is the only secret that is ever kept in Tossa.

Anyone who likes may accompany the pilgrim, but under the same conditions. The walk takes all day, and the night is spent praying to San Sebastián in Santa Coloma. They start back the following day. As soon as it begins to get dark, soon after five o'clock, the Tossa people go out along the inland road to meet the pilgrim and his followers. Then they all go back to Tossa into the church. The pilgrim wears a curious mantle sewn with sea-shells, a felt hat with a large buckle, and carries a heavy staff. He enters the church, followed by as many people as can pack in. When he comes out he carries a lighted taper. All the people of Tossa carry enormous candles and tapers and light them from the pilgrim's. Then they form up in a procession, the pilgrim with the Tossa priests and a gorgeous scarlet figure who is some important prelate from Gerona, then some self-conscious choir boys and then streams of Tossa people. It was quite unimportant whether one had religious or anti-religious convictions; this was a *fiesta* and the most hardened Tossa agnostic, bar Rovira, carried his candle as bravely as any other.

The procession moved slowly through the narrow streets up to the old town, where big bonfires were burning on the battlements. The village lights were out and the glow from the procession lit up the old huddled houses and turned the window-panes red. We watched from the main street as it passed along a parallel street, and it reminded us of a

Reinhardt production as the brilliantly lit procession passed across the tops of the streets opening into the main one. It was like a curious game of hide and seek, watching the soft glow of the candles as the people passed behind buildings then, by running across and intercepting the route, getting a sudden glimpse of the full glory of the scene as the procession came into view again for an instant.

By April the winter was forgotten and the summer *Fiesta Mayor* was the great topic. The village dressmaker was already thinking out new frocks for the Tossa beauties, the tailor getting patterns of green and fawn stripes, or pale blue and mauve stripes on brown, and discussing the padding of shoulders with the young men. I was looking forward to the *fiesta* myself, as I had missed it the year before, but I forbade too much discussion in the kitchen till June.

We were rather embarrassed in early summer by people who came to study the flowers or the birds of Catalonia. They expected us to know so much about them and we never by any chance got the right name for anything. Sometimes people were quite severe with us, but we remained ignorant. Two very nice people spent all day trudging the hillsides with specimen cases and cameras, and they never once asked us the name of anything. We confided in them that we were crassly ignorant of the names of things. Archie made a series of his worst puns: 'I never know vetch vetch is vetch, or wort wort is wort.'

The specimen hunters were out all day and seemed to take little notice of the rest of the guests. After they left they sent me an article one of them had published about Tossa birds, so that I should be able to confound the next person who asked me if we had siskins in our garden, and a delightful poem with a verse about each of our other guests, which showed that the specimen hunters had found plenty to amuse them indoors as well as out.

We often had bursts of literary efforts from our departed

199

guests. A family who spent the winter with us had a small daughter, who endeared herself to the whole household. She sent us an alphabet which started:

A
our Arrival one evening so late
Poor Chico had long in Gerona to wait.

B
for the Blankets, one guest asked for nine
Our hostess replied other places are fine.

C
for the Casa, with its absence of fuss,
Too simple for some folks but perfect for us

I saw a lot of Zügel these days. His family had deserted him. Frau Zügel had gone off with the two children to find a school in Switzerland for them. They had decided against letting the kids struggle with their lessons in Catalan. We missed them nearly as much as Zügel. He was working hard, and all English painters and critics who saw his work tried to persuade him to exhibit in London. The clear Tossa atmosphere had given his wonderful sense of colour new values and his latest pictures were poems of concise design and brilliant tones.

We were amused at the reaction of our guests to the pictures we had in the big room. Most of them recognized the biggest picture was Don Quixote, although one or two suggested the White Knight (it was so queer to waste a lot of paint on anything not English) and one or two said helplessly, 'Yes, very interesting, I'm sure.' One young couple fell in love with and insisted on buying one picture, although they admitted they had only a hazy idea what it was meant to be. But they so loved the colouring and the design that they did not care. I soon learned what value to put on guests' demands to be shown Zügel's studio. He was always delighted to show his pictures to people who had even a vague understanding of what he was attempting to do, but it bored him to tears to have to pull out one picture after another to a chorus of 'How lovely!'

Leonard suddenly decided he would do his part about entertaining lone young women. Whether Archie's obvious success with a very charming German girl encouraged him or whether he just thought it was time he stopped having imaginary Spanish girlfriends that only he knew about, he definitely adopted, not one lone female, but three hearty English girls. He took them to Marcus's every night. He developed a distinct finesse in introducing the surplus two to enterprising Catalans so that whichever one he decided to keep for himself could be shown the beach by moonlight. Leon had always been adorable about his Spanish girlfriends. There was a sort of rule that even the girl herself must never know about it. With the village girls this was sensible, as the village mothers had a firm eye on Leonard, but this strange rule extended to the Barcelona visitors as well. Leon would pick out some nice-looking girl, preferably one that was not already too like her stout mother. He would dance with her and bow politely when they met in the street. That is all the poor girl would know about it. But to Leon, and of course to us, she was his new girlfriend.

However, the affair with the three English girls was different. One of them knew about it anyway. They were all three of the type that foreigners call so English, and although extremely nice girls and probably quite intelligent, they gave the impression of being incredibly stupid. Perhaps we had a strange effect on them so that they were unable to speak when we were there, but the few times Archie and I joined them at Marcus's we were worn out trying to unparalyse them. Leon said they were not so very stupid.

Archie was rather preoccupied with his German girl. She was a dear and I liked her enormously, but she was scared to death of me. She simply could not believe that I did not mind her very mild affair with my husband. I could not explain to her that it was such a very unimportant affair that it did not cause me a moment's anxiety, so that was that. Every time I came into the room where she was, she would look at me in a scared way with enormous blue eyes. I said to Archie that he really must train his women better if he ever wanted to have a secret affair with anyone. I did not mind what he did, but I did object to having anxious looks from people I wanted very much to be friends with.

It was almost too much when one of the three English girls started to do the same thing. She was worse, because she not only looked scared but she smiled ingratiatingly. Whenever I looked I either saw the round blue eyes of the German girl or the wide hopeful smile of the English one. I rushed to Leon.

'Leon, my angel, you know I don't care what you do, but please make your beastly girlfriends understand this too. If you tackle the other two, life is going to be unbearable with a mass of scared women round the house trying to placate me.'

Leon and Archie shrieked with laughter. I threatened I would see what I could do about my young men friends. A houseful of girls unable to face me and men not able to meet Archie's cold Scotch eye would be great fun.

I noticed that neither Archie nor Leon were in the least concerned when their girlfriends had to leave. Leon was so tired from his late nights that I insisted that he go to bed early, stay in bed in the mornings, and let me do the breakfasts for a few days. He said it was against all his principles but I overruled him.

We had a frightful scare with Leon before the *Fiesta Mayor*. The poor lad was so thrilled about the *fiesta* and had ordered his new suit and bought a new shirt to match. Then, ten days before the first day of the *fiesta*, he confessed he was feeling ill. When Leon admits that he is ill, it is a case of immediate bed. There happened to be two English doctors staying with us. They were friends who had come to Spain together. They swooped down on Leon with cries of joy.

At first they thought it was just a slight chill and that a day or so in bed would put him right. Later they began to whisper in corners, and then they took me aside. They would like the Tossa doctor to take a blood test. They did not wish to be alarming, but Leon had the symptoms of para-typhoid! My feelings can be imagined. The two doctors were dears and of course did not say a word to alarm the household, and I had to make up some story for Leon to explain the Tossa doctor and his tests.

The Tossa doctor came up, asked Leon a lot of questions, most of which were so technical that even Leon's knowledge of Catalan and Spanish was inadequate, refused to make any tests, and said Leon had a simple liver trouble which many Catalans had at that time of year. He asked Leon very confidentially if he had ever had - - - - - , using a terrific word of which none of us could grasp the pronunciation, let alone the meaning. Leon, hoping for the best, assured him he had not. The doctor looked extremely surprised and asked: Was Leon absolutely sure about this? Leon, feeling he had committed himself for ever to not having had whatever it was, firmly held to his assertion. The doctor shook his head doubtfully and went away. The next day Leon turned bright yellow and it was found that he had jaundice.

He had it very slightly, but the poor lad felt awful and, of course, missed the *fiesta*. I enjoyed the *fiesta* enormously and danced every *sardanas* and felt horribly mean when I thought of Leon hearing all the music lying in bed. With one of the staff in bed it took some organizing to arrange for us all to have a share in the *fiesta*, but we managed. The fact that nothing would drag our guests away from the *sardanas* until the very last dance helped us to get back up the hill to have the meals ready in time.

Everything was prepared beforehand. One night we were having mashed potatoes with one of the courses. Isabel had boiled and mashed the potatoes before she went down to dance. When she got to her house she had a sudden panic that she had not done enough. So she boiled some of her own potatoes, and when we met in the *sardanas* she told me about it. 'My mother is here with them so that I can take them up with me when we go, and add them to the others.' Isabel's mother, an enormously fat old woman, was standing patiently watching the dancing, holding a bowl covered with a cloth and containing the extra mashed potatoes.

The Casa Johnstone had been open exactly one year. It was an unbelievably successful year and we were very pleased with ourselves. We had been practically full up the entire time, and we were already booked up to capacity as far ahead as the end of September. We had had in nearly every case people we liked, and now we were getting bookings from their friends. Archie had put on weight and was brown and bursting with fitness. He adored hotel-keeping. Leon, despite his recent jaundice, looked much better than when he came to us, so I told him my hounding him to bed early and fussing about his health generally was justified and he must never complain about it again. He had done quite well by coming to us. He had earned far more money the first year than at his other job; he had worked far less; he had prospects of not only earning more money for the second year, for we had decided to give him a bigger percentage, but Archie and I had practically adopted him and had told him that when the whole business was a thoroughly going concern we would hand the place over to him. We had ideas about eventually retiring to a small house somewhere near Tossa and having enough out of the hotel to live comfortably in Spain and a bit over for occasional trips abroad—which meant going further south still. We had no great urge to go back to England. If Leon could allow us enough to do this the rest of the hotel was his to play with.

When Leon first met us he had big ideas. His notion of living was to work and work and make a huge business and go on making more money. His only real doubt about coming to us was that he had thought our schemes too small. We thought the idea of eventually having complete control over the Casa Johnstone and being able to expand to his heart's content would thrill him. A year with us had changed Leon considerably. He saw we preferred to enjoy life and have little money than to spend all our lives working like hell to accumulate a pile of wealth for when we were old. He also learned that one can enjoy life and yet make enough money to live very comfortably.

When I first gave him an idea of our still very vague plans of retiring to a cottage I expected him to fall on my neck with excitement. Instead, he looked at me, his eyes very bright, and asked, 'But you and Archie won't go away very far, will you? You simply must do the correspondence and Archie must look after the back premises!' Leon had learned to do everything else that I did, from the *hors-d'oeuvres* to chivvying Francisca and Quimeta in the housework. I still held out over the letters. I told him that when he spoke and wrote better English than I did he was sacked. He could always spell much better.

For me the year had been more than a successful business year. It had justified the risks I had taken. In nearly every instance where I had defied expert opinions the result had made me even more confident in my own inexpertness. The whole staff, from Quimeta to Archie, were happy. Even Beetle, the black Peke, although she never did care much for so many people all over her house, had settled down to a gorgeous life of free roamings in the woods behind the house and games on the beach. The fact that we all enjoyed our work so much was of much more satisfaction to me than that it was successful from a business point of view. I had never been so well, the 'blonde streaks' in my hair were now lost in general blondeness, which in itself was worth coming to Spain for.

Archie, Leon and I surveyed the past and the future and found it good. Archie, thirty-nine, Leon, twenty-four and I, thirty years old, saw a vista stretching before us of a long peaceful life in the Spanish sunshine.

I spent most of my working time in July writing 'No' letters to people who wanted to come in August and September. We had wondered whether to build an annexe just for the three busiest months, but had decided we would wait one more year. I had definitely struck about ever having thirty-five people again in the house, and we decided to put people in the village only as a last resort when they simply refused to be turned away.

We occasionally got bits of news which might have meant more to people well up in the Spanish and European situation. There had been various rumours from people we knew in Madrid and other parts of Spain that conditions were still very bad among the workers, and Communists were getting restive for a much more Left régime. The murders of a Right minister and a Left civil guard chief, or vice versa, were pointers, but we knew so little of the political upheavals. Several murders were put down to gunmen in Barcelona; one or two people told us they were political gunmen.

We were completely unprepared for the news of a military revolt. In Tossa no one knew at first whether it was a communist revolt within the army. Then we heard that it was a rising of the Right against the government. People said it should have been a military coup but it did not quite come off. There were no posts and no papers. Everyone was extremely vague as to what it was really all about. We shrugged our shoulders and told our guests not to worry. We knew all about revolutions, we said; the last one lasted five days.

Book IV — On the Rocks

1

We did not take the trouble very seriously. We heard something about fighting in Barcelona and even vaguer reports from Madrid and elsewhere. Our guests were quite unconcerned and even a few who were due to go home were not disappointed when they found the trains were not running. Four of these went to Gerona by car to see if there really were any trains or not and came back thrilled because they had sat in a café and drunk beer with some of the Gerona volunteers. We said we expected a few days would see everything back to normal again. In a few days it was obvious that it was a much bigger show than anyone had imagined. News from Barcelona was coming in and accounts of the amazing stand by the people, who cleared the rebel army out of the Hotel Colón, from which standpoint they were sweeping the Plaza Cataluña with machine-gun fire, rushed, armed with knives and such rifles and arms as they could get, in borrowed cars to rout rebel batteries, and in twelve hours had put an entire rebel division out of action. Between the Hotel Colón, held by the rebels, and the telephone building, held by the people, was a fountain, the usual shallow basin with a column spurting water from twisted dolphins. Flattened against the column, drenched with water, Frank Jellinek, who had written us farewell-to-Spain letters from Altea at least twice, watched the battle, his camera water-logged but his journalist eye recording everything for his despatches to the *Manchester Guardian*. Soon it was obvious that the whole of Catalonia was rapidly crushing the revolt. We heard about Saragossa holding out against the Government in Aragón and it seemed only a few days before it must fall. We thought the whole rebellion would be crushed in a week or so at the most.

In the meanwhile our guests were amusing themselves very much as usual. There was no more dancing at the café in the evenings and the atmosphere of the village was changed, but the ordinary visitor, absorbed in his own concerns, did not notice the anxiety and sorrow that the villagers felt. The Catalan is peculiar in that he hates anyone being killed and is just as concerned over a death roll on the rebel side as on his own.

The three of us worked hard to keep the atmosphere of the hotel cheerful. It was not difficult because no one was concerned about the domestic troubles of Spain, and we could with complete honesty assure them that nothing would ever happen in Tossa. There was only one couple who were definitely panicky. They had their own car and we got permission from the mayor for them to leave Tossa in it for the frontier. It would be a tiresome drive, with delays at all the towns through which they passed, but we knew that they would meet the greatest courtesy everywhere, although they left certain of dire happenings.

It was much pleasanter without them and, surprisingly, the day after they left a young man arrived in a car from the frontier. We just stared at him in amazement, but he said firmly that he had said he was coming on that date and he thought he might as well turn up. He was most entertaining about his drive and said that alone he would never have achieved it. He had met a German girl at the frontier who was determined to get back to Barcelona, where she lived, and who made love to all the guards *en route*. He was eloquent about the 'frightful toughs these Communists seemed to be.' We refrained from arguing and later, when he realized that all the most peaceful Tossa villagers looked just the same he admitted that it might just be a national characteristic to look like a Russian bandit.

That was a point we had to drive home to our guests. Every now and then some of our friends in the village would call in on their turn of guard duty, to have a cognac or pass the time chatting to us. We are so used to the unshaved, rough appearance of the villagers that it did not seem at all alarming to us to have them come in bristling with ancient shotguns and rusty dirks and three-day growths to sit down among the guests. I was alarmed by the way they flung their guns to the floor, but that was all. After a bit the guests got used to it and were entertained highly by them.

After a week or so it seemed that it was going to be a longer job than we had expected. Some of our visitors began to get alarmed about getting back to their work. We did our best about getting cars to go to the frontier.

The car-hiring situation in Tossa was peculiar. The two proprietors were deadly rivals and one was very Left and the other very Right. Luckily we had always refused to mix political expediency with business and had hired cars impartially from both. Other people who had patronized only the Right cars were now unable to get one for love or money. To add to the confusion, the Left car owner was the local carrier and, since elections six months previously, the mayor; the Right owner was the postmaster, and the ex-mayor. So the postmaster's cars could not get the permission which had now to be obtained from the mayor before one could leave Tossa. However, soon no one could get permission to use the cars because of a general strike, so there seemed nothing for it but to stay in Tossa and wait. Everyone was very cheerful about it. We were in the lucky position of speaking our guests' languages and therefore could keep them happy. Other English people in the village were, apparently, not enjoying themselves so much. There was an idiotic German journalist,

a visitor, not a resident, who for a time kept alarming everyone by accounts of frightful happenings in various other
villages. Archie gently pointed out to him that even the Tossa
guards might start shooting up scaremongering foreigners if
any case were reported to them.

People began to get uneasy. They wanted to get home. The
English have a horror of any constraint except in their own
country, where they are treated like schoolchildren, but
British freedom abroad must be maintained. We were lucky in
our guests. A party of four had arrived the day the trouble had
started: Mr Townsend and his daughter and Mrs Bain and her
daughter. They were staying for four weeks, so they were not
at all worried about getting home. Mr Townsend looked a
middle-aged man with sparse white hair. We were amazed to
find that he was nearly seventy. He took our hill in his stride,
so to speak, and was one of the few guests not to mention a
funicular. His daughter was rather quiet, obviously quite
unused to revolutions, and was doing her best to keep up with
the emancipated attitude of the rest of the party, who were
frankly enjoying it all. Mrs Bain was worried only by the
thought that her husband in England might be alarmed about
her, and we could not send or receive any letters. Telegrams
still arrived occasionally, but the disorganization of the
revolution combined with the vagaries of the Tossa telegraph
system made this form of communication very unreliable.
Mary Bain, tall, slim and very attractive in a slightly aloof way,
was fascinated by Tossa. All four had a strong sense of
humour, and Mrs Bain was one of the few people who were
interested in the Tossa people and the effect all this would
have on them.

Miss Townsend never did quite get used to the local guards
dropping in on us. The guards were so delightful about these
visits. They really did want to let us know that they were on
our land in case we were alarmed if we heard them at night.
Beetle, who insisted, in her role of watch dog, on sleeping

outside, always greeted them with a noise that would not have shamed a bloodhound, and never could get over the fact that they did not rush away, leaving their guns behind.

It was amusing to see the different reactions of the Tossa lads to this sudden responsibility. The first night any of them came up we heard a noise at the back door and found outside a very shame-faced Jaume, holding his gun behind his back. He felt it was really not quite the thing to go about with weapons, especially to disturb us. However, we persuaded him and his mates to come in for a drink, but they would only stay in the kitchen. Others would come boldly up to the front door, which was always open, and then would be rather shaken to find the room full of English people. They were rather uncertain what to do with their guns. Later, when they realized that we liked having them in for a drink, they would come in more boldly and fling their guns carelessly on the floor.

Besides the Townsend party we had the intrepid young man who arrived after the trouble had started, Mr Hughes by name; a charming American couple who painted and who were rather concerned about getting their boat to New York; and a large party of very noisy young people. All the girls looked exactly alike and so did all the men. I never did grasp which was which, except one rather older man who invariably was helped up from the café by Emilio at lunch time or, if Emilio was busy, was left asleep until his friends joined him again late in the afternoon. Two very earnest young women from Ibiza completed the household. They were very strange and had that handwoven look that English people from the Balearics acquire. As they had lived ten years in Ibiza, Archie and I began to wonder if we would perhaps get like that after ten years in Catalonia.

One was fair and large and strode about Tossa looking for pottery (most of the Tossa pottery comes from Ibiza anyway), or stood entranced at street corners gazing at the picturesque scene; the other had masses of jet-black curls that almost entirely hid her face, and stayed indoors all day writing music. She always worked in the big room and always looked up apologetically every time anyone came in or out, and explained her strange occupation by saying that her publisher never gave her any peace. Neither of them bathed, nor indeed looked at the sea at all. Perhaps they had seen it already in Ibiza.

The 'unrest' among the foreign visitors in the village was growing. There were several people who really had to get back to their jobs. The most responsible of our noisy party began to think seriously that they should be getting home. The American couple became more concerned about their approaching sailing date. We were helpless, and everyone was very nice to us about it. Suddenly, one day after lunch, the mayor telephoned up to say a ship had left Palamós, to the north of us, and was calling at San Feliu and Tossa to take off people who wanted to leave. He had no other information whatever. The ship might be expected at any time.

We thought of all kinds of possibilities. The most probable idea was that it was a cargo boat to take people as far as Port Vendres over the frontier, where they could catch the ordinary train to Paris. There were rumours that it was a racket by an enterprising cargo line to take people round by Gibraltar to England. Everyone was very excited. The noisy party decided to pack and be ready in case it was possible to go. No one else from our hotel was very much interested. We all went down to the café to wait for the ship. After two hours we went back to the house. Just as it was getting dark Mary Bain, who was up on one of the terraces, shouted, 'Ship ahoy!' We rushed out and looked. There, very cautiously entering the bay, was an English destroyer!

By the time we got down to the beach the whole of Tossa was on the sands. It was almost impossible to move. The ship's boats were ages coming ashore; they kept circling round and going backwards and forwards. At last they landed and a very pink and white officer stepped ashore and asked for Mr Johnstone, the British consul. I was standing near, trying to get some luggage through the throng, and answered, 'Mr Johnstone is here somewhere, but he isn't the British consul.'

The little officer looked upset and said plaintively: 'Vice-consul, then.'

'Not even vice-consul,' I said firmly, but added more kindly, as the boy seemed really rather shaken. 'Here he comes now.'

Archie struggled through the people and spoke to the officer. The boy seemed amazed that we were still alive, and still more astonished when we said we were not leaving. He said that he had orders to advise everyone to leave immediately; that this might be their last chance. Leonard took him through the crowds to the mayor while Archie struggled with the suitcase. The American couple decided at the last minute to leave to catch their boat. The officer sent two sailors up to the hotel to wait for and bring down their luggage. Meanwhile there was a sudden panic among the English visitors living in the village. They had heard the officer's advice and decided at the last moment to leave. The congestion on the beach seemed to alarm them still more, and by the time we got down again to the beach with the Americans several people were quite hysterical.

Meanwhile we were having an enthralling time while the Americans did their packing. The two sailors sat in our big room drinking brandy and entertaining us and the remaining guests. The noisy party was already on board. The two sailors gave us their impressions of the whole business, and they were illuminating. The ship had arrived in Tossa bay with decks cleared for action. One of our sailors was a gunner. He had never yet been allowed to fire a gun in anger, and was longing to. The ship's boats had landed that peculiar way because of expected hostile action from the shore. The whole ship's company was tense, waiting for something to happen. The landing party had signalled from the shore and the tension relaxed. We asked the two lads various questions about themselves and their officers. We mentioned the pink-faced young man who was in charge of the landing party.

'Oh, him' said one of them. 'He's the stupidest man in the ship. They always send the stupid ones ashore first.'

'This 'ole business seems silly to me,' vouchsafed the other. 'Only got to Malta two days before, and then off again. Time we get to Marseilles with this little lot and a bit of rough weather, the ship'll be like a Channel steamer. I want a bit of fighting, I do. I ain't never fired that bleeding gun at anything worthwhile.'

We asked for news, but they had come from Egypt via Malta and knew very little. 'We get the news stuck up every day, but that don't mean anything. They puts up what they thinks.'

They were looking forward to getting to Barcelona; they had heard that there was some real fighting going on there. They drank up their brandy and the Americans came down. We asked the sailors if they could get a bottle of brandy aboard. The Americans offered to take it for them. They were very grateful and promised they would find them on board. They collected the luggage and went off, wishing us luck. Archie asked them if they would leave a place like this.

'No blooming fear!'

When we got back to the beach the confusion was indescribable. The beam of the destroyer's searchlight played on the beach, the village and the old battlements, making no doubt a wonderful cinematic spectacle for the people aboard, but to us, almost blinded by the sickly violet glare right in our eyes, it seemed like a definite breach of international good manners. Crowds of Tossa people were still on the beach, and the sailors who were lamp-signalling were having a grand time with the Tossa maidens. But the other English people were by this time convinced that they had escaped death only by the merciful intervention of the British Navy, and they could not get aboard quickly enough.

We managed to fight a way through for our Americans, who were now thinking they would almost rather miss their boat to New York than yield to the general panic. I was trying to keep two of their suitcases from being pushed into the sea while we waited for the boat to come alongside. I was actually standing in the water with my trousers rolled up, pushing the cases back. A huge English woman was shoving behind them. At last I said, 'For God's sake wait a little. The massacre won't start for a few minutes.'

Finally everyone was aboard. The signallers packed up and tore themselves away from the Tossa youth and beauty. The Tossa people stood together quite silently and watched the frenzied departure of their visitors. One old woman asked me what was the matter with them. Another said in amazement, 'They're not afraid of us, surely?'

I was quite unable to answer. I have never felt so little pride in my fellow countrymen.

We went back to the house for dinner, rather depleted but terribly superior. Mr Townsend chuckled all through the meal at remembrance of the sailors' conversation. Mrs Bain was rather concerned about the Tossa people's reactions.

'I hope they won't take it as a reflection on their hospitality,' she kept saying. 'They have been so pleasant to us, I should hate them to feel we had let them down.'

I told her what the women had said to me. She was very upset. 'Do tell them that it was just the English Government's lack of understanding; that the British Navy always sends ships at the least provocation.'

The next day I had the perfect explanation given me by a garage man I met in the village. He had stopped me to ask if we were leaving. I assured him we were staying as long as the Tossa people would allow us. Another man came up and spoke about the ship. Everyone was very upset about it. A ship was bad enough, but a warship! He kept repeating 'warship' to himself as if it was the last straw. The garage man answered with a shrug that only a Catalan can achieve: 'But the English Navy, it is always so hysterical!'

2

In the hotel life went on pretty much as usual. Soon the Ibiza ladies went to Barcelona. They did not know if they could get to Ibiza, as there was some doubt which side had gained ascendancy there, but they thought they ought to do something about their property. Mr Hughes was beginning to wonder whether the trains would be running in time for him to get back to his job. Things were getting normal in Catalonia. There was an entirely new administration in the towns and villages. Instead of the mayor and a town council they now had a central committee composed of the various trade union and political organizations. In Barcelona each group had big headquarters in various large hotels. We had never heard of most of the organizations, and even now I do not know them all. They are known by their initials and cars with FAI or UGT or POUM and many others were to be seen everywhere in Barcelona.

Mr Hughes went into Barcelona by car in his usual enterprising way. He made a collection of the groups of initials he saw. Unfortunately he did not know Catalan, and among the ones he had written down was LLET, which was written on the side of a lorry. 'Llet' is the Catalan for 'milk'.

The FAI were the most prominent at first, at any rate round us. The initials stand for Federación Anarquista Ibérica, and the organization is known colloquially as the FAI, pronounced 'Fie'. Our men were as ignorant as we were about all this, and Isabel assured me quite seriously that the Tossa guards were there to catch any of the FAI who tried to escape. She was hopelessly mixed up with FAI and Fascism. Actually anarchy was a new department for Tossa. As a matter of fact I have never understood what a Spanish anarchist actually is. He is certainly quite different from my idea, laboriously fostered by an English education, of an anarchist. A federation of anarchists sounds as wrong to me as covey of sheep.

However, all this did not affect Tossa very much. The committee was formed and the first thing they had to do was to *Do Something About the Priest*. The strangest rumours flew round. Our chief source of information was Isabel, who, when she arrived panting up the hill every morning, could hardly wait to get her breath back before she poured out her news, usually a very garbled account of a distorted version she had heard. We did finally grasp that the priest was imprisoned in his house. We even saw a very self-conscious guard outside. They had unearthed some money in the church, removed it, and locked up the church. As far as Tossa was concerned it had done its part in the great *Struggle for Freedom*.

The FAI had other ideas. They sent men from Barcelona and the nearer big towns which had proper organizations to investigate whether the villages were taking their responsibilities seriously. Each village had by this time organized its own militia, who took the place of the usual civil guards and coast guards, who had been rushed off to the fighting. The FAI men arrived in Tossa and saw that the church had not yet been emptied of its saints. They professed horror on hearing that the priest was still alive. They arrived about midday, had a look at the church and its contents, and asked where they made the best *arroz catalan* in Tossa. After lunch they took everything out of the church and piled it up in the square outside. Most of Tossa collected to watch. Tossa was interested, but no one offered to help and no one would have thought of doing anything on his own initiative. It was amazing to see the amount that came out of the church. A few children tried to play with some of the gaudy jewels and bracelets on the images of the saints, but their mothers snatched them away and handed them to the mayor, who was a dignified observer of the proceedings.

When the men had finished they were dead tired. They sent for the priest and he arrived, guarded by Tossa militiamen. He was terrified. They marched him into the church and started to deliberate his fate. But they were so tired. Soon they brought him out again and told the villagers to keep him locked up in his house. They said they would be back the next day to burn the things. The villagers, with an unexpected access of initiative, told the FAI men they need not bother, they could do that themselves. The FAI deputation got into its commandeered car and drove off.

The next day the Catalan painter Creixams, nominated by the committee as artistic arbiter, examined the piled-up images and picked out those he thought were worth preserving in the Tossa museum. The villagers decided it was rather dangerous to burn the things near the houses, so three lorries—loaned by three separate individuals, on the principle that 'we're all in this, boys!'—took them down to the beach. The children scampered around the edge of the flames enjoying the biggest bonfire of their lives; the grown-ups stood around with faces that registered exactly nothing.

A few days later we were all on the beach having our morning bathe when another British destroyer arrived. Mary Bain and I went out to meet it on *patinos*. We rather disconcerted the ship's personnel, who were prepared for a more hostile reception. When we at last convinced them that Tossa was extremely peaceful and that there was no chance of shots from the cliffs, some English refugees, who had been kept firmly out of danger below, appeared on deck. We talked to them from our *patinos*, and even persuaded them to get their bathing things and come into the water. They were full of awful stories. They had been picked up at seaside places similar to Tossa further up the coast. I tried to pin them down to details, but there were none. Someone asked if our priest had been killed. I said no, and had the priest been killed in the village they came from? Oh, no, but in the next village all sorts of things had happened. I gathered that none of these people had had the slightest unpleasantness of any sort, but 'there must be something terrible happening somewhere if a warship comes to fetch one.'

When Mary and I got back to the beach we found the officer in charge of the landing party in earnest conversation with Mr Townsend, Archie and Mrs Bain. The officer was exactly like the officer from the first ship, but a grown-up edition. Mr Townsend was saying that nothing would induce him to give up his pleasant holiday and spend an uncomfortable twenty-four hours in a destroyer. Mrs Bain was longing to stay but really worried about her husband in England, who was a colonel in the British Army and therefore would believe the very worst.

We got an idea from the officer how this business was appearing in the English press. We were amazed to hear that we were trapped among wild Bolsheviks, who were howling outside our houses for our blood, while the rebels, tactfully called 'insurgents' in *The Times*, were doing their utmost to arrive in time to save us from *Something Worse than Death*. Mrs Bain was torn between upsetting the Tossa people and annoying Mr Townsend, who declared he would have to go if she left and, on the other hand, the idea of peacefully lying in the sunshine on the beach while her husband had apoplexy in England.

Miss Townsend unexpectedly decided firmly she wished to stay and, of course, Mary Bain seconded her. It was really all a question of when the railways, and consequently the mails, would work again. They appealed to us. If we had not had the responsibility of an hotel-keeper and if they had been just ordinary visitors I would have said at once, 'Stay.' But we were in the difficult position of gaining by their staying, and it was impossible to be unbiased. As a matter of fact, we had begun to realize what a serious thing this revolution was becoming.

We really felt it would be easier to be free agents and not to have to reassure guests and radiate cheerfulness all day. We said we would love them to stay but we felt, as the navy was so insistent, it might be better for them to leave. We added truthfully that we would rather have them than anyone in the house during a revolution but that we could not be responsible for what might happen. They went off to pack, Mr Townsend really annoyed at missing the rest of his holiday. I admired them all enormously because they kept their sense of proportion and refused to find trouble where there was none. Mr Hughes decided at the last moment to go as well. He was due back in three days in any case, and if the trains still refused to run his employers might reasonably ask why he had twice refused a 'lift' from the British Navy.

The officer talked to us very seriously, but we had to pull his leg a little. What amazed us was the way these people thought we would just go away and leave our property to its fate. We invited him up for drink and he had to admit that he would not leave a place like this in a hurry. But I suppose the word 'Communist' would be sufficient to make even the navy quail. It was a mercy the officer did not know about our anarchists, or he would probably never have come as far inland even as our hotel.

We saw the ship go off with mixed feelings. The Tossa people did not bother to come down to the shore. We were sorry the nicest lot of people should have gone, but it was good to have the house empty to enjoy the revolution by ourselves. We celebrated by making as much noise as we liked and taking possession of the front terrace and all the places sacred to guests.

The next day the trains were running again.

We were absolutely amazed when we got our first batch of letters and papers. We had been prepared for a certain amount of nonsense on the part of the diehard press, and we had heard the version of the British Navy, but we were totally unprepared for responsible papers coming out in tacit support of a rebellion. It had never struck us that if it was the Rights who were rebels and the Lefts who were a legally elected government the British Conservative attitude would be 'Up the rebels!'

We proceeded to organize our lives without guests. Thanks to Leonard's cleverness we had made enough our first year to keep us going for a bit, but we laughed at the idea of having long to wait. In any case we started at once to economize. I nearly cried when I thought of how I had struggled to fit people in for August. I wrote letters to everyone saying it was impossible to come at present, but I would let them know how things were. We thought we could probably have guests again in a month. I was surprised to see how many of our intended guests still wanted to come. Several suggested going as far as the frontier and waiting in a French resort until we said it was safe to come here. Others said they would come anyway, but the frontier remained closed for incoming foreigners.

Meanwhile we discussed our position here. We decided that in the advent of a real Communist régime, which seemed unlikely according to reports from people we knew in Barcelona, we might be allowed to live and work in the hotel even if it was taken over by the state. Archie could probably get the job of doing the foreign publicity. We were absolutely prepared to hand over everything, but we wanted to be allowed a living here. Many people in Barcelona seemed to think that at the most there would a very Left democracy. We were beginning to get a vague idea of the ideals of Spanish anarchism, which was represented in Tossa by the FAI. The general idea, we gathered, of trying to run a country on the lines of good-fellowship and on the argument that it is a waste of time and energy to force people to do something against their will seemed sound enough. In any case we were all for joining in any new experiment in living if we were allowed to.

All this time life was very good in Tossa. The weather was

perfect. We took our lunch down to the beach every day and realized what a lovely time our guests must have had. We made long excursions up the coast on our *patino* and tried our hand at fishing, with no success. In the afternoons we went out to the Buen Retiro and played tennis. The proprietor, like all the other refugees, was in a great state of excitement. They could not make up their minds what to do and how everything would affect them. Their trouble was that, for them, a Fascist or a Communist regime was equally disastrous. All they wanted was somewhere where they could live in peace, except among themselves, and make money.

We could do very little to cheer them up. Whenever we said hopefully that this and that might happen and things brighten up all round, they looked at us tragically and said, 'Ah! You are English. You do not know what it is to have no country.' When we suggested that we had invested far more money in Tossa than they had and therefore stood to lose more, they sighed and said hopelessly, 'but you have British passports'. We found it was really better to see as little of them as possible. They spent most of the lovely weather sitting indoors discussing the black future, or else drinking innumerable coffees at the café, listening to the incessant noise of the radio. We had cut out the café because we could not afford it any more. We could understand that things were bad for them, because they had already left one country; but when it came to envying us because we took our lunch down to the beach every day and were determined to enjoy life while we could, we had no patience with them.

They were horrified at the idea of spending a winter in Tossa without very much money. If they had been reasonable people I would have at once suggested that, as our house was the only one in Tossa so situated as to get all the winter sun, and as it was enormous, everyone should come up and live there rent free and we should all share expenses for food, central heating, hot water, etc. If they had been like most of my friends in England it would have worked perfectly well. But with people who expect you to pay for your share in a car at the exact rate of hire in Spain and who think you are slightly mad if you do not act similarly, it would have been impossible. Besides, we were still expected to pay for our tennis, although officially the Buen Retiro was closed and we had to sweep and roll the court ourselves.

We were not absolutely without guests. Journalist friends from Barcelona came out for weekends, and occasionally someone would come for a week or so's rest from the Aragón front. When we could afford it we had one of our women up again. Otherwise I did the housework, helped most efficiently by Leonard and Archie. I cooked completely Catalan now, and we had cut out butter and other foreign luxuries. I had to laugh when I thought of my horror of cooking on a Catalan charcoal fire. I could not have made half our staple dishes on a gas fire.

3

We were all getting used to living in what Archie called 'these very, very anxious times'. The Marcuses and Nicolaus, a friend of theirs who had come to help them in the bar during the summer, were not among the hysterical refugees. We were so relieved to be able to go up to them on the beach and not be received with a salvo of 'What can we do for money?' and 'Where are we to go?' They were the only foreigners in Tossa who did not mention their own future. We were sorry for the two pretty German lads, who really were short of money. They were desperate to get to Paris, where they had friends, but had not quite enough for the fare. However, the British Navy came to the rescue.

The third ship arrived one evening while we were having tea in the sunshine on our terrace. We were now the only English people in the village, and were torn between our duty as hosts and our tea. However, we compromised by sending Leonard to meet the ship's boat, which was obviously quite lost and was landing at the far end of the beach among all the fishing boats. We gulped down our tea and went down to meet the officer. I nearly decided to let Archie go alone—pink naval officers do not attract me much—but at the last moment went with him. We met Leonard taking the officer and another man to the mayor's house. The other man was one of those pale, sandy Englishmen who generally become vice-consuls in small villages. The officer was the most devastatingly handsome young man I have ever seen. He was far less portentous about the whole business than the other two. His eyelashes were very long and curly.

We asked them both to have a drink at the small pub next door to the mayor's house. The sandy Englishman looked very shaken, but the officer thought a beer would be a good idea. The other whispered that he thought it was too dangerous. I asked why.

'The people—they might be unpleasant,' he said.

'They have been wonderful to us,' I replied, rather curtly. 'That is why we have no intention of leaving.'

'They may be all right now, but will it last?' asked the half-wit gloomily. 'You really had much better come with us. It may be your last chance!'

'Will there really not be another ship?' I asked the officer over our beer. 'Every ship has said that it would be the last one.'

'I don't know.' The officer drank his beer with relish. 'We have orders to persuade everyone to leave. There are a good many ships taking people off from other parts of Spain, but they are working overtime. There are some places that are definitely not very healthy at the moment.'

'Of course,' I agreed. 'And I would be the first person to leap into a British destroyer if I were somewhere where they were raising hell. But would you want to leave a place like this when all your property was here?'

'Nothing would make me leave,' admitted the officer without thinking. Then, getting all official again: 'But I really must persuade you if possible. Ours is a very nice ship,' he added reflectively.

The sandy Englishman came over. He had finished his beer and had been having a conversation with Consuelo, who was serving the drinks. 'They seem amazingly friendly,' he said almost reluctantly, but added more brightly: 'You never know what may happen later if they get roused!'

When we got back to the boat we found the two German lovelies waiting, hoping that the ship would give them a free ride to Marseilles. The officer looked rather shaken but said he would ask if that was possible. He then stood on the beach and, looking more like a film star than ever, semaphored the

226

ship, watched by an admiring crowd, including several fascinated children, the German boys, and myself. Evidently the navy fears nothing, for they agreed to take them. I was sad to see the last of the eyelashes so soon. That was the first and last time I have ever contemplated leaving Tossa.

Two days later we got a telegram from a kind but rather exasperating consul in Barcelona to ask if we would like another warship to call. If the Tossa people had not by now been definitely tired of being treated like a hostile tribe I might have said, 'Yes,' in case some more eyelashes appeared. We telegraphed firmly: 'Many thanks, no.' After all, Tossa has its own eyelashes.

We were not underestimating the really marvellous work that the consulate and the navy were doing to rescue people who were cut off in the fighting areas, but it was rather maddening to be persistently treated as if Tossa were a hot-bed of terrorism. There is no doubt that the British Government does things in style, but much needless alarm among foreign visitors in safe areas of Spain could have been avoided by a little imagination. I am definitely in favour of a warship in a crisis, but not a fleet trying to persuade me that there is imminent danger when there is none. In any case I would have preferred to leave quietly by train. If we had been nervous people we would have left in at least the second or third warship, and would have lost our living and all our invested capital. As it is we may lose our invested capital but there is a good chance of being allowed a living, and a sporting chance of losing nothing at all. Of course, there is also a chance of not being allowed to live, but this seems very remote.

The days went on very much the same. We bathed, played tennis, tried to fish, and had our radio tuned up so that we could hear the English news. The *News Chronicle* was the only paper we had except the *New Statesman and Nation*. The *Continental Daily Mail* had been sent to us daily, as we ran an ad in it, but we wrote them a polite postcard asking them to take us off their free list as we were living peacefully among our friends, the Red Terrorists.

Suddenly one day Archie's journalistic blood was roused. At least we say it was that. It was also a chance of prolonging our stay in Spain if he could earn some money. He rushed off to Barcelona, armed with letters from the Tossa mayor to say he was a good supporter of the government and wires from the *News Chronicle* authorizing him to represent them. He spent a day getting his Press permit and another day persuading the authorities to allow him to go to the front, and then disappeared for a week. The village was most excited about it. I was almost a war widow, when Archie suddenly returned with a story and a war wound in the shape of a small scratch on his hand and a hole burned in his trouser leg by his cigarette while he lay beneath the wreckage of his car somewhere near Huesca.

The greatest danger at the front at that time was from the driver of one's car. He either went over the side of a mountain, or else got mixed up in the enemy lines. Archie had both misfortunes. They had driven for miles without seeing a soul and had no idea where they were. Archie was beginning to get rather alarmed in case they would find themselves miles on the wrong side of the undefined front, when they rounded a bend and saw written on a great slab of rock 'Long Live the Arisen Christ!' 'Christ!' said Archie, and they turned round and went back at a rate that was even excessive for the driver, with his strange ideas about speed. Every military driver went as fast as he could while still staying on the twisty roads. Sometimes they went faster than this. Archie's driver did, and Archie found himself lying at the bottom of a ravine pinned in the wreckage of the car, his cigarette burning a hole in his trousers before he was dragged out.

The driver was killed. Archie had to jump lorries or walk after this, and consequently saw far more of the real conditions at the front. He was enormously impressed by the extraordinary spirit at the front, where the men were almost ready to fight among themselves for the privilege of getting to the advanced posts. Archie went to the front again later, and found the atmosphere of rather desultory and cheerful fighting changed. Everyone was much grimmer, but the spirit was still there. It was not a purely fighting spirit, such as one finds in the Irish. It seemed as if the tremendous will of a whole people were concentrated in each man. Archie had been in the Great War in France for nearly three years and knew something about warfare in general. He said he had never seen anything like the determination of these people. They seemed completely indifferent to death, and they refused to be relieved in the line. There were men waiting in thousands to take their place but they only could do so when someone was killed. Man-power and will-power seemed inexhaustible; only rifles were lacking.

Everyone was thrilled when Archie got back from the front, and wanted to hear the latest reports from him. He was to be seen most evenings holding forth in his priceless Spanish to a group of the village elders at the café. A few of the younger refugees had gone off to the front on active service. These were mostly young men who had been active members of Socialist organizations who felt that anti-Fascism was something more than a comfortable, academic attitude of mind.

The situation in the village was curious. The majority of the people were all for a quiet life whatever happened. There were never any really violent politics in Tossa, although in Spain generally politics are as much a national pastime as football is in England. When things settled down after the first disorganization of the revolt, we discovered that extremists on either side were rare. Two of the rich Rights of the neighbourhood disappeared, presumably over the frontier. We waited to see what would happen to the other known

Rights in the village. One of them was the postmaster; several kept various well-to-do shops. Nothing whatever happened to them. The postmaster is still doing his job as badly as ever and the shops are all open. The two men who fled were apparently the only two who were actively Fascist in the village.

Equally, extremists on the Left were very few. One Fortunato, a fisherman who has always been a good friend of ours, and who was always known as one of the few Communists in Tossa, came out with a dazzling red tie with a hammer and sickle painted on it in silver. I admired it and he whipped it off and gave it to me. It is one of the most bourgeois-looking things I have ever seen. Fortunato, even without his tie, was a shining light on the committee, while the head of the whole organization was one Isidor, a waiter. He and a fellow waiter, Bienvenido, were of great importance, as they, with Francisco, the *sardanas*-dancing waiter, were the only people in Tossa belonging to a real syndicate, and so they virtually took over command.

Isidor was a little, dark, repressed creature with sad brown eyes hidden behind enormous horn-rimmed glasses. He invariably had a pipe hanging out of a corner of his mouth, even when on duty. He was very slow-witted, at least when waiting. When he served me in the bar near the beach I was always so sorry for him that I never complained about having to wait for my order or having to repeat it over and over again. His mind always seemed elsewhere. He was not a native of Tossa but came from another part of Catalonia. That, in Tossa eyes, explained and excused all his peculiarities.

Now at last he had come into his own. He still looked an odd, misshapen figure, perhaps more so now that he was bulging with ammunition and had revolvers strapped all over him. He sat every night at the café, a sawn-off shotgun held affectionately under his arm, listening to the interminable flow of words from the radio, smiling dreamily into space.

Bienvenido was always with him, his thin face lined and worried-looking, his brilliant eyes glinting. He was always talking, snapping out words in a nasal Catalan that vied with the radio, gesticulating wildly and thumping the table for emphasis. With them were usually one or two of the members of the committee, or often strange FAI men whom we did not know. Some of the FAI men looked such typical visionary revolutionaries that it was hard to remember that they were representatives of law and order in this through-the-looking-glass revolution.

The most important man in the real management of Tossa affairs was Francisco. Long experience in coping with guests of all nationalities and the fact that he had travelled lifted him above the intelligence of the other committee leaders. While he could be roused to a frenzy of indignation at any suggestion that the Tossa committee's decisions were not supreme, he was the stabilizing influence behind a number of the sensible regulations the committee laid down. He did not seem to have a moment to sit at the café; he was doing the work of an entire committee on his own so that the Tossa committee should have some solid force behind it.

At another table would be sitting the moderates of Tossa. The ex-mayor, who was definitely no longer mayor now that the committee had taken over the whole administration of the village, but who still had to deal with a number of un-military, undramatic difficulties which the committee found beyond them, and his friends among the moderate Left always sat together and listened to the radio or discussed the situation without any heat. They were definitely representative of the real Tossa opinion. There was not enough misery and hardship in Tossa to make for that fierce spirit that was apparent at the front or in the big towns. The people were bewildered. They wanted a Left régime because they were definitely better off under it; also it is an instilled maxim that Catalonia is for the Catalans, and the Lefts were more sympathetic towards Catalan ideals. But everyone, except a few who were definitely thought extreme, had wanted complete autonomy or complete anything.

We found that out in conversations with the lads who formed the village guards. They were utterly unlike the picture the foreign papers had conjured up of bloodthirsty Reds. They did not want to fight at all, but as they thought the alternative to fighting was a Fascist victory and a firing squad, they preferred to shoot the Fascists first. They were on the whole extraordinarily fatalistic. They did not want to die but they might as well die as have Fascism, and Fascism wasn't coming tomorrow, was their attitude. They were definitely against any killing at all, on either side, if possible. One even went so far as to say that he disapproved of any fighting even between nations. This was an answer to one of us who had expressed sorrow at the idiocy of Spaniards fighting Spaniards. He said that he did not wish to fight his brother, but all men were his brothers. It was the same to him whether he had to fight against a foreign foe or his own countrymen. One of the others remarked that that was lucky, as he would have plenty of opportunity to kill Germans and Italians in this war.

They were really amusing about their weapons. Some of them had done their military service, but several of them were still too young. I saw one lad of about seventeen on guard with a rifle that weighed him down. I asked him if he could use it. He confessed he was terrified of it, and then took me aside and shot back the bolt to show me that it was not loaded. He made me promise not to tell anyone.

Another lad was visiting us one night on his round of duty and showed us with pride an aged repeating rifle he had just been given. He pointed it straight at the Zügel picture at the end of the room and demonstrated how it worked. It fired a score of bullets one after another, he assured us. I hoped devoutly it would do nothing of the kind. He jerked back the bolt to show us how the cartridge cases would come out, but nothing happened. He shook it, banged it on the floor, muttered, '*Espere, espere*' ('Wait, wait') to an imaginary Fascist, and at last got it to work. He jerked a stream of bullets all over the floor and was so excited that it really did work at last. He went on until the last bullet shot out, and he and his mates crawled about the floor to retrieve them. It was a fantastic scene, but we were becoming used to fantastic scenes.

4

The refugees were by this time almost past worrying about their money and were concerned only about their personal safety. We could not see the slightest reason for this but, having been told so often that we were British and therefore had no troubles in the world, we dared not protest. We did remark that Leonard was not British, but they seemed to look on him as a definite addition to the Union Jack, and the fact that he was as unconcerned about his safety as we were about ours did not therefore reassure them at all.

They were much more miserable because they did nothing all day except discuss the situation. It was quite useless to discuss anything about which one could know nothing. The rebel radio made it clear that all of Spain that mattered was in their hands; the Government radio was equally positive that all the important places were theirs. English newspapers were nearly as contradictory. The *News Chronicle* would cheer us by favourable Government news; people wrote about seeing in the *Daily Mail* that the rebels—no, insurgents—my error— 'Patriots' was the *Mail*'s effort—that the Patriots had almost succeeded in saving the Spanish church for the Mahommedans, or whatever they were trying to do. It was all much too complicated to follow, let alone argue about. But the refugees talked all day in little groups and worked themselves up into a state of panic. I am certain they must have loathed us because we always refused to believe some frightful story someone had heard from somewhere that the rebels had massacred all the women in some place or other, and therefore if they arrived in Tossa they would do the same, starting, of course, with the foreigners. It was useless to point out that, firstly, it was very unlikely to be true at all; secondly, the probability of rebels reaching Tossa was very remote; thirdly, if they did they would be very unlikely to massacre anyone, and in any case they might even leave the foreigners until last.

It seemed to us that the only thing we could do to help at the moment was to keep unpanicked and cheerful. I would love to describe our bravery and how we hid our terror nobly and went about with glassy smiles, but as a matter of fact it was far easier to be happy than miserable. The weather was perfect and we bathed and sunbathed every day. The only aspect we had of the trouble was the light comedy one. René Clair would have been in his element here.

The committee had taken over the house of one of the Rights from Barcelona, who had discreetly disappeared. It was a lovely old house, with low black beams and beautiful Catalan tiles and plates on the walls. The committee were very proud of their new quarters. They first festooned the doors with notices saying: 'This house is yours, respect it as such', then put a large mat outside the front door and many ashtrays in the large hall. They arranged some armchairs round the radio, and otherwise left everything exactly as it was when they came into the house.

All the foreign residents were sent for to fill in some papers, and we went down to see the new quarters for the first time. We sat round a small table near a window and saw it piled with magazines. They were all years-old copies of the *Sketch* and the *Tatler*. There was a large open cigarette box, and we were told to help ourselves. We felt that even at a dentist's hospitality could go no further. We could see that there was a patio that opened into the room at the far end. One of the militia saw me looking at it and asked me if I would like to see it. I assured him that I would. He escorted me out into a small garden with a door at the end leading into a large patio.

I was just going through the door when another militiaman came out. He was the chief of the coastguards and was now on the committee. He said something I did not understand, rushed back through the door, and other man seized me by the shoulders and turned me round to face the other way. I thought a firing-party at least would appear. After a moment the coastguard reappeared, my escort allowed me to turn round, and they both ushered me into the patio. It was a delightful place, with lemon-trees and a fountain playing. It then transpired that the coastguard had remembered he had turned off the fountain and had rushed back to turn it on again for my benefit. I was not to see the patio without the fountain playing.

When I remarked on the lemons and said that I was surprised they did not sell them, as lemons were impossible to get in Tossa, they were both deeply shocked. These were commandeered lemons, and of course could not be touched. They apologized for not being able to pick me a bunch of the flowers that grew everywhere in the patio, but everything must be left exactly as they took it over.

Back in the big room the atmosphere was rather mixed. The militiamen were listening to dance music on the radio and chaffing Archie and Leonard in Catalan. The refugees sat in worried groups, wondering what the paper was they had to fill up.

At the end of the room was a great carved wooden double door with a roughly painted notice saying 'No entrance except on business'. Another door nearby just said '*No entra*' and another had chalked carefully on cardboard and then pinned with a small drawing pin 'Arms, dangerous'.

We waited patiently. We were all old residents now and were never surprised at waiting for anything. We had waited for long hours outside the *Guardia Civil* offices in the times of the Right régime; we could wait equally well now in the Left régime. We wondered if the Right's having taken our right thumb-print eight times meant that the Left would want our left thumb-print eight times. Suddenly there sounded through the room the dull booming of a gong.

We all jumped. The refugees nearly died. Their worst fears were about to be realized. We all looked at the double doors. I really expected a Chinaman to walk out with a large shining knife. The doors were flung back and little Isidor stood there, blinking through his spectacles. 'Next, please,' he said.

We got used to the gong and no longer thought it at all funny. What was more natural when there was no bell? We got used to the room with its contrast of lovely pictures and scrawled notices. We have now read the papers from cover to cover. What still surprises us is the way the militia still take care of the property they have commandeered. If the owners came back and the committee's property was removed, they would notice very little difference in their house.

Archie went off again to Barcelona to see if he could get to the front again. This time he managed a flight over Huesca, which the Government forces were still attacking fiercely. He was again impressed by the feeling among the men, who were doing their utmost, with very little real equipment, to take this strongly fortified town. He came back to Tossa more enthusiastic than ever and cheered us up enormously. We had heard too much about the rebel advance in the north and not enough about the Government advances elsewhere. It seemed that the Government forces could only just about hold their own instead of sweeping the rebels out of the country, as we had hoped before the Non-Intervention Committee intervened. Yet even when it was quite clear that arms would be supplied to the rebels but not to the Government, the people here did not waver in their determination to fight with whatever weapons they could find.

In Tossa things went on just the same. There was a sudden outcrop of horror stories which were as idiotic as they were untrue. The only people who believed them were the old women who gossiped together over the washing at the river side, or the refugees. There were always a number of big bonfires of old maize stalks at this time of the year, and the word went round that these fires were burning bodies. We never grasped exactly whose bodies, but definitely there was a body in each fire. If anyone went to Barcelona for a week or went away for good, they were rumoured killed and burned. If too many people actually saw them leave, they were immediately reported shot in Barcelona. If one protested that someone had met them in Barcelona, the date of the shooting was postponed.

The burning bodies got to be such a joke to if we did not see some of the refugees for a day or two we decided that they must have been killed and burned, and would point to a minute fire in a field and say, 'Poor so and so, he or she was so charming.'

One day Archie and I were crossing the stream and saw a figure in the distance whom we thought was one of the refugees we had not seen for several days.

'Oh,' said Archie, 'old Schroeder hasn't been shot after all.' Then, as the figure came nearer we saw it was a Catalan we did not know. 'Oh yes, he has,' added Archie unconcernedly.

The stories were so fantastic that no one who was not so scared that they were prepared for anything could have credited them. Anyone who was seen talking with a FAI man or who went down the street with a militiaman on each side was immediately as good as dead in Tossa opinion. The extraordinary thing was that we never did learn of anyone being really shot in Tossa. There were occasions when little Isidor got over-excited and did peculiar things. One night we heard the sound of revolver shots below our house and found afterwards that Isidor had rushed through the vegetable gardens shooting at the cabbages in the moonlight. On another occasion he drove a car through the outdoor café among the tables and threatened us all with his sawn-off shotgun. Someone gave him a drink and he calmed down. He was definitely not right in his head. The nearest anyone got to being killed was a girl who was talking to some of the Tossa guards when one of them threw down his gun and a charge of shot missed her by inches. It blew a big hole in the plaster behind her. A guard was showing a friend his revolver and shot him clean through the shoulder, luckily a flesh wound that was not very bad. Those are all the casualties to date. Isidor disappeared eventually and stories flew round about his fate. They ranged from the usual body-burning to prison in Barcelona. He probably went off to the front.

Bienvenido now became head of the committee. He was more stable than Isidor, but liable to sudden brainstorms. He could get into such a frenzy of rage that he screamed his words and stamped like a child in a tantrum. On the whole he was sensible enough, and we got on very well with him.

The committee had strange ideas about its duties. One evening we were sitting in Marcus's bar with a bunch of guards and some people from Barcelona. In our party was a pretty girl who worked on the committee. It was late and we were all dancing and drinking happily when the door burst open and Bienvenido strode in, followed rather sheepishly by another member of the committee called Pla. Bienvenido strode up to the girl and shouted at her and a man who sat near her to come with him at once. He did not greet us at all. They both stood up. Bienvenido yelled at them to get out, and he and Pla lined up behind them and marched them out. We stayed absolutely amazed and half expected to hear that they were put up against the outside wall and shot. We heard nothing. Most of the other Spanish visitors were really concerned and did not know what to do. Presently one of the Spaniards, who realized that we might be worried, came to tell us what had happened. It appeared that the girl's parents were fussing because their daughter was out so late. Pla, who was thinking about getting engaged to the girl, was asked if he had seen her, and he said he would find her. Someone told him she was at Marcus's bar with another man. Pla ran to the committee in a great state and asked for help. Bienvenido went off with a bang to fetch her.

The next day I met Bienvenido and asked him about it. He was in a good mood. He said he was not going to allow this Barcelona night life to corrupt the Tossa village maidens.

We were sad because Zügel decided to go away. He was lost in Tossa without his family and could not paint. He had very little outside news, of course, and as he did not speak a word of Spanish or Catalan he felt cut off from everything. He was very funny about how he understood what was going on. He could not really follow a single sentence, but he would make up stories to himself. He assured me that he could tell exactly what had happened on the Huesca front by the expression on the Tossa doctor's face when he met him fetching his letters from the post. He was full of strange theories about the people of Tossa. He had invented a sort of Tossa superman, a simple working man with the deep insight into human nature that Zügel thought he himself possessed, and with the intellectual ability which Zügel really did possess. Zügel often spent hours talking German with fishermen, who understood nothing except that here was someone obviously trying to be friendly and, being the friendliest people on earth, had responded heartily in Catalan. Zügel, convinced that he had been having an intellectual conversation in Catalan, would come away delighted at the understanding and intelligence of the Tossa folk. He excused the not particularly brilliant work of some of the committee members by saying that these were the unintelligent people, and the Tossa supermen, or Zügelmen, were biding their time.

Zügel was horror-stricken by reports of atrocities on either side in the revolt. He had idealized Spaniards, and it was equally abhorrent to him whether they massacred people or lost his letters in the post. Both smacked of Prussianism and German bureaucracy. When he found that even in Spain he had not found a land where he could paint as he wished, he left.

5

We were now learning how to live in Tossa as Tossa people. We had never found living especially cheap, because we had had many things that were definitely only for foreigners. No one in Tossa ever dreams of eating butter; they dislike it. The favourite Tossa meal at any time of the day was a large hunk of a long loaf soaked in water and rung out, then covered in olive oil and half a tomato rubbed over it. This, with plenty of salt and pepper, was preferred by our women to any English delicacy we offered them. They ate little meat, and then generally bought small bits for stews and soups. Dried beans and peas they liked and, of course, fish. When they were not eating hunks of bread and tomatoes at their house doors they were eating hunks of bread with grilled fish on their doorsteps.

We decided to go all Catalan. I reserved the right to modify our diet provided it did not cost more. Garlic, the staple diet of the Catalans, was definitely out except in pharmaceutical quantities. I insisted on cooking with the oil hot instead of having everything soaked in lukewarm oil. We found out some really exciting things about food. There were lots of large white mushrooms growing on our hill. They were not in the least like English mushrooms, and it would never have entered our heads to eat them. We found that all Tossa went into the woods to gather fungi of every sort and ate them without any ill effects, so we asked about our white ones and were told they were delicious. We certainly had qualms when we took the first mouthful, and were rather apt to wait for each other to try them first, but after one taste we entirely forgot about danger. In fact we did not care much if we did die after them. They tasted rather like the tenderest pork cutlet imaginable. We cooked them in hot oil and served them with fried parsley and crisp onion rings.

We tried various other kinds of fungi. The guards often brought us basketfuls. We liked our own best, and next to them flat red ones with white spots, which were fried and served with garlic sauce. Controlled garlic, of course. The little brown ones like those in fairy-tale pictures we ate stewed in a wine sauce.

We found that sweet potatoes were good both as a savoury and a sweet. Ordinary potatoes were temporarily rather short owing to so many being sent off to the front, but there were plenty of sweet potatoes. We had them *sauté* and made into omelettes. I found one egg would do for the three of us in this way. We were beginning to see what it was to have friends in the village. We could nearly always get potatoes, and even eggs. Instead of Leonard having to queue in the butcher's for Beetle's liver, the butcher woman kept him a small piece concealed in a draw so that he could come in at any time and get it.

There was no real food shortage at all in Tossa. Certain things, especially eggs, were difficult to get because of lack of distributing organization elsewhere. Potatoes were only temporarily scarce. Every available spare bit of land was green with them. There was plenty of fish. We found that fresh sardines, split open and marinaded like herrings, were good. It was a brain wave, because we could always buy dozens at a time and then get no more for a few weeks until the next big catch.

We had a menu something as follows: coffee and rolls for breakfast, with honey or arbutus jelly. This was an invention of mine and was a great success. Arbutus bushes grow everywhere, and it is very little work to fill baskets with the orange and red berries. They have to be boiled and then sieved through a very fine mesh to get rid of the thousands of tiny pips, and then the pulp is made into jelly with sugar and lemon juice. It tastes like something between quince jelly, strawberry jam, and medlar jelly. For lunch we had rolls and brown bread and a salad with lettuce or endive, tomatoes, and any vegetables left from the day before. We had our marinaded sardines, or tinned sardines. Sometimes we had a potato omelette, or our mushrooms, or sweet potatoes made into rissoles and fried. We often had figs, picked from trees on the hillside, or our own grapes.

Tea was definitely a luxury. We used up our stock of it, and then had coffee. We had a large store of biscuits and we felt comfortably plutocratic every afternoon about five o'clock.

In the evening we had our more solid meal. We had soup, Catalan soup full of bits of things, or a vegetable course and a meat course. I found braising meat in oil over charcoal in a closed dish was a delicious way of coping with the wiry Catalan sheep or athletic pig. So-called veal, cut very small and cooked slowly in oil with potatoes and a seasoning of cinnamon and saffron is a heavenly mixture. I got more and more enthusiastic about the Catalan charcoal stove. I no longer minded filling my kitchen with smoke and bits of ash every time I wanted a fire. It was worth it.

We kept our budget very carefully. We found after several weeks that we were spending about fifty pesetas a week—a little over a pound a week for three people. The only other expense was the electric power for pumping our water up to the house, which was negligible. The meter for the lighting had long since refused to record anything. We felt that if this would only continue we might almost get the money back that had been forced out of us by the strange business methods of the electric company.

We needed to spend nothing on clothes. Even if the revolution lasts so long that our clothes are worn out one needs nothing more than a thick pair of corduroy trousers, costing about seven shillings and sixpence, a few shirts costing two-and-six each made to measure, and a fisherman's jersey, which can be made for a few pesetas. I have turned every available bit of wool in the house into socks and, with rope-soled *alpargatas*, these are our footwear. In really bad weather one wears wooden clogs. This is, of course, for winter, when clothes are expensive compared with summer trousers and shirts.

In December in Tossa one has breakfast outside in the sun, one has lunch outside in the sun. At five o'clock the sun is down and a log fire can be lit. Wood is cheap and pine logs burn well. We had central heating for our guests, but we really do not miss it. With the sun pouring down all day the house is warmed through, and it is only a question of remembering to shut the windows at sundown.

Those were a few of the reasons why we did not wish to leave Tossa. We could not understand the refugees. They were all supposed to be desperate for money, but they were happily talking of leaving what must surely be one of the cheapest places they could find. We were completely indifferent as to whether they left or stayed, but they seemed to expect us to take over their possessions for them. There was a grand idea that we should pretend to buy the Buen Retiro, have all the responsibility for it during the revolution, and than hand it over intact when all was over and the owner had returned from a sojourn in, of all places to choose at this time, Italy. It did not seem to strike any of them that perhaps it was not such a simple matter to rush away at the first sign of trouble, pass the winter comfortably in some peaceful spot away from wars and revolts, and then come back when everything was settled to claim their property.

Again they would not have been so irritating if they had not made such a fuss. It did not matter to us if they preferred giving up their property to facing the still remote possibility of future discomfort. What was annoying was their groans and moans and complaints that they had no money, that they had lost everything, that life was treating them so badly. The

Spanish revolution, 1936, was engineered for the express purpose of allowing Hitler to get one back at them. They were so convinced that they were of sufficient importance to be singled out for special attention from both sides that everything had a sinister significance. Never did one of them go to Barcelona without something highly suspicious happening to him. One of them was sitting alone in an outside café, an unusual thing for a woman to do in Barcelona, and a German in militia uniform came up and spoke to her. According to her story he asked her many questions, said he knew all about her and her political activities, and left her almost hysterical. Another was roughly accosted by two strange men, and if he had not shown great ingenuity in shaking them off he was certain that he would have been languishing in a Spanish prison. Another went to the German consul and found him having an interview with the Italian consul—obviously working out a plan to deal with Tossa refugees.

We began to think about these coincidences. It was so strange that nothing ever happened to us when we went to Barcelona, or indeed anywhere. Then Archie remembered an occasion when he had been walking along the Ramblas late one night and a couple of slightly drunk volunteers had come up and taken him by the arm, one on each side, and had walked him off to a nearby café for a drink. They were cheery souls, and Archie had enjoyed himself. Of course, if it had happened to any of the refugees they would have immediately put their hands up and expected to be shot. Leonard was sent for by the Tossa committee one morning because a man from Barcelona was there searching for someone called Leonard. He was questioned for hours, and finally convinced the man that he was not the right Leonard—or the wrong Leonard—or the Right Leonard. The whole committee vouched for him and said what a nice boy he was. We were rather amused, but we began to realize that a refugee would have considered it a personal attack. I was walking along over one of the big hills surrounding Tossa, looking for mushrooms, when four FAI men jumped out of the bushes with levelled rifles. They thought it the funniest joke they had ever heard of. I did not think it so funny but luckily, having pretty steady nerves, I did not mind so much. A refugee would have had a heart attack. We then saw that they were always looking for trouble and, not unnaturally in these times, they found it everywhere.

So they began to melt away. The owners of the Buen Retiro went first. We refused to take the place over. With great fuss they got their permits and stamps and wired back to their friends that they had *Safely Crossed the Frontier.* We could not see what difficulty there might be crossing the frontier, but we had reckoned without the refugees. The next lot were stopped, kept in Port Bou prison for the night, and sent back to Barcelona the next day. The committee here were tele-phoned to and there was great excitement. The reason was that one of them, an architect, had tried to take out the plans of a house he wanted to build in Tossa. If he had taken it to the Tossa committee before he left, explained it, and got them to stamp it, there would probably have been no trouble. But he just tried to get it over on his own—plans in the middle of a war!

The Baroness left to winter in Nice. Others, feeling greater need to earn money, went to Geneva to try to get jobs as interpreters. If there was, by any chance, no opening for an untrained interpreter in Geneva, one of them was going to start a farm in South America. He was a photographer by trade.

Gradually they disappeared from Tossa. They all did it the same way. With breaking hearts they found themselves thrown upon the cold unkind world. We tried hard to see why. They were all amazed that we stayed. At last Nicolaus and the Marcuses, and a French poet and his wife, were left.

Nicolaus came up to live with us. We had always said we

would love to have anyone up if they were reasonable people, and Nicolaus was definitely that. He agreed absolutely with us about staying in Tossa. The Marcuses were happy in their small house or they would probably have come up as well. They often came up to our sun terrace. The French poet and his wife seemed also quite content. The wife was known by us as Madame Salud, as she was always violently asserting her loyalty with the villagers, who invariably forgot to say the new greeting of *salud* instead of *adiós*. Madame Salud did not like us much. She was one of the 'discovers' of Tossa and did not like any other foreigners at all. She watched with eager joy the refugees one by one fade away. We must have been a disappointment to her.

One night we were all sitting round our fire after dinner when we heard an aeroplane. It was the first time we had heard a night-flying plane over Tossa. We went out to look at it and just saw its light over the sea. It was brilliant moonlight, and the lights of Tossa hardly showed. Suddenly they all went out. At the same time our telephone rang and the committee ordered us to put our lights out. We were just going to bed so it did not matter very much. Nicolaus went down into the village to find out what was happening and came up with the news that there was either a bombardment in Rosas, a coast town about fifty miles away, by an enemy warship, and an attempted landing, or an air raid by Italian aeroplanes. We went to bed feeling that there was very little chance of any trouble in Tossa and slept soundly. The next day it appeared that there really had been some shots fired at Rosas from a rebel boat far out at sea, and a boat in Rosas harbour had been damaged. The aeroplanes we heard were, of course, from Barcelona, going to the rescue.

The excitement in Tossa was intense. The war was really getting nearer. Most of the Tossa women had no idea what a ship or an aeroplane could do and were inclined to be scared. The fact that there had been no attempt at a landing, and that it was obviously only a raiding ship trying to scare people, meant nothing to them. All the lights had been put out in Tossa and that was enough. The next night and thenceforth the lights were on again, but we were asked to keep the shutters down as our house faced the sea, and to put the lights out if we saw the town lights were out. A large siren was installed in the market square. They tested it and we found we could not hear it from our house, but it does not concern us very much. Madame Salud and family left the next day.

6

We had by this time given up our idle way of living and were all three working hard. I was doing the cooking and the household washing; I had never before realized how enormous a sheet can be when it is wet, nor how lovely it is after it has been dried in the sun, spread over rosemary and lavender bushes. Archie and Leonard swept the tiled floors and made beds. Leonard did the morning shopping and made the breakfast coffee. He also added to the household finances by giving English lessons to Spanish visitors to Tossa. Archie gardened and wrote the household letters. I added to everyone's labours by writing this book. We had only one typewriter, so I usually wrote all the morning while Archie subbed the previous chapter. Leonard would type the previous chapter in the afternoon while I okayed Archie's subbing ready for Leonard the next day.

All very complicated, and not made any simpler by having to answer questions about Chapter VII when trying to write Chapter XI. The beginning of the book was easy, but the last part was made very difficult by the fact that there was no end. Obviously the artistic ending and the one which would ensure the book being a success was to have me, if not all of us, shot by either side, but we all agreed that this going rather too far. The other really good ending was to finish the revolution and fill the Casa Johnstone again with guests, and leave us smiling on our terrace ready to start the upward curve of the Johnstone graph once more. This, alas, also seems unlikely. At the moment I have no other ideas, and can only go on from day to day hoping for the best, or worst.

The village had their last Sunday evening dance to give a send off to the Tossa boys who were called up to be soldiers.

They all had previously volunteered, gone off to Barcelona with great *éclat,* and then had all been sent home again because they were not yet wanted. It was rather hard luck that they were now being called up as conscripts. The system seemed to be to call up the men who had done their military service in 1932, 1933, 1934 and 1935. Everyone was very cheerful and the dance was a great success. We all went. Archie and I were rather anxious to show ourselves a bit more in the village to contradict rumours that we were leaving. We were inclined to stay all day up on our hill in the sunshine, and people were beginning to think we were afraid. Some of the departed refugees had virtually barricaded themselves into their houses and had only crept out after dark. We have no idea why. So we put on our best clothes and went to the dance. Archie was reluctant to wear shoes again, and it took a long while to get the mould off his one suit, but we felt we, too, must suffer for the cause. Actually he loved it when he got there, and would sit in corners comparing adventures at the front with tough FAI men. We both felt that when we were dressed up we were a credit to the British Empire in a revolution.

Everyone I danced with asked me why we did not put a Union Jack up over our house. Apart from the fact that we had no Union Jack, we felt that we really could not bear to live quite so much under the wing of something we cursed about every time we heard the British news. The attitude of the British Government was making us keep very quiet about our nationality. I became more Irish than ever and Archie rolled his r's with greater emphasis. Leonard, of course, was disowned by Germany anyway, but the villagers considered him a Catalan. No one ever asked him if he was leaving.

At the dance everyone was very gay and, in keeping with the Spanish and Catalan temperament, decided to enjoy things while they could. I assured all inquirers that I was not at all afraid. I was repeating this almost mechanically by this time to an ex-workman of ours, one of the few Tossa Communists. To my surprise I had said quite the wrong thing. He looked at me very severely and said, 'Well, you ought to be. These Fascists are very bad people. If they come here they will kill everyone, every man, woman, and child.' I was a little shaken and said I was sure he might be right, but what I meant was, they would not come to Tossa. He looked at me darkly and said 'Wait' in lugubrious tones. I did not dare to cheer him up in case I was accused of being pro-Fascist, so I left it at that. He looked with strong disapproval at me for the rest of the evening for being such an unwomanly woman.

The general opinion among the lads of the village was that if they were going to die they might as well enjoy themselves first. Only one with whom I danced was really hating the idea of going off. He would pull himself together and smile and talk while dancing, but at the end of each dance he would sigh and shake himself, as if each dance was a step nearer the end. As a matter of fact none of them was going direct to the front. They were being sent first to Gerona to relieve more trained soldiers.

Chico was in great form. He by this time considered himself an old soldier, as he had been driving lorries with supplies to the front for several weeks, and was now back on leave. Archie told him I was writing a book about him. He was very shaken, and, of course, we pulled his leg and said we had written all about his love affairs with the English visitors. He got very excited and said he was now a Spanish non-commissioned officer and could not have anything written about him. He threatened to have me shot. Then he decided he would write a book in Spanish all about me, so that we would be quits. Leonard could translate them both.

Señor Moreno was dead tired. He was slightly superior about the village politics and the revolution generally. One felt that he really should have been directing operations in Barcelona, that he was wasted in a small place like Tossa. It was difficult to suggest anything to him in the way of improvements in the Tossa régime because he was inclined to treat us as children who had been reassured that all was well. So we gave it up.

Francisco was not at the dance. He sometimes was to be seen flying through the village, or his head would appear round a bar door looking for someone, but he was up to the eyes in work. He was now in charge of the police activities. Tossa being in the war area, as was the whole coast, constant vigilance was necessary. The heads of the provincial police, realizing that they had someone who would be capable of making decisions on his own, left Francisco a good deal of responsibility. It was in great measure thanks to his common sense and restraint that wilder and less experienced members of the Tossa administration were calmed down and everything ran so smoothly. Certainly we, as foreigners, could be grateful for having someone in command whose outlook had been broadened by travel and education.

Archie spent a long time trying to convince one of the FAI men that the car he had seen smashed up at the front was not the one Archie had crashed in. Archie's accident had happened at an entirely different place and the front was strewn with crashed cars, but the FAI man was certain it must have been the same one.

Leonard was usually rather distant to us at the village dances, but as this one was in a revolution he considered himself in our party. Leonard always looked very German and smart among the Tossa boys. His well-cut London suit contrasted with the Tossa fashion of green suits with broad stripes, huge shoulders, and swinging trousers. At close quarters he definitely diffused the Tossa barber's latest scent from Barcelona, and towards the end of the evening no German would have owned him. The refractory curl was back in its place over one eye, he had removed his tie, and except that he held his partner as if she might bite him instead of in the impassioned grip of one of the repressed Tossa swains, he looked as Catalan as any in the room. Leonard's native caution stood him in good stead in Tossa, where he ranked possibly as *Eligible Youth No 1*. There were many mammas who counted the number of times their daughters danced with him and who had dark designs.

I enjoyed dancing again with the lads of the village. I am amazed afresh every time I dance or talk with them how perfectly charming they are. As children they are allowed to do exactly as they please, and may scream and play all round grown-ups trying to work or talk. No one restrains them in the least. Yet they grow into the most thoughtful, most charming people imaginable. They have perfect natural manners and no self-consciousness at all. I snatched a moment to rest my feet, unused to high-heeled shoes, and looked round the dance floor. Crowded rows of Tossa mothers sat on chairs round the floor, some with daughters on their knees; others complacently watched their daughters swinging by in the dance.

In the adjoining bar the older men, or the married men whose wives did not allow them to dance, sat at tables and drank, and ate olives and anchovies. They were all very cheerful and forgetting the war for the time being. Archie was deep in conversation with Jaume. The boy who delivered our bread every day offered me some olives from his plateful. The Tossa lads, earnest in the serious intricacies of the tango, had solemn expressions as they moved with the Catalan's incredible grace. It seemed impossible that English newspapers could be describing these people as Reds, but if a party of rebels had suddenly arrived in the village and had tried to take control, every one of these lads would have fought rather than be shot against the market-square wall. Then the British public would have read about the savagery of the cornered Reds.

It was at the Tossa dance that I heard what I think is one of the best stories of the revolution. It was told me by one of the party involved, and from what I know of the Spanish temperament I am sure the story is true. This man was one of a column, a small self-contained unit, sent to the front. There was some misunderstanding and the column could not find where they were supposed to be. They wandered round for a week, being pushed on from each village, which was already feeling the pinch of being in the war area and did not want to feed a strange column. At last they arrived at a village where there was obviously a *fiesta* going on. (As *fiestas* are in honour of the various saints they were at a discount at this time, but one village near Tossa got out of the difficulty by having a *fiesta* of Comrade Augustin!) In the war area there seemed to be no excuse at all for a *fiesta*, and the column pushed forward to see what it was about. It was a real *fiesta*, and everyone was dancing and oblivious of the war. The newcomers were astonished to see a number of men from the enemy side among the dancers, and were then told the story.

The Government forces had learned that a rebel party was going to descend on the village. They were detailed off to occupy the village secretly and to ambush the rebels as they came through a valley into the village. They prepared the ambush and waited. Presently the first of the rebels was sighted. A man on the outpost of the ambush suddenly jumped up, rushed out towards the enemy and flung his arms round the neck of the first man. It was his brother, who had been doing his military service at the time the revolt broke out, and who was now fighting on the side of the rebels. They both forgot all about the war in their delight at seeing each other again. The other men on both sides felt that this was such a touching scene that it was absurd to fight any more, so they all went into the village together and had a *fiesta*. The lost column joined in.

Another story with a very mixed moral is about a firm in Barcelona that started making war equipment. The firm was taken over by the workmen, one of whom told Archie that, thanks to a new method, they were making articles at a cost of two pesetas which the Government was buying for four pesetas. He slapped Archie on the back. 'They say we workers can't run a business ourselves! And here we are making 100 per cent profit!'

Tossa was away behind all that. The committee tried various reforms, such as shop closing hours. There was a great outcry from the shop-keepers and the shoppers. They were used to buying things at any hour, Sundays included, and no one liked the new arrangements. The committee, probably on Francisco's advice, had the good sense not to press the matter. The most they could do to keep up appearances was to buy up potatoes outside Tossa when the shortage was no longer acute and sell them in the ex-church. Tossa women responded nobly and queued up for hours to buy potatoes. The fact that they could be bought quite normally in the market-square without any bother at all did not concern them. There was a war on and Tossa must play the game.

We were justifiably but rather meanly amused when some FAI people from Blanes came to commandeer four cars from Tossa. There were any number of cars still at large, so to speak. We found that someone unknown to us, who had evidently heard of the commandeering party had, in the darkness, parked his car well up our drive. We very smugly reported it to the committee, who were not interested, as the four cars had already been seized. The first to be commandeered belonged to the departed owner of the Buen Retiro. We had tried to point out to the refugees that to leave one's property in such times was tantamount to giving it away at once. We tried to feel sorry for the poor car owner.

Our reflexes are now going through a conditioning process that even Pavlov could not have bettered. There has been an outbreak of blasting all round us. This is going on all along the coast, as the whole district is virtually in the war area. Luckily, our house is just sheltered by a brow of hill from the nearest operations, so that we do not have to dodge bits of flying rock all day. We only have to keep a weather eye open when we go down the drive.

The constant bangs do not even make us blink, and even Beetle has been persuaded that it is not a series of new thunderstorms. She is terrified of thunder. The villagers do not bat an eyelid at the most terrific explosion, and they handle the dynamite with a careless *bonhomie* that is frightening. Leon was at the committee when some new revolvers had just been unpacked. They were handed around, admired, and loaded ready to try outside. One went off and blew a hole in the soft plaster of the wall. Just below the hole was a box. When the members of the committee had recovered from their surprise one of them walked over and examined the hole. Then he opened the lid of the box below and chuckled.

'*Mire!*' he said. The box was full of sticks of dynamite.

With their own lethal weapons they are careless, but they have a great respect for anything savouring of danger from the enemy. It is firmly rooted in each Tossa mind that Franco is attacking Madrid only as a preliminary to his real objective, Tossa. Any enemy ships ranging the coast are only interested in bombarding Tossa. It is useless to argue that the enemy have no interest in wasting ammunition on a completely unimportant village; that they would not attempt to land in quite the most difficult point of the whole coast; that although shots may have been fired from enemy ships at important harbours within earshot, still the possibility of anyone bothering about Tossa is remote. It is still more useless to try to explain just what it means to destroy even a small village. These people have no conception of the limitations of aeroplanes or battleships. One bomb or shell would lay waste to the village, they are sure. One enemy bullet could kill several Tossa people easily, but their own weapons are handled with a complete disregard of life and limb.

I was sitting writing on the front terrace. The bright December sunshine warmed the bent backs of the men working in the vegetable plots below. Fishermen were rolling up their sardine nets, the big *seine* nets were spread out, covering most of the yellow sand with a brown film. Every few yards an old Tossa grandmother squatted, busily mending, their umbrellas, like great black mushrooms, shading them from the sun. Some children were playing about on the distant football field. In the stream Tossa women scrubbed and gossiped. Some of them, the washing finished, were already toiling up the hill on the far side of Tossa, balancing their wooden wash-boards piled with wet bundles on their heads, to spread the clothes on the lavender and thyme bushes in the blazing sun. A man directly below our terrace was beating *fesols* (dried beans like butter beans) out of their crackling yellow pods. The clickety-click of his two sticks beat in time with the women thumping their washing. Blasting was going on intermittently on the far side of the cliff. Boom, boom-boom-boom, boom. Archie came running out of the house.

'That wasn't blasting,' he said.

'Rubbish, of course it was.' I went on typing. 'Do go away and let me work.'

'That was shell-fire.'

Boom, boom-boom-boom-boom.

'Look!' Leon came out, and we all saw puffs of white smoke high in the air far away over the headland. We heard the self-important roar of one of the little flying-boats that patrol the coast, and one flew past, very low in the water. I looked at Tossa. One or two of the men working below in the plots had stopped work and were looking up. The fishermen were standing in groups on the beach. The women in the stream were silent. The man went on beating his *fesols* and the children were still playing.

'Look there,' called Archie, who had climbed halfway up the hill above the house to see better.

A sinister grey cruiser slipped silently past Tossa bay. She had no flag that we could see. A small seaplane flashed over her. The cruiser spat angrily at the plane. Boom boom boom. The plane rose, swooped away, shot off towards Barcelona. The cruiser continued her extremely leisurely course. She was close inshore and quite unruffled. As far as we could gather she must have been an enemy ship, and the seaplane presumably from Barcelona, but as this war is a real one, things are not so well arranged as in cowboy films, where the hero always has a white horse.

By this time, when the cruiser was well past, having ignored Tossa entirely, the Tossa people were beginning to realize that there might have been some danger somewhere. The men working the blasting came streaming down from what we should have imagined was one of the safest spots, as they must have been somewhere near the earth's centre by this time. The gardeners had set off for the village at the double. Even the *fesols* man was staring uncertainly towards the disappearing backs. The women left the stream and were rushing towards their homes and happy, unconscious children, shrieking at the tops of their hearty Catalan voices. The children on the football field were standing in a bewildered huddle. The fishermen had disappeared from the beach, and the Tossa front was held only by the row of old women under their black umbrellas.

For the next two hours Tossa went through the motions of being under heavy gunfire. The women and children streamed out into the hills in accordance with the defence regulations posted in all coastal villages. The men rallied in the market-place. One or two kind souls, seeing me writing on the terrace, called to me to come with them out of danger. We were in a rather difficult position. We knew that the fraction of danger that there might have been was long past, but that no amount of eloquence could possibly persuade the Tossa people of this. It seemed too superior to wave from the terrace and say in effect 'Thanks very much, you run along off to the hills and have fun playing at bombardments. I am not going to be so childish.'

The Catalan mentality is so opposed to every English tradition which decrees that no matter how terrified one may be one keeps a stiff upper lip, chaps. How many colonies have sprouted from stiff upper lips? The Catalans are not interested in upper lips. They like living, and it is only when they are not allowed to live as they like that they get roused and are willing to risk dying. When a Catalan is frightened by a mad dog, a Fascist, or a runaway horse he says so quite frankly. He takes every possible precaution, but that does not prevent him form being just as efficient in a crisis as a stiff-lipped Englishman.

We think that the Catalan Government owes the rebels a vote of thanks. A few more rehearsals and the coast towns will take no more interest in a passing warship than in the blasting. The blasting makes much the most noise.

So we remain on our terrace, a credit to our Empire. Only the Union Jack is lacking. Bravely we face the future. Starting again with nothing but our bare hands we try to wrest a living from the soil. We are not even allowed that. Tonet saw us digging and said, 'Please,' he would do it for us, he did it so much better. He has planted green peas and broad beans. Rovira wants to give us some rabbits. The electric meter is still not working. We have decided we like living under anarchism. So, despite the general exodus of foreign residents we have decided to stay here.

For further information please apply to Casa Johnstone, Tossa de Mar, Gerona, Spain.

259

ALSO AVAILABLE FROM THE CLAPTON PRESS

MY HOUSE IN MALAGA by Sir Peter Chalmers Mitchell
While most ex-pats fled to Gibraltar in 1936, Sir Peter stayed on to protect his house and servants from the rebels. He ended up in prison for sheltering Arthur Koestler from Franco's rabid head of propaganda, who had threatened to 'shoot him like a dog'.

BRITISH WOMEN AND THE SPANISH CIVIL WAR by Angela Jackson — 2020 Edition
Angela Jackson's classic examination of the interaction between British women and the war in Spain, through their own oral and written narratives. Revised and updated for this new edition.

BOADILLA by Esmond Romilly
The nephew that Winston Churchill disowned describes his experiences fighting with the International Brigade to defend the Spanish Republic. Written on his honeymoon in France after he eloped with Jessica Mitford.

SOME STILL LIVE by F.G. Tinker Jr.
Frank Tinker was a US pilot who signed up with the Republican forces because he didn't like Mussolini. He was also attracted by the prospect of adventure and a generous pay cheque. This is an account of his experiences in Spain.

SPANISH PORTRAIT by Elizabeth Lake
A brutally honest, semi-autobiographical novel set in San Sebastián and Madrid between 1934 and 1936, portraying a frantic love affair against a background of confusion and apprehension as Spain drifted inexorably towards civil war.

MARGUERITE REILLY by Elizabeth Lake
First published in 1946, Marguerite Reilly is the fictionalised story of four generations of Irish immigrants struggling to make good in the Victorian and post-Victorian era, from the days of the Great Hunger up to the end of the second world war. Harrowing at times but always entertaining, this is a must-read for anyone with Anglo-Irish heritage.

ALSO AVAILABLE FROM THE CLAPTON PRESS

NEVER MORE ALIVE: INSIDE THE SPANISH REPUBLIC
by Kate Mangan, with a Preface by Paul Preston
When her lover, Jan Kurzke, made his way to Spain to join the
International Brigade in 1936, Kate Mangan went after him. She
ended up working with Constancia de la Mora in the Republic's
Press Office, where she met a host of characters including WH
Auden, Stephen Spender, Ernest Hemingway, Robert Capa,
Gerda Taro, Walter Reuter and many more. When Jan was
seriously injured she visited him in hospital, helped him across
the border to France and left him with friends in Paris so she
could return to her job in Valencia.

THE GOOD COMRADE, MEMOIRS OF AN INTERNATIONAL
BRIGADER
by Jan Kurzke, with an Introduction by Richard Baxell
Jan Kurzke was a left-wing artist who fled Nazi Germany in the
early 1930s and tramped round the south of Spain, witnessing
first-hand the poverty of the rural population, later moving to
England where he met Kate Mangan. When the Spanish civil war
broke out in 1936, Jan went back and joined the International
Brigade, while Kate followed shortly after, working for the
Republican press office. Many of his fellow volunteers died in the
savage battles on the outskirts of Madrid and Jan himself was
seriously wounded at Boadilla, nearly losing his leg. This is his
memoir, a companion volume to *Never More Alive.*

IN PLACE OF SPLENDOUR: THE AUTOBIOGRAPHY OF A
SPANISH WOMAN by Constancia de la Mora,
with a foreword by Soledad Fox Maura
Constancia de la Mora was the grand-daughter of Antonio
Maura, who had served under Alfonso XIII as Prime Minister.
She was one of the first women to obtain a divorce under the
fledgling Spanish Republic. During the civil war she became a
key figure in the Republic's International Press Office, moving to
the USA and Mexico after the war was lost. This is her
remarkable memoir, with a detailed history of the build-up to the
conflict.

ALSO AVAILABLE FROM THE CLAPTON PRESS

**NEVER MORE ALIVE: INSIDE THE SPANISH REPUBLIC
by Kate Mangan, with a Preface by Paul Preston**
When her lover, Jan Kurzke, joined the International Brigade in
1936, Kate Mangan followed him to Spain. She found a job with
the Republican Press Office, meeting a host of characters
including Auden, Spender, Hemingway, Robert Capa, Gerda
Taro, Walter Reuter and many more. When Jan was seriously
injured she helped him across the border to France and left him
with friends in Paris so she could return to her job in Valencia.

**THE GOOD COMRADE, MEMOIRS OF AN INTERNATIONAL
BRIGADER
by Jan Kurzke, with an Introduction by Richard Baxell**
Jan Kurzke was an artist who fled Nazi Germany in the early
1930s and tramped round Spain, witnessing first-hand the
poverty of the rural population. When the civil war broke out in
1936, Jan joined the International Brigade. Many of his fellow
volunteers died in the battle for Madrid and Jan himself was
seriously wounded at Boadilla, nearly losing a leg. This is his
memoir, a companion volume to *Never More Alive.*

**IN PLACE OF SPLENDOUR: THE AUTOBIOGRAPHY OF A
SPANISH WOMAN by Constancia de la Mora,
with a foreword by Soledad Fox Maura**
Constancia de la Mora was the rebellious grand-daughter of
Antonio Maura, who had served under Alfonso XIII as Prime
Minister. She was one of the first women to obtain a divorce
under the fledgling Spanish Republic. During the civil war ran
the Republican Press Office. This is her remarkable memoir, with
a detailed history of the build-up to the conflict.

**BEHIND THE SPANISH BARRICADES
by John Langdon-Davies, with a Prologue by Paul Preston**
First published in 1936, *Behind the Spanish Barricades*
chronicles the early months of the Spanish Civil War through the
eyes of a seasoned journalist well acquainted with Spanish and
Catalan cultures. Arriving on a second-hand motorbike, he
experiences the exuberant atmosphere in Barcelona during its
short-lived proletarian revolution, as well as the horrors of war
as he visits Toledo during the siege of the Alcázar.

ALSO AVAILABLE FROM THE CLAPTON PRESS

FIRING A SHOT FOR FREEDOM: THE MEMOIRS OF FRIDA STEWART with a Foreword and Afterword by Angela Jackson
Frida Stewart drove an ambulance to Murcia to help the Spanish Republic and visited the front in Madrid. During the Second World War she was arrested by the Gestapo in Paris and escaped from her internment camp with help from the French Resistance, returning to London where she worked with General de Gaulle. This is her previously unpublished memoir.

STRUGGLE FOR THE SPANISH SOUL & SPAIN IN THE POST-WAR WORLD by Arturo and Ilsa Barea, with Introduction by William Chislett.
Arturo and Ilsa Barea worked for the Spanish Republic's Press and Censorship office and later sought refuge in the UK. These two essays, both written during the Second World War, called on the democracies of Europe to unseat Franco; both fell on deaf ears. Together the two essays present a horrific picture of the early years of the dictatorship., which endured until 1975.

THE FIGHTER FELL IN LOVE: A SPANISH CIVIL WAR MEMOIR by James R Jump, with a Foreword by Paul Preston and a Preface by Jack Jones
Aged twenty-one, James R Jump went to Spain to join the International Brigade. This previously unpublished memoir, based on his diaries, brings back to life his time in Spain and the tragic course of the war he took part in, while the accompanying poems reflect the intense emotions sparked by his experience.

SINGLE TO SPAIN & ESCAPE FROM DISASTER by Keith Scott Watson
The author was one of the first British volunteers to join the International Brigades; within a couple of months most of the British in his battalion were dead and he had been chased out of Spain as a deserter. He soon returned to Spain and was one of the first journalists on the spot to report on the bombing of Guernica in April 1937. *Single to Spain* is his memoir of his experiences in the siege of Madrid, first published in 1937. *Escape from Disaster* is his report on the fall of Barcelona and his desperate dash for the border in January 1939.

Milton Keynes UK
Ingram Content Group UK Ltd.
UKHW020721061024
2026UKWH00039B/348

9 781913 693169